TECHNOLOGY
TOGETHER

Whole-School
Professional Development
for
Capability and Confidence

RENATA PHELPS
ANNE GRAHAM

International Society for Technology in Education
EUGENE, OREGON • WASHINGTON, DC

TECHNOLOGY **TOGETHER**

Whole-School **Professional Development** for **Capability and Confidence**

RENATA PHELPS and ANNE GRAHAM

© 2013 International Society for Technology in Education
World rights reserved. No part of this book may be reproduced or transmitted in any form or by any means—electronic, mechanical, photocopying, recording, or by any information storage or retrieval system—without prior written permission from the publisher. Contact Permissions Editor: www.iste.org/learn/publications/permissions-and-reprints.aspx; permissions@iste.org; fax: 1.541.302.3780.

Director of Book Publishing: *Courtney Burkholder*
Acquisitions Editor: *Jeff V. Bolkan*
Production Editors: *Tina Wells, Lynda Gansel*
Production Coordinator: *Emily Reed*
Graphic Designer: *Signe Landin*
Proofreader: *Kathy Hamman*
Indexer: *Pilar Wyman, Wyman Indexing*
Book Design, Cover Design: *Kathy Sturtevant*
Book Production: *Tracy Cozzens*

Library of Congress Cataloging-in-Publication Data

Phelps, Renata.
  Technology together : whole-school professional development for capability and confidence / Renata Phelps and Anne Graham. — First editon.
    pages cm
  Includes bibliographical references and index.
  ISBN 978-1-56484-325-8
  1. Educational technology—Study and teaching. 2. Information technology—Study and teaching. 3. Teachers—Training of. 4. Teachers—In-service training. I. Title.
  LB1028.3.P474 2013
  371.33—dc23

2012036910

First Edition
ISBN: 978-1-56484-325-8
Printed in the United States of America

Cover Art: © iStockphoto.com/derrrek
ISTE® is a registered trademark of the International Society for Technology in Education.

About ISTE

The International Society for Technology in Education (ISTE) is the trusted source for professional development, knowledge generation, advocacy, and leadership for innovation. ISTE is the premier membership association for educators and education leaders engaged in improving teaching and learning by advancing the effective use of technology in PK–12 and teacher education.

Home to ISTE's annual conference and exposition, the ISTE leadership conference, and the widely adopted NETS, ISTE represents more than 100,000 professionals worldwide. We support our members with information, networking opportunities, and guidance as they face the challenge of transforming education. To find out more about these and other ISTE initiatives, visit our website at www.iste.org.

As part of our mission, ISTE Book Publishing works with experienced educators to develop and produce practical resources for classroom teachers, teacher educators, and technology leaders. Every manuscript we select for publication is carefully peer-reviewed and professionally edited. We value your feedback on this book and other ISTE products. Email us at books@iste.org.

International Society for Technology in Education
Washington, DC, Office:
    1710 Rhode Island Ave. NW, Suite 900, Washington, DC 20036-3132
Eugene, Oregon, Office:
    180 West 8th Ave., Suite 300, Eugene, OR 97401-2916
Order Desk: 1.800.336.5191
Order Fax: 1.541.302.3778
Customer Service: orders@iste.org
Book Publishing: books@iste.org
Book Sales and Marketing: booksmarketing@iste.org
Web: www.iste.org

About the Authors

Renata Phelps, PhD, is employed at Southern Cross University, Australia, as a senior lecturer in the School of Education and a research associate with the Centre for Children and Young People. Her main areas of research and teaching relate to educational information technology with a focus on teacher professional development and the integration of ICT in primary, secondary, and tertiary education environments. She has a particular interest and passion for learner-centered pedagogy and fostering self-regulated learning through metacognitive approaches. Renata enjoys supporting teachers through action learning and action research as they strive to innovate in their practice and best meet the learning needs of their students. Renata has published in the area of complexity theory in education, and the organization and management of research. With her partner Don and numerous dogs, ducks, and chickens, Renata lives on a large rural property in northern New South Wales (NSW), Australia. She is involved in rainforest reforestation and the rescue and care of Australian wildlife such as wallabies and possums. She aims toward a sustainable and self-sufficient lifestyle with a big vegetable garden and lots of fruit trees.

Anne Graham, PhD, is a professor of childhood studies and the director of the Centre for Children and Young People at Southern Cross University, Australia. She was previously head of the School of Education and has many years' experience working in undergraduate and postgraduate teacher education. Anne's research, publishing, and professional interests include teacher learning, children's social and emotional well-being, participation and engagement in schools, and ethical issues in researching with children and young people. Over the past 15 years, Anne has developed and implemented in schools a range of professional development programs based on experiential learning approaches that place teachers' experience at the center of the learning process. Anne has four adult children and lives by the beach on the beautiful north coast of NSW. When not at work, she enjoys swimming, walking, traveling, and spending time with family and friends.

Acknowledgments

We would like to acknowledge the contributions of the school communities in New South Wales who collaborated in the development of the Technology Together project:

Xavier Catholic College, Ballina; St. Mary's Primary, Bellingen; St. Mary's Primary, Casino; St. Augustine's Primary, Coffs Harbour; Mt. St. John's Primary, Dorrigo; St. Anthony's Primary, Kingscliff; St. Brigid's Primary, Kyogle; St. Joseph's Primary School, Laurieton; St. Carthage's Primary, Lismore; St. Joseph's Primary, Maclean; St. John's Primary, Mullumbimby; St. Joseph's High School, Port Macquarie; Mary Help of Christians Primary, Sawtell; St. Joseph's Primary, Tweed Heads; St. Francis Xavier Primary, Woolgoolga; and St. James Primary, Yamba.

The research would not have been possible without the support of all those teachers who participated, particularly the school leaders and companion mentors who facilitated the process within their school. This team demonstrated exceptional vision and commitment to improvement of ICT learning outcomes for teachers and students alike. We would like to acknowledge the contributions of the following people:

Sharon Barrington, Sue Beacroft, Bernadette Birchall, Tony Boyle, Michelle Bratti, Sharon Brennan, Tanya Buckanan, Terry Cahill, Michelle Campbell, Carolyn Carrigan, Lisa Conte, Suzie Coster, Ann Dawson, Helen Day, Paul Edgar, Sue Fern, John Fitzgerald, Andrew Frawley, Michael Fuhrmann, Jo Gallagher, Jason Holmes, Tony Hurley, Christine Jeffrey, Mick Kennedy, Grant Lawler, Eric Littler, Col Mackay, Jake Madden, Kath Maginnity, Tom Maginnity, Mark McDonald, Christine Mulherin, Anne O'Brien, Anthony O'Brien, Damian O'Bryan, Vince Powell, Paul Riedy, Haley Rogusz, Greg Ryan, Michelle Scott, Therese Seymour, Amanda Smith, Stacy Smith, Chris Speirs, Jenni Thomson, Patrick Tierney, Jenny Triglone, Mary Walsh, Vanessa Walters, Liz Watts, Peter Watts, Tony Watts, Brian Wills, and Mark Wilson.

We would particularly like to thank the Lismore Catholic Education Office staff for co-funding, supporting, and promoting the research over many years—Dianne Marshall, Anne Wenham, Cath Bryant, Andrew Burgess, Sr. Berenice Kerr, and Lee MacMaster. In particular, our deep appreciation is extended to Paul Thornton, who played a key role in ensuring the success of the Technology Together model—we thank Paul sincerely for his commitment, leadership, and vision, and for traveling side-by-side with us on the journey. Thanks also to additional members of our initial advisory group: Peter Bailey, Mick Howell, Ron Fletcher, Michael Cunningham, Sharon Ison, Rosemary Cureton, Paul Edgar, and Ian Walton.

ACKNOWLEDGMENTS

We also extend thanks to our colleagues, all highly respected classroom practitioners, who provided feedback on our final draft of the book: Lesleigh Altmann, Kate Battiston, Andrew Maslen, and Charlie O'Sullivan.

Finally, a very special thank-you to Carrie Maddison, Emma Fountain, and Wendy Britt for their tireless support behind the scenes in the administration, management, and analysis of data associated with the project. Without the input and enthusiasm of all these people, this publication would not have been possible.

Contents

PREFACE xi

INTRODUCTION 1
    Quotes and Resources 3
    Chapter Summaries 3
    Technology Together at a Glance 4

CHAPTER 1
Technology Together: A Whole-School Teacher-Learning Model 7
    Why Develop a Whole-School Approach to ICT Learning? 8
    What Is Technology Together? 11
    Capability- versus Competency-Based Approaches 14
    Focusing on Teachers' Values, Attitudes, and Beliefs 15
    Technology Together Works 16
    How Technology Together Differs from Previous Approaches 18
    Acknowledging Technology Learning as a Complex Process 20
    Technology Together as Evidence-Based Action-Oriented Practice .. 25
    The Technology Together Website 27

CHAPTER 2
An Overview 29
    The Eight Foundational Pillars 30
    Introducing the Metacognitive Approach to Technology Learning .. 36
    The Three Metacognitive Dimensions: Affects, Motivation, and Strategies .. 37
    Reflection *on, in,* and *for* Action over Time 41
    The Visual Model 42
    Technology Together as Learning Journey 44

CHAPTER 3

Planning for Implementation 47

Step 1 – Deciding Who to Involve and When 48
Step 2 – Introducing Technology Together to Your School 49
Step 3 – Considering Your ICT Vision 51
Step 4 – Allocating Roles 52
Step 5 – Conducting a School Analysis 59
Step 6 – Facilitating Goal Setting 67
Step 7 – Planning Your Mentoring Strategies 69
Step 8 – Managing Release Time 74
Step 9 – Embedding Strategies for Reflection and Discussion 76
Step 10 – Planning to Showcase and Celebrate Achievements 82
Checklist for Implementation Planning 83

CHAPTER 4

Mentoring within a Metacognitive Framework 87

Why Technology Together Mentoring Is Different 88
Mentoring to Develop Capability 89
Mentoring with Mindfulness toward Affects 94
Mentoring to Foster Motivation 102
Mentoring to Develop Appropriate Strategies 108
General Advice for Mentors 124

CHAPTER 5

Supporting Teachers' Teaching 127

Six Strategies to Challenge Pedagogy 128
Strategy 1 – Reflecting on Objectivism, Constructivism, and Connectivism 129
Strategy 2 – Reflecting on Authenticity in Teaching and Learning 131
Strategy 3 – Reflecting on Students as Digital Natives 134
Strategy 4 – Reflecting on Whether Students Need to Be Taught ICT Skills 137
Strategy 5 – Reflecting on How ICT Can Transform Teaching 139
Strategy 6 – Developing Students' Metacognition 144
Learning *with* and *from* Students 146

CHAPTER 6

Goals and Initiatives ... 149

- Helping Teachers Set Goals ... 150
- The Goal-Setting Structure ... 151
- Whole-School Goal Setting ... 152
- How to Use This Chapter ... 154
- Metacognitive Goals ... 156
- Leadership Goals ... 157
- Recreational Goals ... 157
- Skills-Based Goals ... 158
- Foundational Computer Skills ... 159
- Hardware Skills ... 160
- Word Processing Skills ... 162
- World Wide Web Skills ... 163
- Communication Applications Skills ... 165
- Spreadsheet Software Skills ... 167
- Presentation Software Skills ... 168
- Multimedia Skills ... 170
- Database Software Skills ... 171
- Interactive Whiteboard Skills (Flipchart Software) ... 173
- Mobile Applications Skills ... 174
- Pedagogy Goals ... 176
- Classroom Management ... 177
- Authentic, Connectivist Online Learning ... 179
- Showcasing and Celebrating Achievements ... 186

CHAPTER 7

Bringing It All Together and Making IT Happen ... 187

- Scheduling into the School Year ... 188
- Advice from the Front Line ... 197
- Where to Go from Here: Sustaining the Process ... 205

CONTENTS

APPENDIXES
Appendix A – **List of Resources** 207
Appendix B – **Student and Teacher Surveys** 213
Appendix C – **NETS for Coaches (NETS•C)** 225

GLOSSARY 229

BIBLIOGRAPHY 235
References 235
Further Reading 239

INDEX 243

Preface

The Technology Together model had its early foundations in teacher education programs at Southern Cross University in New South Wales (NSW), Australia. We faced the challenge of preparing individuals with very diverse ICT backgrounds for a career of continued technological change. Our hunch was that the best way of helping teachers to survive and thrive in this context was for them to develop confidence and effective learning strategies. Through a series of action research cycles conducted over several years, a metacognitive approach to computer technology learning was developed, evaluated, and continuously refined, to best meet the needs of teachers (Phelps, 2002, 2007; Phelps & Ellis, 2002a, 2002b). As this book stresses, a metacognitive approach was seen as central because it is concerned with teachers learning to think about the *how* and *why* of what they do. The approach builds teachers' knowledge and awareness of their own thinking processes in relation to ICT as they identify goals and learning strategies.

The potential of such an approach was recognized by a regional school system that partnered with Southern Cross University to provide an accredited postgraduate-level professional development course for teachers in primary and secondary schools, based on the metacognitive approach. After an initial pilot of the course with 40 teachers, a further four groups of 40 teachers (200 teachers in total) participated (Phelps, Graham, & Kerr, 2004).

Our interactions with these practicing teachers highlighted that the metacognitive approach was very beneficial for many teachers, particularly those who lacked confidence with computers. However, we recognized that not all teachers want to take university courses, and those who might most benefit from engaging in ICT professional learning aren't always the ones who volunteer to attend. We also acknowledged that teachers' ICT learning, and their capacity to integrate technology in their teaching, relied on them having a supportive ICT learning culture in their school. The full potential of the metacognitive approach, we felt, could only best be realized within the context of a whole-school implementation model.

In partnership with the Catholic Education Office, Lismore, NSW, we applied to the Australian Research Council (ARC) under the industry linkages program. Our application was successful, and in 2004 the Technology Together research project began. This research sought to develop a holistic and flexible approach to information and communication technology (ICT) professional development for primary and secondary school teachers, an approach that was not only about ICT skills training but also acknowledged the importance of leadership, school culture, and meeting all teachers "where they are at" on the technology learning ladder.

Underpinning the research was a focus on developing teachers' capability—their ability to continue learning and adapting to technological change. Briefly, the research aimed to do the following:

- Document the metacognitive influences on teachers' use of ICT,
- Determine the effectiveness of the metacognitive approach in supporting teachers' ICT professional development in a whole-school context,
- Develop and refine practical approaches to schools' implementation of the approach,
- Understand the role of school administrative leaders in influencing teachers' approaches to technology use, and
- Produce professional development resources that could support schools' approaches to teachers' ICT professional development.

We adopted an action research approach because we perceived it offered the most scope for engaging teachers in a change process. As such, the Technology Together project involved two macrocycles conducted over two school years, with seven schools participating in 2005 and nine different schools participating in 2006. Of these 16 schools, 14 were primary schools and two were secondary schools, and they ranged in size from a small 10-teacher school to a large 33-teacher primary school and a 39-teacher secondary school.

Following an initial workshop, each school engaged in three term-long microcycles (in Australia three terms is equivalent to three-fourths of a school year) of planning, implementing and evaluating a range of initiatives and strategies considered consistent with the metacognitive approach. What was learned by schools in the first year was built on by schools in the second year. As both partners and facilitators we visited the schools each term, providing explicit opportunities to reflect on and revise activities. Participants worked closely with us to develop, implement, and refine metacognitive approaches within their school contexts. The processes were facilitated in schools by key staff, referred to as *companion mentors* (CMs), who also played a role as co-researchers, helping us to collect and analyze data. A Reconnector Workshop (held in 2007 with representatives from most schools) shared and discussed findings and recommendations for the final project report and the resulting professional development resources.

From this project we gained considerable insights into the complex and dynamic influences that impact on the day-to-day integration of ICT in schools and classrooms. We learned a great deal about teachers' learning in relation to technology and how school communities can best support and encourage teachers—new and old, confident and hesitant—to continue to learn with and from their students.

Most schools participating in the development and trials of the Technology Together project experienced considerable benefits and positive outcomes. As we describe in Chapter 1, the approach to ICT professional development that we developed and refined was considerably different from approaches that schools had previously employed. Further, school leaders reported benefits from involvement that extended beyond ICT integration to a general enhancement of teacher professionalism and teaching quality. Although the technologies continue to change and new hardware and software have since made their way into the schools we worked with, what we learned together is just as relevant now as it was then—if not more so.

Introduction

Sometimes it is important to state up front what something is not. The Technology Together approach, the topic of this book, is not a product. Rather, Technology Together is a process, a collection of tips and hints and a way of perceiving professional development. It is not a rigid technology program or project that you complete step by step—it is a flexible framework for ongoing information and communication technology (ICT) integration and professional development.

It was never our intention to produce a step-by-step process guaranteed to work for all teachers in all school contexts. Rather, the Technology Together model is conceived of as a general approach to teacher professional learning, designed to be flexibly adjusted to individual school contexts. Every teacher, every class, and every school context is acknowledged as unique and distinctive; therefore, the processes we suggest are adaptable to the culture and context of each school. The implementation of the model will be shaped by a range of factors, including leadership styles, school size, backgrounds and interests of the staff, history of previous ICT professional development initiatives, and hardware and software resources.

So why have we developed and written about such an approach? Teachers in primary and secondary classrooms face ever-increasing expectations and greater levels of accountability. Rapid developments in ICT and much espoused assumptions about how such technology will change learning environments remain among the major professional challenges faced by the profession.

Over the last decade, ratios of computers to students have decreased in many countries, and an increasing number of schools use 1-to-1 computing (one computer or mobile device per student). Interactive whiteboards (IWBs) have found their way into a large number of classrooms, and the power and potential of mobile technologies have begun to be recognized. New communications systems not only enable messages to be distributed instantly to all teachers, students, and/or parents, but also allow collaborations between classes in different schools and even different countries, as well as interactions with local, national, and international subject experts. Virtual worlds create new environments for learning that we are only just beginning to imagine.

INTRODUCTION

In any one school, we typically find teachers and students with diverse levels of experience and confidence with technology. Some are creative and skilled with their ICT use, while others resist, resent, or fear the challenges that technology represents. Even those who are using existing technologies will face the prospect of needing to continually learn and change.

Professional development for teachers in ICT thus remains a major educational imperative, presenting significant financial and strategic challenges to school systems and governments internationally. Numerous studies point to the limitations of traditional professional development approaches, which focus on skills-based training within competency-oriented frameworks. This research instead emphasizes the importance of a positive attitude toward integration, enthusiasm, lack of anxiety, and approach to teaching and learning as key factors in ICT adoption by teachers (Ertmer & Ottenbreit-Leftwich, 2010).

Effective ICT professional learning requires the development of attitudes, values, and beliefs that foster confidence and an openness in teachers toward ongoing learning and adaptability to change. It also requires changes in school cultures and established understandings of the way teacher learning is approached. There is a strong case for ICT professional development approaches that promote lifelong technology learning where teachers are more self-directed in identifying what they need to learn and in undertaking the actual learning process.

The approach to teacher professional development we describe in this book and on our website, http://technologytogether.scu.edu.au, incorporates such an emphasis. The Technology Together model offers guidance to those who support and assist teachers as learners. It inspires confidence to challenge the teachers with whom you work—and particularly to recognize the benefits of fostering learner independence rather than dependence.

Technology Together: Whole-School Professional Development for Capability and Confidence is intended to guide teachers and schools toward becoming capable technology users so that new and emerging ICT can be integrated into classrooms in creative, purposeful, student-centered ways. The Technology Together website provides a wide range of resources to assist you to implement the model in your school and to support the learning of your colleagues. Together, these resources detail the philosophy, theory, principles, and practices that make up the Technology Together process, providing opportunities for you to consider how these ideas can best be applied in your own school context.

Quotes and Resources

Throughout this book we place a strong emphasis on maintaining the teachers' voices and sharing comments, feedback, stories, and suggestions from participants who have been directly involved with implementing Technology Together in their schools. This book contains numerous quotes from participants. Quotes throughout the book made by teachers and school leaders who participated in the development of Technology Together appear in italicized paragraphs such as this one:

> *Participation in the Technology Together project has led to a cultural change in our school.*

There are more than 70 resources in *Technology Together: Whole-School Professional Development for Capability and Confidence*. Throughout this book you will see **Resource** set in boldface. **Resource** alerts you to a figure, a table, a form, or a display that is keyed to the List of Resources in Appendix A. Some of the resources are downloadable from the authors' website.

Chapter Summaries

Chapter 1 explains why a whole-school approach to ICT learning is so important and how the Technology Together model addresses this need. We describe what it means to be a capable technology user and why a focus on values, attitudes, and beliefs is beneficial. We present feedback from teachers who have developed and implemented the Technology Together process to explain how it can benefit school communities. We also discuss the theoretical foundations of the approach, grounding the metacognitive approach firmly in contemporary understandings of learning and educational change. Finally, we explain how the Technology Together website, used in conjunction with this book, can support your school to implement Technology Together.

Chapter 2 provides an overview of the eight foundational pillars—key ideas serving as a framework for Technology Together—including an introduction to the metacognitive approach that underpins the process. We also explore the metaphor of ICT learning as a journey, an image we have found valuable in supporting our fellow teacher-travelers. We explore how this metaphor can assist teachers to navigate the complex landscape of ICT learning and see their journey as an adventure and process of cultural discovery.

Chapter 3 provides guidance that schools need to get started in planning to implement the model. We divide this process into 10 steps and provide a checklist to help ensure you have everything in place.

Chapter 4 focuses on the very important process of mentoring within the metacognitive framework. We explain what makes the model's mentoring different from mentoring that normally occurs in schools and, particularly, how mentors can focus on developing capability as distinct from competence. The chapter provides guidance to mentors on being mindful to affects, fostering motivation, and developing appropriate learning strategies.

Chapter 5 places a specific focus on challenging and supporting teachers' pedagogy. We present six strategies for stimulating teachers to reflect deeply on their pedagogical beliefs and on how ICT can most effectively support student learning.

Chapter 6 focuses on the process of working with teachers to set learning goals and to implement ICT initiatives in their classrooms. We scaffold the process with a series of stimulus resources focused on metacognitive goals, leadership goals, recreational goals, skills goals, and pedagogical goals. We conclude the chapter with suggestions for showcasing achievements—both of students and teachers.

Chapter 7 brings all the elements together, providing a suggested schedule for how Technology Together can be structured across a school year, while emphasizing the importance of flexibility and continuous evaluation and refinement of the process. We also include a section with advice on avoiding potential pitfalls and sustaining the process.

Technology Together at a Glance

An at-a-glance chart for implementing the Technology Together approach follows. This chart indicates which chapters are especially well-suited for getting started (Chapters 2 and 3) and which chapters are well-suited for the ongoing implementation of the process (Chapters 4–6).

In the at-a-glance chart (next page), note that a four-term system (typical in Australia and South Africa) and a two-semester system (used in parts of the U.S. and Canada) have a first cycle, two mid cycles, and a last cycle. A three-term system (typical in the U.K., Canada, and the U.S.) has a first cycle, one mid cycle, and a last cycle.

INTRODUCTION

Technology Together Model at a Glance

DECIDING TO GET INVOLVED
School leaders hear about Technology Together, read this book, and decide to implement Technology Together in their school.

Optional decision to involve an external Technology Together partner (See Chapter 3)

Typically end of prior year

ANALYSIS
School undertakes an analysis process
(see Chapter 3)

PLANNING
School decides who will play key roles and what strategies will be used
(see Chapter 3)

INTRODUCTION
Technology Together is introduced to staff, potentially through a staff development day
(see Chapter 2)

FIRST CYCLE
Teachers set goals and are supported to implement learning strategies (see Chapter 6)

Discussion of a range of elements influencing teacher and student learning
(see Chapters 4 and 5)

Reflecting on and celebrating learning achievements (see Chapter 6)

Typically first quarter of school year

Evaluating and refining the process

MID CYCLE/S
Teachers set goals and are supported to implement learning strategies

Discussion of a range of elements influencing teacher and student learning

Reflecting on and celebrating learning achievements

Typically second and third quarters of school year

Evaluating and refining the process

LAST CYCLE
Teachers set goals and are supported to implement learning strategies

Discussion of a range of elements influencing teacher and student learning

Reflecting on and celebrating learning achievements

Typically final (fourth) quarter of school year

Sustaining the process into the future

TECHNOLOGY **TOGETHER** | Whole-School Professional Development for Capability and Confidence

CHAPTER **1**

Technology Together: A Whole-School Teacher-Learning Model

If you are reading this book, you probably already realize the importance of information and communication technology (ICT) for you and your school. You are not alone. Teacher professional learning for ICT integration is a major priority and challenge across the globe. Some people view technology learning as a problem for individual teachers—with the onus on the teachers themselves to be responsible for "keeping up." Other people view technology professional learning as the responsibility of a school or school system to ensure their staff continue to learn in a changing educational environment. Yet others recognize that teacher professional learning is a collaborative, collective, and complex phenomenon, particularly when it comes to technology. If you share any of these views, then this book is for you.

Why Develop a Whole-School Approach to ICT Learning?

The rationale for ICT integration in classrooms is two-fold. First, the ability to utilize emerging technologies has become the new, essential literacy for the 21st century. For future generations to maximize their capacity to operate within competitive and technologically driven economies, it is critical to foster students' technology abilities at every level of schooling. Second, and perhaps most importantly, the pedagogical integration of ICT across the curriculum provides many opportunities to maximize student motivation, engagement, independence, and individualization in teaching and learning, as well as to enhance student achievement, create new learning possibilities, and extend interaction with local and global communities (see for example, Dwyer, 2007; MCEETYA ICT in Schools Taskforce, 2005; Passey, Rogers, Machell, & McHugh, 2004).

Yet, despite years of focus on ICT integration, research continues to highlight issues related to teachers' ICT skills and level of confidence, as well as the limited ways most teachers use technology (Lundin, 2002; Russell, Finger, & Russell, 2000). Redmond and Brown (2004) observe that "While the ICT pioneers continue to traverse unmapped areas, the middle and late adopters are finding it difficult to continue without knowing their destination" (p. 14). More recently, Ertmer and Ottenbreit-Leftwich (2010) point out that technology is still not often used to support the student-centered instruction believed most beneficial for facilitating learning, and that even among teachers who claim to have student-centered, constructivist practices, technology use is generally not innovative. These authors argue that good teaching is effective only when combined with relevant ICT tools and resources—that we should expect teachers to use the most appropriate technology tools in the same ways that we expect other professionals, such as doctors, mechanics, and police, to do so.

Achieving appropriate, creative, and pedagogically sound ICT integration in a school curriculum, however, presents significant systemic challenges. Focused efforts and funding to support teacher professional learning has often lagged behind a push to infuse hardware and software into classrooms. Many developed countries have an aging population of teachers, the majority of whom did not receive preservice training in computer use. These teachers face considerable challenges in integrating new and emerging technologies across a diverse range of classroom situations.

Some people suggest that young, beginning teachers will be change agents, expecting that they—similar to the much-discussed "digital natives"—will already be confident with technology. Because new teachers have had exposure to ICT integration ideas in their preservice education, the assumption is they will carry these ideas into their classrooms and be well-placed to spread knowledge, skills, and practices to more experienced teachers. Although this may partially be the case, there are several problems with this thinking. First, research suggests that young, beginning teachers moving into the profession with new ideas often meet with a teaching culture that actively discourages such innovation (Ertmer & Ottenbreit-Leftwich, 2010). Second, this proposition assumes that all young people are confident and capable with technology—something research and personal experience suggest can be a misleading stereotype (we discuss this in Chapter 5). Young, beginning teachers may be more familiar with technology than their grandparents and parents, but not all of them pick up new skills and acquire knowledge easily. Additionally, the technologies young teachers have become familiar with in their youth may not necessarily be the same as those they find in their future classrooms. Beginning teachers, like all teachers, are going to need to keep learning. Will young teachers also become complacent about the technologies and pedagogies they now use? How will they cope with continual change?

We can be certain that technological change is continual and inevitable and that most of this change will be unforeseen and largely unpredictable. Twenty years ago the widespread use of interactive whiteboards and laptop computers, as we now have in many classrooms, was unimaginable. While laptops roll out en masse, a further revolution is underway, as handheld mobile devices and tablets saturate workplaces and homes and become set to provide the next major opportunity (and challenge) for schools. What the next wave of technological change will bring is the subject of much speculation:

> Learning about technology is equivalent to asking teachers to hit a moving target. Teachers will never have "complete" knowledge about the tools available, as they are always in a state of flux. (Ertmer & Ottenbreit-Leftwich, 2010, p. 260)

The entire field of technology and education is characterized by change, imagination, and a vision about the future. As Strudler (2010) has poetically claimed:

> It's about the dreams of what could be, the realities of what is, and the efforts to whittle away at the gap between the two. The dreams, of course, are dynamic and change with the field; the realities, however, are laden with challenges and have evolved more slowly than many of us might have hoped. (p. 221)

There will always be new technologies to challenge the ways teachers think about and approach classroom pedagogy—always another itch to scratch! So, how well do the cultures within our schools support teachers, young and old, beginning and experienced, who want to innovate in their use of ICT? And how well do our schools support teachers who are not eager to innovate—those who are nervous or hesitant about technology integration as a whole?

Traditionally, schools and school systems have either not responded at all, or have tended to provide directive-style training to introduce specific technologies (hardware or software) or new teaching ideas. However, with computer technology evolving so rapidly and the availability of diverse highly beneficial software, hardware, web-based resources, and new teaching ideas increasing exponentially, such approaches become problematic and unsustainable. Directive-style training not only becomes outdated quickly, but it often results in a low retention and implementation rate as teachers have difficulty transitioning skills and teaching ideas from a training context to their daily workplaces (Phelps, Graham, & Kerr, 2004).

Professional development in ICT is often offered to teachers on a voluntary basis, and it rarely requires demonstrated application of what has been learned. As a result, teachers who are highly motivated to learn about ICT are most likely to benefit from professional development, while those who are anxious, hesitant, or apathetic are left further behind. Opportunities for more systematic support and encouragement of all teachers to be involved in ICT professional learning frequently rest within schools' daily processes and practices rather than in formal training approaches.

Some approaches to teacher training and professional development focus primarily on enhancing teacher knowledge. The TPACK (technological pedagogical and content knowledge) model (American Association of Colleges for Teacher Education Committee on Innovation and Technology, 2008; Mishra & Koehler, 2006), for example, is gaining prominence in educational contexts. This model focuses specifically on three primary forms of knowledge: technological knowledge (TK), pedagogical knowledge (PK), and content knowledge (CK).

The need for knowledge is relatively easy to address—knowledge can be shared and exchanged and passed from teacher to teacher via books, websites, workshops, staff meetings, and so on. However knowledge, while important, is only part of the picture in terms of teacher professional learning. Teachers need to value technology as an instructional tool and have the willingness, openness, and capacity to adopt and adapt their teaching practices. For many teachers, this is not an easy journey:

> ICT in the classroom fundamentally challenges a person's psyche. It makes you question who you are and what you are doing. This is both profound and threatening. This understanding clarifies the reasons behind the "avoidance" behaviors … and encourages us to not be dismissive of the conflicts faced by individual teachers. It is not techno-fear, it is disempowerment and a loss of the sense of self. (Lloyd & Yelland, 2003, p. 93)

A significant body of evidence now suggests that teachers' attitudes toward ICT and their pedagogical beliefs influence whether and how they will embrace ICT (Ertmer & Ottenbreit-Leftwich, 2010; Judson, 2006; Levin & Wadmany, 2006–2007).

A school's culture, context, and structure can significantly influence whether, and to what extent, teachers perceive a benefit in using ICT, are motivated to learn, are encouraged and supported, or feel anxious. Schools are fundamentally social organizations and implement reforms and innovations through localized social processes. How change is viewed and approached is very much influenced by school culture—the norms, values, beliefs, traditions, and rituals that build up over time and shape how people think, feel, and act in schools (Howard, 1999). Each school, and even each team of teachers in a school, has norms that guide behavior, and instructional practices and peer pressure can both positively and negatively affect outcomes in terms of ICT integration (Ertmer & Ottenbreit-Leftwich, 2010). The cultures and practices at work within schools can either reinforce a belief that ICT is a separate part of the curriculum and "someone else's responsibility," or they can promote a context in which ICT is seen as integral to teaching and learning and, therefore, part of all teachers' responsibilities. School cultures can support continual learning, change, and risk taking, or they can discourage or simply fail to embrace it.

For these reasons we see technology learning as integrally entwined with the cultural practices at work in a school. To be effective, a whole-school approach is needed—one that considers the complex interplay of a range of factors that affect technology learning and hence integration.

What Is Technology Together?

The Technology Together model is a holistic and flexible learning process that can be implemented in primary and secondary schools to help all teachers embrace and integrate ICT effectively into their pedagogy. The approach has been developed by teachers for teachers, through an action research initiative. Ideally, the approach is adopted by a school for a 12- to 18-month period and is best approached as an ongoing learning process rather than a project in the sense that it will become embedded into the schools' regular planning and functioning.

The Technology Together approach is based on eight foundational pillars:

1. Technology learning is different from technology training.
2. Technology competency is different from technology capability.
3. Adoption and integration of technology is influenced by teachers' attitudes, beliefs, values, motivation, confidence, and learning strategies.
4. Technology (ICT) learning is complex and is influenced by school culture.
5. A whole-school approach maximizes student outcomes.

6. Leadership is important in establishing a supportive school environment.
7. How teachers learn is just as important as what teachers learn.
8. Technology learning can enhance teacher professionalism and stimulate change in school culture.

We explore these pillars in some detail in Chapter 2.

At one level, the approach aims to increase teachers' confidence in using technology and to enhance and diversify teachers' ideas and knowledge about how to integrate ICT into the classroom and across the curriculum. However, Technology Together is not only about learning specific skills. Rather, it aims to empower teachers to take control of their own technology learning, and it seeks to build a supportive, whole-school environment rich in teacher reflection and dialogue. Technology Together is about lifting the profile of professional learning and making ICT integration a priority in the school. As one Technology Together participant commented:

> *Technology Together provides a foundation to convince people that they are capable and confident to do new things—you need to have this before we can create real, new change.*

Technology Together provides ideas and resources that act as stimuli to support individual teachers and whole schools in setting ICT implementation goals and adopting appropriate strategies to achieve those goals. Because Technology Together is grounded in experiential learning, encouraging teachers to experiment with initiatives in their classrooms, it results in immediate change and benefits for both teachers and students.

The process is not intended as a quick fix or a one-size-fits-all model, but rather as a responsive, highly flexible process that can be adapted to local needs and specific classroom contexts. Central to the approach is the recognition that every school, teacher, classroom, and student is different. Only you, in your own specific context, know what is best for you and for the teachers and students with whom you work. Technology Together acknowledges the central importance of school culture in influencing change and recognizes that schools need to adapt their approaches in response to their school culture. In this way, Technology Together is as relevant for schools that have had extensive ICT implementation in place for many years as it is for those schools that are still struggling to engage with new technologies. The process meets individual teachers "where they are" on the technology-learning ladder and focuses on developing teachers' capability—their ability to continue learning and adapting to technological change.

Although Technology Together focuses on technology, the Technology Together principles have shown it to be a process with broad benefits that extend beyond ICT. The process helps teachers better understand change and the need for ongoing, lifelong learning, which not only can transform their approach to broader professional learning and development, but also can help reinvigorate their understanding of students' learning.

To summarize, the Technology Together model has the following six principles:

1. **Prioritizing whole-school development.** Its focus is not on individual teachers alone, but on helping all staff within a school (teachers, support staff, and administration) to work together as a community.

2. **Creating a climate for learning.** It aims to develop a school culture that supports teachers' professional learning—a culture where dialogue among teachers is increased and teachers come together to support one another.

3. **Acknowledging and accepting change.** It helps individuals come to terms with the constant and rapid rate of technological change and encourages all teachers to accept and embrace this change and become independent, confident ICT learners.

4. **Increasing teachers' confidence and motivation to use technology.** It is founded on the premise that ICT adoption and integration is influenced by teachers' attitudes, beliefs, values, motivation, confidence, and learning strategies. It focuses as much on these influences as on development of specific skills.

5. **Emphasizing immediate learning outcomes for students.** It stimulates teachers to engage in creative and innovative ICT integration activities in their classrooms. It works to diversify teachers' ideas and knowledge about how to integrate ICT and implement their learning in the classroom, with immediate outcomes for students.

6. **Enhancing teachers' professionalism.** Its approaches are those advocated and promoted in many professional contexts and by many professional bodies. They are recognized as enhancing quality teaching.

The Technology Together motto, "I can–You can," emphasizes the strong focus on building teachers' confidence with ICT integration. **Figure 1.1** represents the collaborative and supportive underpinnings of the model, with teachers working together to build a stronger school culture for learning.

Figure 1.1   The "I can–You can" motto from the Technology Together logo

Capability versus Competency-Based Approaches

Technology Together makes an important distinction between competence and capability. We are all accustomed to ICT learning contexts that use directive-style training and focus on developing specific skills. It is easy for organizations, schools included, to send staff for training on how to use specific software programs or new systems. This type of training typically requires teachers to sit in a computer lab or training room for an hour, three hours, or a whole day (or more) as they are walked through details on what to do, when to do it, and how to do it.

Learning the steps to operate software or hardware is helpful in raising our awareness of what is possible and introducing us to what we need to do. But how much of this learning do we retain, transfer, and use after the training is finished? The ability to use software or hardware under controlled conditions and with readily available support may heighten our enthusiasm and yet give us a false sense of security and confidence. We may feel like we know all we need to know and then become disillusioned when we return to our workplace and encounter problems or difficulties that the training did not prepare us for.

The implications, however, may be more significant than this. Research shows that directive-style training can, at times, have a diminishing impact on individuals' confidence with technology, and it can limit flexibility and responsiveness to technology integration. Such training can unconsciously reinforce our dependence on others to teach us, that is, position us as novices while others are experts. When the next new software or hardware becomes available, or even a new version of familiar software, we look to training to show us how to use it.

Our approach is premised on the notion that, although it is important to be able to perform specific computer tasks, have specific skills, and be competent in ICT use, it is much more critical to strive toward technology capability. Capability indicates the confidence to try new things, to be adaptable, to problem solve, and to engage in continual, lifelong technology learning. The Technology Together approach thus focuses on helping teachers become more self-directed in identifying what they need to learn and in undertaking the actual learning.

The distinction between competency and capability is as much about values, attitudes, and beliefs as it is about a particular approach to technology learning. So while implementing Technology Together will no doubt include skills-based training, its balance with more authentic approaches to learning and its unique focus on the role of teachers' values, attitudes, and beliefs in learning sets Technology Together apart from most other approaches to teacher professional development in ICT.

Focusing on Teachers' Values, Attitudes, and Beliefs

The Technology Together approach is founded on the understanding that ICT adoption and integration by teachers (and students) is greatly influenced by their attitudes, beliefs, values, motivation, confidence, and learning strategies. The model therefore employs a metacognitive approach that encourages teachers to think of themselves as technology learners. We believe the metacognitive approach develops teachers' confidence with computers and their willingness to try new integration ideas. It can also significantly influence their understanding of how students learn and how they can support students to become strong, metacognitively aware learners themselves. Some teachers find such substantial value in the metacognitive approach that they adopt it as a teaching strategy with their own students (see Chapter 5).

When teachers are prompted to think about their values, beliefs, and past experiences, they often start to recognize factors that affect their learning. This recognition can bring key insights into how teachers help themselves change. It can help teachers to realize the strengths and limitations of various learning strategies and to change their perspectives and behaviors. Technology learners can also be prompted to see that becoming a proficient technology user relies more on attitudes and learning strategies than on having a magic personal quality or skills set, as explained by one Technology Together participant:

Generally, teachers observe others with computer skills and think that they somehow attained the skills by magic. They think that they deserve the same dose of magic. They need to be convinced that they can get there if they approach the situation with a positive attitude.

The metacognitive approach (discussed in more detail in Chapter 2) encourages teachers to think of themselves as technology learners, to move outside their comfort zones, and to try new strategies with their students. Reflecting on values, beliefs, and experiences can also prompt teachers to think more critically and constructively about their pedagogical practices. The model thus aims to help teachers reach an "*aha* moment" of understanding—a belief that if "I can, You can."

Technology Together Works

This book's Preface outlines how Technology Together has been developed through research and informed by empirical evidence as to what helps teachers with diverse ICT backgrounds engage in sound professional learning. This research suggests that a metacognitive approach can greatly benefit many teachers, particularly those who lack confidence with technology. Technology Together has been developed by teachers, for teachers, to reflect the real needs and contexts of schools. However, the best way of gauging whether the model works is through the words of teachers who have participated in the process. These teachers have told us that the Technology Together process can

- Motivate teachers to experiment and try new things

  [These] strategies empowered staff to become more playful, engaging with the technology in a safe and comfortable environment that allowed them to be more confident risktakers. Through playfulness and exploration, teachers were able to commence their journey at their level, in their comfort zone, and as confidence increased they then extended their capabilities.

- Increase teachers' confidence to learn

  The capability approach to ICT learning has far surpassed our previous competency based approach. In contrast to our previous checklist mentality, teachers are now more open to problem solving with ICT, taking risks with software and hardware, and more than this, teachers are excited about the huge potential for ICT to enhance the educational outcomes of their classroom.

- Create a "can do" attitude

Through feeling valued in participating in this project, some teachers changed the way they view many things about school. With increased confidence they were able to look at most problems around the school with an attitude of "I know there is a solution" rather than "I give up."

- Build a learning community

More staff members are suggesting strategies to others to help solve their problems.... Teachers do not feel isolated—there is always someone to talk to regarding ICT issues.

- Change teachers' general attitudes toward professional learning

Participation in the Technology Together project has led to a cultural change in our school. The executive teachers have previously been hesitant at implementing some professional development because experience has shown that it was rarely accepted as important and often met resistance. This project has provided the platform to approach other whole-school development opportunities with enthusiasm and a sense of collegial growth.

- Enhance school leaders' relationships with teachers

The opportunity to work with a broad range of staff in a professional yet non-threatening situation has resulted in a greater awareness of where people are at, the needs of the community, and how best they can support staff in an active and vital manner.

- Change teachers' relationships with their students

Staff members recognize that students are often highly skilled in ICT and keen to share their knowledge with teachers. This is a highly significant shift in the perception of good teaching practice at our school. No longer is the teacher seen as the receptacle of all ICT knowledge.

- Lead to change in school culture

> *Technology Together has proved to be an outstanding success at (our school).... The attitude of teachers toward ICT in general terms has undergone a momentous change. It is now taken for granted that ICT is a part of everyday teaching and learning at our school. ICT enjoys a much higher profile, and discussion surrounding it is commonplace.*

That said, we acknowledge the complex range of factors that influence teachers' ICT learning. In fact, this very complexity led to developing the process around a metacognitive approach. No two individual teachers are the same, nor are any two school communities. The Technology Together model can provide you with a framework, ideas, tips, resources, and suggestions, together with stories and real-life examples of teachers' experiences. However, ultimately it is your interpretation and experimentation with how it will work best in your own school environment that will contribute most to its success.

Teachers need to have ownership over the learning process and be motivated and engaged. In developing the Technology Together process we recognized that such enthusiasm and commitment cannot be assumed. This book provides guidance on how to introduce and implement the learning approach in a way that respects the particularities of your school but also builds motivation and enthusiasm. However, there will always be some staff resistant to ICT integration or to ongoing professional learning and change. Technology Together endeavors to cater to these circumstances by providing guidance and tips on how to gradually and subtly engage all teachers. Nevertheless, we also acknowledge that teachers (just like students) cannot be made to learn. By influencing school culture, the process aims to ensure that even the most reticent teacher will be attracted by the conversations and activity that emerge as colleagues learn together without fear of being exposed as deficient or unable to keep up with changing technologies.

How Technology Together Differs from Previous Approaches

If you are a school leader or teacher at a school where technology has been a feature of the learning environment for some time, you will likely have already tried many different forms of professional development and be asking yourself whether Technology Together is relevant or can add value to your school.

As we have discussed, technology is rapidly changing as new hardware, software, resources, and integration possibilities are constantly emerging. How well are your teachers placed to embrace, and thrive on, this change? Even if all teachers in your school are confident technology users, Technology Together can further invigorate a culture of embracing and sharing ideas and of collaboration and mutual support. It can also challenge and nourish teachers' professionalism and further build positive relationships with students.

The schools involved in developing Technology Together report that it is substantially different from previous ICT professional development approaches implemented by their schools. Typically, schools say that their previous approaches emphasized acquisition of skills or performing specific tasks and that they were initiated by corporate directives, driven by ICT experts, and founded on a "just in case" philosophy. Often these approaches involved sending teachers out of school for training of questionable long-term value. Technology Together was identified as contrasting with previous approaches by

- Reaching a greater number of staff,
- Supporting people to get involved and to try new things,
- Acknowledging that each teacher starts from a different place,
- Encouraging identification and pursuit of personally relevant goals,
- Putting teachers in charge of their own learning,
- Giving teachers choice over their strategies and the people who support them,
- Prompting more discussion and sharing about technology,
- Building confidence by encouraging novices to teach each other,
- Allocating time on the basis of expressed need,
- Breaking down perceptions of one person as expert,
- Emphasizing the value of reflection and acknowledging feelings,
- Building collegiality and collaboration, and
- Actively prompting celebration of teachers' achievements.

Technology Together was also found to have a wider impact on school culture. Schools reported increased enthusiasm and willingness to learn new things and a realization by teachers that support was available and they did not need to feel isolated or judged. Participants commented on an increased willingness to learn with and from students and an increase in collaborative work and learning within and between grades. Overall, schools reported changes in teachers' attitudes toward professional learning and a higher level of professional discussion related to pedagogy:

> *Historically, reflecting on teaching and learning has never been a part of the school culture. This was reflected in lack of professional discussion, and … very few teachers*

evaluated practice.... There is now a commitment to ongoing reflection and professional development by executive and staff.

Acknowledging Technology Learning as a Complex Process

Most of us as educators readily acknowledge that teaching, learning, and education itself are very complex—many factors affect our work and students' learning. Some of these factors we can influence, but others are beyond our control. Sometimes we do not even recognize these issues and how they shape our work as teachers until after they have made an impact—if we recognize them at all.

At one level, this acknowledgment sounds quite obvious. However, for most of modern history and even into the present day, our school systems have been largely shaped by very different understandings. Our factory model of mass education has tried to ensure identical and measurable outcomes for all students—particularly with regard to the three Rs. This factory model represents an attempt to treat learning like an assembly line when, in fact, learning does not always happen in smooth, forward steps. As Loader (2007) describes, schools have been seen as separate from homes, workplaces, and even society; roles in schools are delineated (learners, teachers, administrators, aides); knowledge is compartmentalized into discrete disciplines (history, geography, mathematics); and there is a conceived "right way" to follow, according to curriculum and assessment.

In recent years, however, some very different theories and ways of thinking have begun to influence educational research and development. A body of thinking often referred to as complexity science (see, for example, Kauffman, 1995; Waldrop, 1992) questions our traditional models of education and challenges us to rethink whether we can understand all causes and effects and solve problems with simple remedies. It stimulates us to think differently about the dynamics at work in our classrooms and the ways we approach our teaching and learning (see, for example, Fullan, 2007; Hargreaves, 1998).

Complexity science is not one single idea but a group of theories that, when combined, provide an alternative understanding of human environments, such as schools and classrooms. These theories can be applied to many different open, nonlinear systems, of which schools and classrooms are examples. Complexity science acknowledges the difficulties in attempting to explain a whole system (like a school or a society) through an understanding of each part of a system separately. Complexity science aims to understand the interactions of the parts and focuses on the "small chance" changes that can influence the behavior of such systems (Stacey, Griffin, & Shaw, 2000). In schools, for instance, complexity science would suggest that we cannot reach an understanding of what works and what does not by focusing only on curriculum or teaching methods. Rather, students' learning is influenced by a complex interplay—a continual "dance" of many system components—teachers, students, families, and curriculum at one level and, at another level, community, business, popular culture, media, and so on.

As Davis and Sumara (2005) describe, "the goal of complexity is neither reduction nor certainty, but enhanced understandings of the common features of complex systems, while preserving the particularities of those systems" (p. 455). Thus, although complexity science does not attempt to predict or confidently claim that "if we all do X, then it will result in Y," it does help us to understand under what circumstances X will lead to Y, why X might not lead to Y, what else X might lead to, and challenges us to consider whether we really want Y to always eventuate from X in the first place. Complexity science might seem a little esoteric; however, the ideas from complexity science have recently begun to creep into mainstream educational thinking and practice, as well as the vernacular of everyday society. Take, for example, the idea of tipping points. This phrase, now in common usage in the media and society more generally, has particularly become popular when discussing the environment and climate change. Search the contents of any major scientific magazine (such as *New Scientist*, *Nature*, or *Scientific American*), and the headlines regularly speak of tipping points and draw on ideas from complexity science.

Another metaphor from complexity science is that of the butterfly effect—the idea that a flap of a butterfly's wings can create tiny changes in the atmosphere that might ultimately alter the path of a tornado. This metaphor, derived from the meteorological modeling of Edward N. Lorenz (Waldrop, 1992), is used to illustrate the notion that a small change at one place in a complex system can have large effects elsewhere.

So what value is complexity science to educators and school leaders who are interested in supporting ICT integration in classrooms? And how can these ideas possibly help us to enhance and support students' and teachers' learning?

Complexity science helps us to recognize that there are many factors that influence teachers' technology learning and that these factors all interact in unpredictable ways. The presence, for example, of highly supportive ICT experts within a school is not, in itself, any guarantee of a progressive ICT-using school culture. Sometimes quite the opposite can be true. Teachers, and in fact the whole-school community, can (in some circumstances) become overly reliant on such a person and therefore tend to avoid responsibility or the need to develop enhanced ICT skills. Similarly, having a supportive and encouraging school management team is in most cases very positive, but sometimes such encouragement can be interpreted less positively, leading to reticence and resistance. Sometimes schools have a very good hardware infrastructure in place, yet the hardware receives little or limited use. Some schools provide staff with lots of formal, well-planned professional development opportunities but find that teachers do not carry through with what they learn and do not progress beyond the basics. Other schools, however, rarely provide such training opportunities and yet have lots of incidental, ad-hoc, self-directed, and self-motivated learning happening every day. Some teachers and whole schools remain stuck with particular patterns of technology use while others, given the right conditions, can radically and rapidly transform themselves into an ICT-using community.

Now let's consider the notion of "sensitivity to initial conditions"—the idea that processes are critically dependent on initial conditions, the complexities of which may be unrecoverable or unknowable. Complexity science suggests that for us to effectively facilitate learning within a school or classroom setting, we need to acknowledge and at least partially understand and engage with the history of the system and the complex interaction of agents (teachers, students, parents, and school leaders, but also teachers' family and friends, and other influences, such as media and industry).

In the context of technology professional learning, sensitivity to initial conditions helps us to recognize that delivering training to all teachers in the same way will not result in the same outcome for each teacher. Some teachers with negative experiences in technology training contexts will bring these along as baggage that influences their attitude and confidence. Other teachers will be bored, and resentful of training, thus affecting the dynamic of the group. Of course, teachers' reactions may not be all negative. One teacher in the group may spontaneously comment on a past experience, and suddenly a previously reluctant, nervous, or resentful group of teachers transforms into a learning community—sharing success stories and creative ideas, supporting the less confident, and capitalizing on the most confident. The trainer is not likely to have been able to create this type of dynamic, even by following a formula.

The idea of sensitivity to initial conditions, then, posits that the starting point for any professional development within a school system must be an acknowledgment of these complex histories and the unpredictable influence they have on both individual and collective responses to change. This is not to assume that individuals or collectives are likely, or even able, to be aware of all these factors. They cannot. But reflective activities, such as journaling, can help stimulate the building of a holistic picture where the interplay of teachers' past experiences with their current and emerging state as technology users becomes better understood. In this way, reflective practice can assist us all to understand the influence of initial conditions and the complexity of change processes.

Complexity science views development and change as natural and evolutionary—neither imposed nor random (Doll, 1989). Change is associated with adaptation and, in particular, learning is viewed as adaptation to environment based on experience. This learning is not only an individual experience, but a shared experience of interaction and alignment within and between individuals or collectives to create new understandings, assumptions, or practices. These ideas are very fitting with the technology-learning environment, which requires continual and constant adaptation to new hardware, new software, and new and evolving ideas and practices.

Importantly, complexity science recognizes that change does not always occur in the direction of best practice or improvement. Sometimes things change and evolve simply because they do, and the processes and outcomes are not better or worse—only different. Some people believe that we should introduce new technologies or techniques only when they have been demonstrated to improve educational outcomes. Complexity science challenges this idea—and certainly the notion that any technology or technique will have the same outcomes in all educational settings. Complexity science instead focuses on the evolution of ideas and practices—trying things out to see if they work at a point in time—while emphasizing that the process of learning and adapting to change is critical in its own right. In other words, if things do not work the way we envisage, what is most important is the learning experience we have had along the way.

Another cornerstone of complexity science concerns difference and diversity. Complexity science focuses on what is atypical in systems—on instances when something does not work as expected. This focus is quite different from traditional scientific and educational practice, which center on controlling variables and on what works for the majority, ignoring any outliers. Similarly, where something does work well, complexity theorists look to the rich, complex, and often nuanced range of factors that come into play in influencing that success, rather than seeking simple, causal connections. Complexity science thus suggests that we pay attention to diversity and differences in each school and the complex interplay of factors, such as leadership, staffing patterns, hardware configurations, and individual and collective dynamics, including levels of commitment and enthusiasm regarding ICT use.

Complexity science emphasizes that both redundancy and diversity are required for a system to be healthy. Redundancy ensures that we all have things in common and a sense of unity, but diversity is critical because new evolutionary possibilities emerge from differences. Technology Together does not, therefore, seek to ensure that all teachers develop the same knowledge or skills sets. Nor does it seek to establish consistent learning goals across a school or to impose any one form of learning strategy on a group. Rather, teachers are encouraged to identify and celebrate their existing skills and knowledge, to set their own goals (individual or collective), and to reflect upon the most appropriate strategies to assist them (with capability in mind). Differences and diversity within the whole school are celebrated and recognized as influencing the system in unexpected ways.

To understand how complexity science can help us develop an effective ICT learning culture within our school, we also need to turn our attention to another concept associated with complexity science—that of homeostasis, or the tendency of a system to maintain a stable, constant condition in the face of changing circumstances because that condition embodies their histories (Davis & Sumara, 2005, p. 455). All school communities develop relatively stable patterns of happenings—traditions develop for approaching technology, and a comfort level develops among staff as to their level of usage. Although some impetus to continually learn is part of most school cultures and contexts, often the rate and nature of change and growth is more or less stable.

Occasionally, however, something happens that makes a major difference for a school. Maybe a chance happening leads to rapid and significant transformation in values, attitudes, beliefs, and practices within a school. Or maybe one teacher leaves the school and another arrives, or a teacher visits another school, sees how something is done, and brings back a new idea. These events cannot necessarily be predicted or caused, but they make an enormous difference in the dynamic within a school. Complexity science refers to these happenings as bifurcation points, or tipping points, as mentioned earlier. Tipping points occur when a system moves from one form of stability to another, prompted by conditions that may or may not be known, thus "expanding the space of the possible" (Davis & Sumara, 2005). Tipping points (bifurcation points) help explain how new patterns can spontaneously arise and evolve without leadership or plans.

The idea of bifurcation underpins much of the Technology Together process. As we elaborate in Chapter 4, the model seeks to enable circumstances that assist transitions (bifurcations) from the competency path of technology learning to the capability path. Further, the model places an explicit emphasis on teachers' recognizing and sharing *aha* experiences, which, in complexity terms, are often significant bifurcation points for teachers in relation to their learning (Phelps, 2005). For example, a realization by a less confident ICT-using teacher that learning a computer skill can be achieved independently through exploratory processes might, for that teacher, be a highly significant moment. The act of sharing this breakthrough with other teachers can profoundly influence the whole school. Creating a context where such events are acknowledged and valued is a critical part of Technology Together.

In summary, then, what does complexity science tell us about ICT professional learning for teachers? It helps us see that in designing and initiating any professional development in schools it is critical to acknowledge the complex interplay of factors that influence ICT integration, particularly the diverse histories, cultures, and contexts of each school. It is also critical to recognize that commonly employed professional development approaches may not necessarily influence teachers and schools in predictable ways. Effective ICT professional development can only be understood and achieved through a respectful recognition of the differences that exist within and between school cultures—differences that can either enable or constrain change. This recognition will inevitably mean that professional development approaches underpinned by a philosophy of "one size fits all" will likely falter because they fail to take account of the nuanced and complex differences that exist within and between schools.

The take-home message here is that ICT professional development needs to be about occasioning learning rather than assuming traditional training mentalities. We should not seek simplistic or generalizable approaches nor expect quick fixes that can be directly transferable to different contexts. We also cannot expect to rely on best practice models or think that what works for one classroom or school will work for another. Rather, we need to view classrooms and school communities as organic wholes and go with the flow of evolving with technologies together.

Technology Together as Evidence-Based Action-Oriented Practice

Technology Together has been developed through a rigorous and extensive process of participatory action research. The principles and practices of action research are also central to the process itself, although schools adopting the approach are more likely to conceive of the process as *action learning* rather than *action research*.

Action research is a form of collective, self-reflective inquiry undertaken by participants to improve their own social or educational practices, their understanding of these practices, and the situations in which these practices are carried out (Kemmis & McTaggart, 1988). Simply put, action research is intended to produce both change and improvement (action) and new understanding (research). Action learning embodies all the same principles of action research but puts less emphasis on making an original contribution to knowledge (as is usually required for research).

Action research and action learning are participatory and collaborative in that teachers shape a project's direction, decide its goals, set its pace, judge its success, and make decisions

Figure 1.2 Action research diagram illustrating the cyclic process of planning, acting, observing, and reflecting

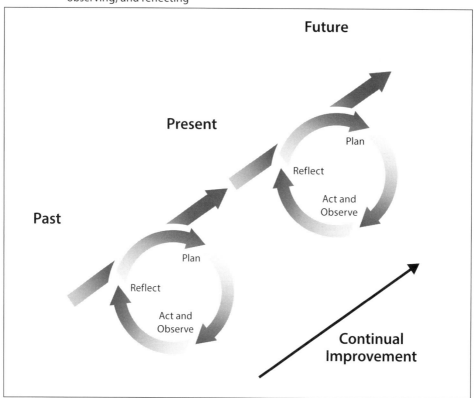

about future actions. Action research and action learning are envisaged as involving cycles of inquiry (typically, planning, acting, observing, and reflecting, followed by improved or refined planning, acting, observing, reflecting), as indicated in **Figure 1.2**.

What teachers learn in each step of the process will inform decisions and actions in subsequent phases. The process is systematic and rigorous and involves sound planning and considered collection of evidence upon which improvement is based. The process also involves discussion, reflection, and a focus on building a community of learners and enhancing teacher professionalism, including learning partnerships and critical friends. Technology Together, for instance, will be most effective if implemented over at least three cycles, with each cycle typically representing a school term (see the at-a-glance chart in the Introduction).

Some schools will choose to make the action learning or action research aspects of Technology Together explicit to teachers, particularly when research is accepted and embraced by the school community. Other schools may decide to place less emphasis on this process. However, we believe it is most vital that all schools approach Technology Together as an evidence-based, action-oriented practice.

For any initiative that a school chooses to implement, it pays dividends to collect good data to evidence and evaluate resultant change. Collecting data in Technology Together is important because it can directly inform the activities of school leaders and mentors. It can also provide stimulus for a school discussion about what works and what does not, as well as enable a school to share its experiences with other schools. For some schools, data collection will be an important means of providing accountability for resourcing and for reporting to school administration authorities, parent groups, and other stakeholders.

One means of providing this evidence and accountability is by documenting how far teachers travel in their ICT professional learning. This information, however, is not only for the purpose of reporting program outcomes. More importantly, it provides a way of celebrating achievements of individuals, groups, and the whole-school community. The stories about what happens in a school can be a very powerful means of sharing experiences, conveying progress to others, and celebrating achievements. As part of the Technology Together website (see the following section) we provide you with resources to help you collect both pre- and post-implementation data and other forms of evidence of learning as you go along.

The Technology Together Website

As indicated in the Introduction, the Technology Together authors host a website:

>   http://technologytogether.scu.edu.au

The Participants' Zone of the Technology Together website provides access to a range of resources and support materials for schools that are implementing the Technology Together approach. In the Participants' Zone you will find

- **Planning and data collection documents.** A range of resources, including the school analysis scaffolds and surveys that we discuss in Chapter 3;
- **Reflection stimuli.** Electronic versions of a range of handouts and pinups for supporting teacher reflection;
- **Staff meeting resources.** A range of PowerPoint presentations that you can use to

introduce Technology Together to your staff and to scaffold staff meeting discussions around elements of the metacognitive model. Most presentations are designed to take from 5–15 minutes.

- **Goal-setting scaffolds.** Resources that prompt teachers with a range of ideas to integrate ICT in their teaching and stimulate teachers to set goals, as discussed in Chapter 6.
- **Community.** Feedback from past participants indicates that schools value sharing their ideas and experiences with others. This section of the website provides a means of communicating with other Technology Together schools to share your ideas and tips.

Access the Participants' Zone is password protected. You will be directed to set up a user name and password. Access to some resources requires you to register your school. Directions and guidelines are provided on the website.

CHAPTER **2**

An Overview

In Chapter 1, we presented a rationale for the Technology Together program so that you could more readily identify what makes this professional development process distinctive and why such an approach offers significant potential in the current educational context. However, before you decide whether Technology Together is right for your school, it is important to explore in more detail the key underlying principles of the approach. In this chapter, we orient you to the "eight foundational pillars," or ideas, that make this approach unique. We then explain the particular metacognitive approach to technology learning that is so central to the process.

The Eight Foundational Pillars

For Technology Together to be most effective in your school, it is critical that all staff understand the eight foundational pillars that define it as a unique professional development process. These are the eight pillars:

1. Technology learning is different from technology training.
2. Technology competency is different from technology capability.
3. Adoption and integration of technology is influenced by teachers' attitudes, beliefs, values, motivation, confidence, and learning strategies.
4. Technology learning is complex and is influenced by school culture.
5. A whole-school approach maximizes student outcomes.
6. Leadership is important in establishing a supportive school environment.
7. How teachers learn is just as important as what teachers learn.
8. ICT learning can enhance teacher professionalism and stimulate change in school culture.

These eight pillars are explained in detail in the following sections. The Technology Together website provides access to resources to help present these ideas to your staff.

Pillar 1
Technology Learning Is Different from Technology Training

The Technology Together philosophy and approach has a degree of resonance with the old Confucian proverb, "Give a man a fish, and he will eat for a day; teach a man to fish, and he will eat for a lifetime." As a professional development process, Technology Together is not a short-term fix for immediate ICT needs, but an approach that focuses on building lifelong technology learning. Technology Together is based on research that clearly indicates that one-shot workshops without ongoing individual support often fail to meet the specific needs of most teachers.

It is understandable that technology learners want "quick fixes" and "ready answers." They are usually very happy when shown how to do something on a computer, but some are even happier if someone does a task for them. Technology learners often feel elated after they have completed a training session and been shown lots of "neat things." The problems often arise, however, when learners return to their own computers and find that things are different or do not go as planned. Often technology learners quickly become discouraged and do not use their new skills. A few days, weeks, or months down the road, they realize they cannot remember what they were shown. These learners will likely lose confidence and come to perceive themselves as "just not good with technology."

This is not to say that such training sessions do not have an important place—they do. However, the way technology learners perceive the training is critical to its value. If learners perceive these sessions as the place where "real" learning occurs and expect that they will know or be able to perform a skill after attending the training, they are often disappointed:

> *I've found it difficult to remember and retain learning, and consequently found it very difficult to implement anything successfully back in the classroom. This paradigm had many negative consequences, but most significantly it undermined my confidence regarding ICT, and I saw myself slipping further behind.*

The Technology Together approach recognizes that directive-style skills training has limitations in terms of flexibility and responsiveness to technological change and, for some learners, this type of training reinforces learning dependency rather than independence. Technology Together takes a more holistic approach to technology learning, helping teachers to identify and use strategies that support long-term outcomes—for them and their students. In other words, technology learning is a journey—not a destination.

Pillar 2
Technology Competency Is Different from Technology Capability

As mentioned in Chapter 1, Technology Together makes an explicit distinction between supporting teachers to become competent technology users versus supporting them to become capable technology users.

Competency-based approaches are widely employed in the teaching of computer skills in industry, technical and vocational education, and in schools. Under the competency-based system, importance is placed on learning and demonstrating specific and defined skills. These specific skills are taught within a controlled environment, such as a computer lab, with all learners using the same software, the same computers, and the same set of steps. Learners are then assessed as competent when they can perform these skills.

Capability, in contrast, "represents an integration of knowledge, skills and personal qualities used effectively and appropriately in response to varied, familiar and unfamiliar circumstances" (Cairns, 2000, p. 2). Many self-taught technology-using teachers may be seen as capable. These teachers use technology out of their own specific necessity and enthusiasm without substantial training. They are comfortable learning any software, willing to "have a go," and generally not intimidated by ICT. Capable technology-using teachers adapt well to rapid and ongoing change. They employ self-directed learning strategies and are willing to experiment with new software and hardware. They recognize and embrace appropriate avenues for classroom ICT integration and are prepared to persevere and problem solve when things do not go to plan.

Competency is, of course, an ingredient of capability. However, capable people are those who can operate in unknown contexts and with new problems. Capability is thus a much stronger attribute than competency in contexts of rapid change, such as is the case with technology. These ideas around capability, and how we can utilize them to help teachers in their technology learning, are explored in more detail in Chapter 4.

Pillar 3
Adoption and Integration of Technology Is Influenced by Teachers' Attitudes, Beliefs, Values, Motivation, Confidence, and Learning Strategies

Technology Together is founded on the premise that adoption and integration of ICT by teachers (and students as well) is influenced by their attitudes, beliefs, values, motivation, confidence, and learning strategies.

As such, Technology Together employs a metacognitive approach that encourages teachers to think of themselves as learners. In simplest terms, metacognition means "thinking about thinking" or "learning about learning." We believe that, for teachers, metacognition helps them develop confidence with technology and fosters motivation to try new integration ideas. Moreover, it can influence teachers' understanding of how their students learn and how to best support them to become strong, metacognitively aware learners.

When teachers are prompted to think about their values, beliefs, and past experiences, they often start to see a story emerge around the factors that have shaped their learning. In turn, this recognition can bring key insights into what needs to change. It can, for instance, assist teachers to realize the strengths and limitations of long-held assumptions about themselves as learners, of the learning strategies they employ, and of the attitudes and behaviors they display when faced with learning something new or challenging. By positioning themselves as technology learners, teachers can also be prompted to see that becoming proficient relies more on their attitudes and learning strategies than on having a "magic" personal quality or skills set.

Even for teachers who are relatively confident with technology, a metacognitive approach can prompt them to move outside their current comfort zones and try new things with their students.

We will return to the metacognitive approach and explore its value for Technology Together in more detail later in this chapter.

Pillar 4
Technology Learning Is Complex and Is Influenced by School Culture

Unarguably, technology integration brings significant change to schools and education as a whole. How schools view and approach this change is very much influenced by their school culture—the norms, values, beliefs, traditions, and rituals that build up over time. School culture, in turn, shapes how people think, feel, and act in schools and it has a significant impact on school improvement and how the school deals with change.

Technology Together recognizes the complexity of factors that influence ICT integration in schools. As outlined in Chapter 1, we acknowledge that there are no single linear or fail-safe approaches to supporting teacher (and student) learning and that not everything can be preplanned. Rather, the approach builds on the notion that reflective school communities can be supported to more readily embrace learning opportunities as they arise.

Technology Together builds on the idea that when individual teachers become more conscious of their values, attitudes, and beliefs about technology use, the culture of learning within a school will change as the collective values, attitudes, and beliefs around technology use evolve. We believe that changing the school culture to become one that values, embraces, and actively discusses ICT can lead to significant teaching and learning outcomes.

Pillar 5
A Whole-School Approach Maximizes Student Outcomes

Most schools will already include key teachers who are motivated and committed to ICT integration. However in many schools, if not all, there will also be a group of teachers who are either not confident or not motivated to integrate ICT.

Technology Together views ICT integration as the responsibility of *all* teachers, not only specialists or motivated teachers. We view ICT not as a separate subject, but as a tool that enhances education while also transforming and revitalizing it. Many schools come to recognize that it is not equitable for some students to experience ICT integration in their learning when others do not. When individual teachers also come to this realization, they will likely be motivated to make real changes in their teaching practice.

> *I thought I had missed the era of computers until I realized that my students hadn't, and if I wanted to be an effective teacher, I had to learn and use these new and fast-changing ideas in my classroom.*

Technology Together works within a collegial framework of school staff supporting each other's learning, rather than a model of "outsiders" coming in or of recognizing experts as the main or only source of assistance. The approach embodies sound principles of mentoring, but we use the term "companion mentor" to emphasize the dynamic of mentoring as "keeping company with," where teachers of equal or similar standing support each other to build self-confidence and capability.

Mentoring can also be a means of supporting change in a school's culture. It can build school community and collegiality and be valuable in supporting teachers to teach in ways that are new to them. Mentoring is critical to effectively integrate ICT across the school and to support the learning outcomes of students.

Pillar 6
Leadership Is Important in Establishing a Supportive School Environment

For teachers to effectively integrate ICT in learning and teaching, their school cultures need to be supportive, not only in resourcing technology access, but in encouraging teachers to continually learn and experiment. Teachers need to be encouraged, but not pressured, and supported, but not over-assisted. Although teachers need to be stimulated with ideas and given adequate resources, school cultures need to avoid promoting an impression that resources alone will be sufficient for effective ICT integration.

The school principal and other administrative school leaders play a key role in establishing and shaping school culture and vision, influencing which behaviors are acceptable and which are not. It is vital for school leaders to embrace ICT integration and the Technology Together process itself, since it is only with their support that real change will be possible. However, there are many other key leaders in schools: IT coordinators, individual teachers, parents, and students themselves can all affect a school's ICT culture and context. Technology Together thus establishes structures and processes to engage all key players in roles that will motivate, engage, and lead the school community.

Pillar 7
How Teachers Learn Is Just as Important as What Teachers Learn

Technology Together builds on the idea that *how* teachers learn is just as important as *what* they learn. For this reason, Technology Together is based around two components: initiatives and strategies. These two components go hand in hand in building teachers' ICT capability.

Technology Together schools identify and focus on initiatives that are most relevant to their own local context. They engage in goal setting as a whole school or with individual staff or both. No matter what initiatives individuals take on, the process encourages all teachers to challenge themselves. Some teachers undertake a one-year initiative while others choose a series of smaller initiatives, one per week or per term. Examples of initiatives might include anything from integrating spreadsheets into a lesson, creating digital stories, establishing a class wiki, or creating a digital photography exhibit.

The strategies implemented by individual teachers and schools are guided by the Technology Together process and underpinned by a metacognitive approach. At a school level, Technology Together might involve regular, informal teacher discussions at staff meetings, weekly or biweekly meetings, or similar small-group processes; blocks of side-by-side work with individuals or small groups, such as grade levels or key learning areas (KLAs); and time for sharing or celebrating achievements across the school. At an individual level, teachers will be encouraged to develop strategies for exploratory learning, problem solving, and appropriate help seeking within a context of collaborative and self-directed learning.

We talk more about initiatives and strategies throughout this book, providing many examples, ideas, and stimulus resources to support the process in your school.

Pillar 8
Technology Learning Can Enhance Teacher Professionalism and Stimulate Change in School Culture

Technology Together embodies a range of principles that contribute to effective professional development (Downes et al., 2001). As a professional development program, Technology Together is

- Rigorous, sustained, and adequate for long-term change of practice;
- Directed toward teachers' intellectual development and leadership;
- Designed and directed by teachers, incorporating the best principles of adult learning and involving shared decisions designed to improve schools;

- Experiential, engaging teachers in concrete tasks of teaching, assessment, observation, and reflection that illuminate the process of learning and development;
- Grounded in inquiry, reflection, and experimentation that are participant-driven, collaborative, and interactive, involving knowledge sharing among teachers and a focus on teachers' communities of practice.

In this sense, Technology Together is not only about professional development in relation to ICT. It is also a process that enhances teachers' professionalism by encouraging them to think deeply about the nature of teaching and learning. It engages them in professional dialogue and collaborative practice and promotes linking theory with practice. We encourage teachers to reflect critically on their own teaching practice and to document learning progress to provide an evidence base for their professional development.

Summary

The eight pillars described here provide the foundation of the Technology Together process. Although Pillar 3 points explicitly to the critically important role of a metacognitive approach to learning—that is, the central importance of thinking about thinking in order to learn how to learn—the other pillars are also tied to this premise. We turn now to a more detailed consideration of what a metacognitive approach is and what it potentially offers for improving technology integration in schools.

Introducing the Metacognitive Approach to Technology Learning

As previously mentioned, metacognition involves active control over the thinking processes involved in learning. A metacognitive approach is highly beneficial for ICT learning because it promotes lifelong learning by encouraging teachers to perceive themselves as learners and to realize that technology learning has no beginning and no end. Metacognition helps technology learners identify what influences their ICT use, both positively and negatively, including both past and recent experiences. The approach guides teachers to articulate their own learning goals, supporting them to be self-directed in identifying what they need to learn and how they go about the learning. It also encourages teachers to celebrate their learning achievements.

A key benefit of the metacognitive approach is that it assists teachers to effectively support other teachers' learning. Most of us enjoy helping other people—assisting them and making their learning easier. After all, that is our job as teachers, and it makes learners happy and makes us feel liked, wanted, and needed. Yet, as we will explain in Chapter 4, it is often when learners encounter difficulties that long-term learning occurs. This reality presents a challenge for all of us in our teaching practice, and particularly in our work with adult technology learners. The metacognitive approach challenges mentors and facilitators to move away from the (sometimes) more comfortable role of making learning easy and, instead, challenges teachers toward the realization that the difficulties and problems they experience are where their "real" learning occurs.

As well as supporting teachers' ICT learning and ability to support each other, a metacognitive approach can also have direct spin-offs for students. Some teachers find a metacognitive approach so valuable they employ it in their own teaching (see Chapter 5). They might employ a metacognitive approach in relation to ICT integration but also more generally as part of their overall pedagogical practice. By explicitly engaging students in thinking about their own thinking and learning about their own learning, teachers will foster lifelong learning capabilities for their students as well as themselves.

A metacognitive approach can also prompt teachers to reflect more critically on the nature of students' learning. This reflection is particularly valuable when teachers seek to find out how students best learn with and from technology—ideally through consulting with the students themselves.

The Three Metacognitive Dimensions: Affects, Motivation, and Strategies

The metacognitive approach assumes that learning is influenced by three key dimensions: affects (can I do this?—feelings, attitudes, and beliefs); motivation (why do I do this?); and strategies (how do I do this?).

Within each of these dimensions, research informing Technology Together has identified a range of elements as influencing technology learning. In the discussion that follows we provide a brief introduction to both the dimensions and these elements. In Chapter 4 we elaborate on the various elements, providing practical advice on how these ideas can be practically applied.

Affects

Affects refers to our feelings, attitudes, beliefs, and assumptions. Affects play a significant role in an individual's approach to technology and can also influence the whole culture of a school.

Much research over the past two decades has focused on the role of self-efficacy in technology learning (see, for example, the early work of Compeau & Higgins, 1995). Self-efficacy refers to individuals' beliefs in their capacity to perform on a particular task. It is not so much concerned with the skills you have, but with your personal judgment of these skills. Self-efficacy is different from self-esteem, which is a generalized evaluation of the whole self. Rather, self-efficacy is specific to a particular task or context. For instance, someone can have high self-efficacy as a singer but low self-efficacy as a technology user. Computer self-efficacy, then, is not about technology skills per se but rather individuals' beliefs about their skills, knowledge, and abilities.

When considering affective aspects of technology learning we also need to consider computer anxiety. Again, much research has documented and attempted to understand what might be defined as irrational, emotional distress experienced by an individual when using or considering the use of computer technology (Igbaria & Iivari, 1995). Quite obviously, people who are less anxious (technophrenics) are much more likely to interact with technology than people who are more anxious (technophobics).

Learned helplessness is another important affective element and is when learners, faced with challenges or difficulties, abandon problem-solving strategies. Put simply, such learners fail to help themselves and become "failure accepting" to avoid the implication of low ability. People who demonstrate learned helplessness often employ self-handicapping tactics, such as procrastination and blaming others in an attempt to circumvent responsibility for their lack of success or fear of failure.

Learned helplessness often relates to attribution; in other words, people's explanations for the causes of events in their life. The basic premise of attribution theory is that individuals' beliefs about what causes these events influence their expectations, which, in turn, influence their behavior. Typical attributions in relation to success include ability, effort, hard work, or luck/chance. Attribution can get in the way of good learning and sometimes is used as an excuse for not integrating ICT at all.

Motivation

The second metacognitive dimension is motivation. It seems fairly obvious that teachers need to be motivated in order to effectively integrate ICT in their teaching. Motivation has traditionally been considered as either extrinsic (driven by factors outside the individual) or intrinsic (driven by factors within the individual). In the case of ICT integration, extrinsic motivation might include curriculum requirements, school or department directives, or social and parental expectations. Intrinsic motivation might include teachers' personal interests or passions for ICT, teachers' beliefs in the importance of students learning to use technology, or teachers' observations that ICT engages and motivates students. Affective dimensions such as anxiety and self-efficacy influence motivation, shaping individual choices, goals, emotional reactions, effort, coping, and persistence.

For many people, perceived usefulness is one of the most important factors influencing their approach to technology. The term "perceived" is used here because it is not an objective matter of whether individuals actually would benefit from using technology, but whether they perceive there is a benefit. Perceived usefulness has an enormous influence on teachers' motivation to engage in technology learning and on how much a teacher will retain from learning contexts.

For teachers, perceived usefulness is relevant in two contexts: personal perceived usefulness (usefulness of technology in individuals' professional or recreational lives) and pedagogical perceived usefulness (usefulness of technology in the classroom). In working with teachers, it can be beneficial to consider both these contexts. Once we start to enhance teachers' personal perceived usefulness, this can also lead us to engage teachers in reflecting on their pedagogical orientation—their values, attitudes, and beliefs about what constitutes "good" teaching and learning.

Another key element related to motivation is goal orientation. In order to assist teachers to take control of their own learning, they need to be supported to realize that the first step is to personally take on some goals. Many new technology users fail to become capable simply because they do not strive to develop new skills or knowledge—they are not motivated to become goal orientated. Goal orientation also relates to the third dimension of the metacognitive approach: strategies.

Strategies

In the previous section, we considered the important role that goal orientation plays in motivation. Teachers need to be motivated by and through goals. Goal setting can thus be used as a strategy to foster, promote, and reinforce good technology use—and can be learned and practiced in order to improve teaching and learning outcomes.

A metacognitive approach encourages teachers to identify and reflect on role models for technology learning. Conventionally, many people think of a role model as someone who has an influential position, such as a parent, teacher, supervisor, or mentor—someone who provides an example for individuals to imitate. However, a role model can be anyone who provides us with stimulus for reflection on what we would like to be or, perhaps, not like to be (in this case, a negative role model). Role models can be used to actively construct our "ideal" or "possible" selves based on our needs and goals (Gibson, 2002).

Although all learning strategies play an important role in technology learning, a metacognitive approach focuses on those that promote capability rather than only competency. In particular, Technology Together encourages teachers to reflect on the strengths and weaknesses of different "pathways to learning" (namely, group instruction, individual instruction, self-directed learning, and peer-group learning) because expectations about their ability to learn in each context can significantly influence teachers' confidence with technology.

Some teachers, for instance, think that the only real way to learn a new computer skill is through formal training or by being shown how to do it—they have never given themselves permission to try learning new things on their own. Other teachers who already learn through self-directed exploration can believe that independent learning is somehow inferior. The realization that most proficient technology users do a good deal of self-directed, exploratory learning can be a big breakthrough (an *aha* moment). The concern of many novice technology users, that they will damage their computers if they explore, is one of the beliefs that can most stand in the way of ongoing learning. Technology Together actively promotes exploratory learning and "playfulness" and argues that such strategies can be taught to, and practiced by, technology learners.

Other elements of learning that Technology Together problematizes are memory and retention. Many novice technology users approach learning from a perspective of needing to memorize things. This is not surprising because technology is shrouded in jargon, and training often requires introducing learners to numerous "facts" and "terms," not to mention "steps." While memory does play a role, technology learners struggle when they focus on memorization as a learning strategy. Research surrounding memory and retention of learning (for example, Bjork, 1994) very convincingly indicates that when learning involves a degree of difficulty, it leads to long-term learning outcomes. Hence, training contexts that learners find to be too easy can be less effective than contexts that introduce a level of difficulty.

In any case, problems and problem solving are (unfortunately or fortunately) an integral part of technology use. Many novice technology users feel that problems only happen to them because they lack knowledge, skill, or experience and that problems never happen to experts. In fact, most experienced technology users will tell you that the more you use technology, the more likely it is that you will encounter problems. The ability to problem solve with technology is something that takes time, experience, patience, and perseverance—but most of all it requires the right attitude and applying the appropriate strategies. Gaining confidence to work through problems will only happen when teachers experience a few successes, and these successes will only occur when teachers have a go at problem solving. Metacognition can play a critical role in supporting this process.

Another key strategy element in the metacognive approach is volition and the related issue of attitude toward time. Volition refers to "sticking power" or the tendency to maintain focus and effort even in the face of difficulties and distractions. Time is usually acknowledged as one of the biggest influences on teachers' technology learning, and of course it is. Most teachers lead very busy lives and are drawn between many and varied commitments. However, time in itself is not a simple consideration and is closely associated with priority and motivation. School culture can exert a big influence on teachers' attitude toward time, particularly whether time spent learning ICT is perceived as an investment or a waste.

While exploratory learning, problem solving, and volition are all important strategies to support effective technology learning, there are times when all of us need to seek help. Help seeking can be a very appropriate strategy to deal with distraction, frustration, or a risk of giving up. However, some learners' conception of seeking help is to find an immediate answer, while others seek tips on how they can move their own learning forward. Helping teachers to better understand when, how, and why they seek help is also a key part of the metacognitive approach.

Reflection *on, in,* and *for* Action over Time

We have considered that a metacognitive approach focuses on three key dimensions that influence technology learning—affects, motivations, and strategies—and that each of these dimensions is made up of a range of interconnected elements. A metacognitive approach encourages reflection on these dimensions over time, prompting teachers to consider how each element has influenced their use of technology in the past, present, and future. In this way, Technology Together encourages teachers to reflect on and discuss the following questions:

- What past experiences have influenced your values, attitudes, beliefs, motivation, confidence, and learning strategies in relation to technology?
- How does your present context affect your values, attitudes, beliefs, motivation, confidence, and learning strategies?
- What are your possible, probable, and preferred futures with technology? How do you go about actively pursuing your preferred future?

When prompted to think about past and present computer use, it can help to confront the reality of current approaches to technology. It can be beneficial to identify the origins of your values, attitudes, and beliefs, and the strengths and limitations of the various learning strategies you have used and/or are using. Reflecting on the past and present is also an opportunity to affirm achievements and to put difficulties or lack of success into perspective.

Thinking about the future and where you see yourself as a technology user can help you engage more actively in creating that future rather than waiting to see where life takes you. In other words, recognizing that you can make a difference in your own learning is empowering. Most importantly, reflection provides a stimulus to change perspectives and behaviors.

A key part of Technology Together, then, is reflecting on the past, present, and future. However, this is not a static, "one-off" process. Rather, reflection is best approached as part of an ongoing learning process. Consistent with the action research/action learning framework that drives Technology Together, teachers are encouraged to engage in cycles of planning, doing/acting, observing, and reflecting. However, reflecting on action does not only occur at the end of each cycle. Rather, we also encourage teachers to reflect both during action and for action.

The Visual Model

Sometimes a visual model or diagram can help explain or communicate ideas effectively. However, it is always difficult to use a two-dimensional diagram to represent a very complex, dynamic, and ever-changing process. Although far from ideal, a visual model of the metacognitive approach may help you better understand and explain to school staff the ideas underpinning the approach.

This model, **Resource 1** | **Figure 2.1**, illustrates the triadic influence of affects, motivation, and strategies on teachers' technology learning. **Figure 1.2**, page 26, illustrates that a metacognitive process encourages teachers to reflect on these three influences in terms of their technology learning in the past, in the present, and what they would like for the future. (See also the Technology Together website for visual models.) Through cycles of planning, acting, observing, and reflecting, teachers strive toward their preferred futures. Throughout Chapter 4 we build on this model with specific ideas about how we can work with school staff to develop a capable ICT-using school community.

Resource 1 | **Figure 2.1** The visual model of the metacognitive approach to technology learning

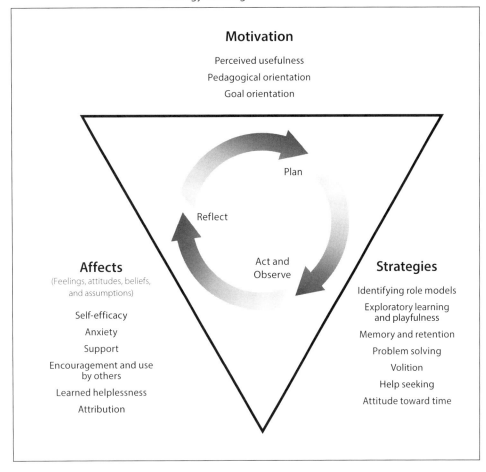

Technology Together as Learning Journey

Before concluding this chapter, we wish to introduce one final concept that helps with understanding the Technology Together process. Metaphors can play an important role in capturing teachers' interest and understanding of the process and the metacognitive approach more specifically. Metaphors play a central role in our construction of social reality and are embedded in our communication systems at cultural and societal levels (Lakoff & Johnson, 1980). Metaphors can challenge our understandings and learning approaches and transform our beliefs, values, and assumptions.

One metaphor that has proved useful is that of technology integration as "journey." This metaphor can provide meaning and support to learners because it assists them to view their learning as an ongoing, lifelong process—an adventure with ups and downs along the way.

As technology "travelers," teachers bring both luggage (affects) and a sense of their preferred direction (motivation) to the journey of technology integration. As travelers, they usually require a means of transport and some navigation strategies to reach their various destinations. If they pack wisely and cast off inappropriate "possessions" (feelings, attitudes, beliefs, and assumptions) along the way, the travelers can make room for new possessions and so enhance their journey.

Travelers need to know the broad direction in which they are heading and why they are going there (their goals). That said, some of the most exciting traveling adventures start from only a broad sense of direction with the main goal being adventure itself. However, without conviction that their journey is worthwhile, travelers are unlikely to go far.

Travelers also need some means of navigation: a map to guide their travels (metacognition). They may start with a large-scale map to provide broad direction, but as travelers progress they need more detailed maps to facilitate their journey. Transport, the method they choose to progress through their adventure, needs planning, acting, and evaluating, and if travelers find one form of transport ineffective or one route inaccessible, they should choose another. Through reflection on our experiences, we learn which approaches are better than others in certain circumstances. So, too, in the technology domain, we need to develop understandings of which learning strategies are best employed in each context.

Along the way, travelers will experience many cultural encounters—experiences that teach them something about themselves and others whom they meet. Such encounters influence the luggage they carry, the direction they take, the navigation they use, and ultimately their journey's destination. We gain from our journeys the photos and memories of our experiences, which combine, through reflection, to teach us about our present situation. These memories and reflections also provide the impetus and excitement to continue our traveling adventures in the future.

CHAPTER **3**

Planning for Implementation

In this chapter, we will get down to details about planning your school's approach to implementing Technology Together. There are many ways you can implement the process—there are no "rights" or "wrongs." We believe the approach you adopt must be right for your school and that it can be adapted as you progress on the learning journey in response to your observations about what works and what does not.

Here we provide guidance on issues for you to consider as you plan to introduce Technology Together to your school. The chapter is organized to help you navigate 10 steps that require close consideration as part of the planning process.

- Step 1   Deciding who to involve and when
- Step 2   Introducing Technology Together to your school
- Step 3   Considering your ICT vision
- Step 4   Allocating roles
- Step 5   Conducting a school analysis
- Step 6   Facilitating goal setting
- Step 7   Planning your mentoring strategies
- Step 8   Managing release time
- Step 9   Embedding strategies for reflection and discussion
- Step 10   Planning to showcase and celebrate achievements

We conclude the chapter with a summary checklist.

Step 1
Deciding Who to Involve and When

Technology Together is a whole-school approach that aims to involve *all teachers* in a school. However, some schools that have been involved in the process recommend involving all school staff, including administrative staff and support staff, because they often have roles that involve ICT. In many schools, for example, teachers' aides work with students with disabilities and often support these students through the use of assistive technologies.

Most schools viewed it as highly beneficial to introduce Technology Together to the whole-school community at one time and to bring everyone along on the learning journey together—reflecting the intent of Technology Together. However, some larger secondary schools reported that in retrospect they would have rolled out the program over a period of time, working with particular grade levels or specific curriculum departments and gradually growing the reach of the process.

One of the biggest factors to influence the success of Technology Together is the timing of implementation. Although no time is ever a quiet time for schools, some terms or semesters and some school years bring with them major commitments or pressures that can make the implementation process more difficult. Major school reviews, the introduction of momentous policy directives, or significant staff changes can all create distractions and excessive pressures on the implementation process. Such pressures often arise without forewarning and are an unavoidable part of school life. However, if you know there will be intensive pressures and deadlines for your school in a particular year, it may be beneficial to delay the implementation of Technology Together until a period with fewer immediate and competing demands.

Past participants recommend that Technology Together be implemented as part of a school's strategic planning process (whether this be annual or more long term). This timing allows you to set technology as a focus, engage the whole school in discussing its ICT vision, develop budgets, and make implementation an explicit priority. Involving all staff in implementation planning increases the likelihood of whole-school ownership of the process.

Keep in mind that Technology Together utilizes an action-learning framework to foster ongoing engagement, development, and learning. As such, the process should involve at least two, if not three or more, clearly defined cycles of planning, acting, observing, and reflecting. Typically, these cycles would thus occur across multiple school terms or semesters, and ideally a period of 12–18 months is needed. We provide a suggested schedule for implementing Technology Together in Chapter 7.

Step 2
Introducing Technology Together to Your School

It is important to introduce Technology Together to your school community well ahead of implementation and invite involvement and commitment. How and when Technology Together is introduced can have a significant bearing on staff support for the process. Our experiences suggest some important considerations.

As mentioned in Step 1, there are benefits if ICT integration is positioned as a priority for the school, based on recommendations of a school review or other whole-school planning process. Staff should agree on the need for improved ICT learning rather than perceiving it as a directive from management or an external policy requirement. Technology Together is *for* teachers and needs to be owned *by* teachers—it should be viewed as a process that the school has chosen to be involved in, not one driven by outsiders. It is critical that school executives promote the process to staff with enthusiasm, rather than as an extra requirement to be met.

It is also important to be mindful that some teachers may find the thought of extending their technology skills anxiety producing. If your staff have a wide range of abilities (as most will), it can be helpful to emphasize that Technology Together will meet all at their own level. Some schools have found it beneficial to use the metaphor of a ladder with everyone starting on different individual rungs, but all taking steps up. Another valuable metaphor is that of a journey—we explored this metaphor in Chapter 2.

Teachers are always looking for practical ideas and outcomes. Technology Together generates these. Focusing on the goal-setting process up front and helping teachers to see that their own personal goals can be met through the process is important. Building on informal word-of-mouth discussions is another way to motivate and engage teachers. Target key players because enthusiasm can spread!

All this said, introducing Technology Together can (and perhaps should) also convey a degree of expectation, including that staff do have some responsibilities. For some schools the accountability that Technology Together provides is a critical success factor, while at other schools accountability can be met with resentment and resistance. You can best judge how to navigate these dynamics in your own school.

Some schools view introducing the Technology Together process as important enough to warrant a staff development day, as this provides a focused time for unpacking the key underpinnings of the process and moving directly into goal setting and strategy planning. If it is not possible to allocate a full or partial staff development day, then a sizable section of a staff meeting should at least be made available. Introducing the foundational ideas of Technology Together (see Chapter 2) is best undertaken by a school's staff rather than by outside experts because this reinforces a sense of school ownership. A range of resources to assist you in introducing the program to staff are provided on the Technology Together website.

A major question to consider when introducing Technology Together is how explicitly to discuss it in a theoretical sense—particularly as it relates to the metacognitive approach. Some teachers are averse to theory as their primary interest and motivation is to improve their practice—they do not immediately recognize the links between the two. Again, prevailing school culture will be a strong influence on this consideration. In our experience, some teachers initially resist engaging with the idea of metacognition because they interpret it as too theoretical. However, such teachers become significantly more open to what it offers once they understand its relevance to their everyday practice with students and recognize that they have probably used metacognitive approaches with students already. Inquiry-based learning approaches, for example, are strongly grounded in metacognition.

Exposing teachers to the dimensions and elements of the metacognitive approach is important and so, where possible, these are best presented in a way that speaks to the experience of teachers in your school. Generating conversation around metacognition early in the process might work well in some schools, while in others it may need to follow some goal-setting activities to generate reflection on affects, motivation, and strategies in a practical, authentic context. In either case, Chapter 4 provides much guidance on this, and the Technology Together website provides support resources.

Step 3
Considering Your ICT Vision

School communities rarely explicitly discuss their educational vision. In fact, future visioning generally gains very little attention in mainstream educational settings. Yet, having a shared vision for technology integration can serve as a driving force for a school, overcoming barriers and providing teachers and school executives with a focus for communication (Hew & Brush, 2007). Engaging in discussion about what education might look like in two, five, ten, or even fifty years' time is important—not because any vision is guaranteed to eventuate but because such a visioning process helps individuals and groups embrace change and play a proactive role in moving toward the vision they prefer.

The interdisciplinary field of futures studies actively engages individuals in envisaging and discussing possible, probable, and preferred futures. *Possible futures* require individuals to think creatively and imaginatively and to consider futures that emphasize differing aspects of continued existence—some dystopian and others utopian. *Probable futures* require individuals to think logically and consider the connection between current conditions and envisaged futures. While it is generally assumed that the future is not fixed and that a variety of alternatives are possible, some futures are seen as more feasible than others. *Preferred futures* require individuals to choose among alternative futures while being clear about the criteria, values, and ethics they use to differentiate among them. In all these ways, futures studies acknowledges the limitations of prediction, instead recognizing the importance of exploring alternative and plural futures rather than arriving at one monolithic future.

As part of your planning for Technology Together, it can be valuable to engage staff in discussions about their possible, probable, and preferred futures for education—particularly as these futures relate to technology. While having a shared school vision can be a useful source of cohesion and unity and may be a powerful impetus for group learning and change, it is not essential. What is more important is the process of individuals' sharing their future visions and negotiating (perhaps even debating) which are probable and which preferred. Our website provides stimulus resources to support staff engagement with these ideas.

Step 4
Allocating Roles

Technology Together works within a framework that is built on staff supporting each other's learning, rather than a model of "outsiders" coming in. While all staff in a school will play a role in the learning process, for Technology Together to be successfully implemented, you need to identify some key "movers and shakers" and discuss with them the specific roles they might play. Those staff most closely involved in operationalizing Technology Together in the school will likely find themselves in one or more of the following roles:

- School management team (or school executive),
- Technology Together facilitator,
- Companion mentor (sometimes abbreviated to CM), and/or
- ICT expert.

We emphasize that facilitators and companion mentors do not need to be ICT experts and, in fact, they are more likely not to be. In some small schools, one person may play multiple roles, while in larger schools it will be essential to share responsibilities. Discussing these key roles explicitly with your whole-school staff is very important. Although the roles will evolve as you proceed, being conscious of what needs to be done, and by whom, is always beneficial.

In this section, we provide guidance in relation to these roles, based on our experiences implementing Technology Together. We also consider the pros and cons of one other role—the external partner—and provide advice on whether you should seek out such a partner to support your school. Our website provides resources to assist you to discuss these roles with staff.

An additional resource that schools may find valuable is ISTE's NETS for Coaches (NETS•C). This document (see Appendix C or www.iste.org/standards/nets-for-coaches.aspx) provides a set of statements about the roles that coaches, technology facilitators, and technology integration specialists play when supporting teachers to integrate ICT. The document can provide an additional stimulus for consideration when allocating roles, but it can also serve as a stimulus for discussion by school executives and teachers as they reflect on what works and what does not in supporting teacher learning.

School Management Team/Executives

School executives play a critical role in leading their school—including in relation to the future visioning previously outlined. While many principals have not had personal experience teaching with new technologies, it is critical that they are willing to provide appropriate leadership to develop and support a vision of pedagogically sound ICT integration.

School executives have unique insights into the direction of the school, the specific needs of individuals, and the availability of resources that classroom teachers may not have. The direct involvement of school executives in Technology Together is essential, and preferably the school principal will be directly and visibly involved as a leader *and* a participant. However, the role school executives play can vary considerably among schools and be influenced by school size and the nature of leaders' engagement with staff. In some schools, leaders will play a more hands-on role, while in other schools, leaders will focus more on facilitating the involvement of others. In any case, school executives, particularly principals, should not underestimate the value of actively setting goals and learning alongside staff—this will model risk-taking behavior and actively encourage and praise staff who do likewise. Be active in the integration process yourselves. You are learners, too!

It is not essential for school leaders to possess well-developed ICT knowledge and skills; however, it is essential that they understand the foundations of Technology Together, including the metacognitive learning process. In some instances, the most effective form of leadership may be to delegate facilitation of the process to a team and empower others to take the lead, supporting their activities and initiating regular meetings to keep in touch with progress and any concerns or issues.

The school management team has a particular influence over the way discussion and reflection is perceived and received within a school. School executives need to value the process of reflection and dialogue and afford it a high priority, for instance, by allocating regular, quality time at staff meetings. Ideally, school executives will also assist the process through appropriate allocation of resources, in the form of hardware, software, and staff release (e.g., providing substitute teachers for "release time").

In summary, then, school executives play a key role in the following tasks:

- Promoting a shared vision for ICT integration;
- Providing strong support for the Technology Together process;
- Introducing Technology Together to staff and encouraging them to be involved;
- Participating in the planning process;
- Allocating resources to the integration process, including release time (see Step 8);
- Supporting the facilitators and mentors and acting as a sounding board and critical friend;

- Providing opportunities (e.g., staff meetings) where teachers are encouraged to discuss, reflect, share, and celebrate achievements;
- Expecting some degree of accountability; and
- Modeling being ICT learners themselves.

Facilitators

Technology Together facilitators are responsible for operationalizing the process at the grassroots level and keeping Technology Together on track. They have an important role to play in planning, implementing, and evaluating the learning cycles; engaging and motivating staff; ensuring that time is set aside at meetings for discussion and reflection; and providing accountability.

Facilitators do not need to be ICT experts, and they do not need to work side-by-side with teachers. It does, however, help if they bring the following qualities to the role of facilitating:

- Good rapport with, and respect from, other staff;
- Commitment to teacher learning and school improvement;
- Sound understanding of Technology Together, including the metacognitive approach;
- Commitment to ICT integration across the curriculum; and
- A reasonable degree of assertiveness to get the process going and keep it running.

The successful implementation of Technology Together critically depends on identifying the right person or people to act in the facilitative role. It is also critical that the facilitator, above all others, is not overcommitted and has the time and energy to help Technology Together succeed.

Companion Mentors

The role of the companion mentor sometimes overlaps with that of facilitator, but in some contexts the roles will be played by different people. In any case, the facilitator and companion mentor need to work closely together. The companion mentor's relationship with other staff is based on support, sharing, and collaboration, and the companion mentor has a key role to

- Provide "side-by-side" support to individual teachers, not only in relation to technical or skills-based support, but also in terms of affects, motivation, and strategies;

- Work with teachers as they set their goals, and prompt them to be ambitious;
- Discuss and suggest learning strategies that are consistent with the metacognitive approach; and
- Encourage teachers to document, share, and celebrate their achievements.

Companion mentors are not necessarily more senior or more experienced teachers, nor are they necessarily the most ICT-literate teachers in the school. Our experience reveals the significant benefits of involving less technologically literate but highly supportive staff. Remember, the mentor relationship is not only about training. However, companion mentors do need to bring the following qualities to the role:

- Patience and calmness when working with other teachers;
- A positive outlook and a good sense of perspective;
- The ability to be supportive without doing everything for ICT learners;
- A deep understanding of, and commitment to, the metacognitive approach;
- Preparedness to try mentoring strategies that are consistent with the metacognitive approach; and
- A willingness to be self-reflective and to critique their own helping strategies.

It is important for a school to identify an appropriate number of companion mentors. Large schools, in particular, need to take care that responsibility does not fall to one mentor alone. The most successful structures in larger schools have involved having a companion mentor for each grade. Such a mentor plays a key role working with staff for that grade but with overall coordination from the Technology Together facilitator.

Some Technology Together schools reported choosing not to adopt the title "mentor," preferring a title such as "learning partner," particularly where companion mentors felt less secure in their skills and knowledge and did not want to be perceived as professing to know all the answers. Other schools decided not to identify specific companion mentors, preferring instead to promote the idea that all teachers support one another. Both of these strategies can work well, and both are consistent with the metacognitive approach as they reinforce the idea that no one knows everything and that everyone is learning together.

> *The term mentor was rarely used, not for any particular reason but mainly because by not labeling one particular member of staff as the mentor, other members of staff were comfortable to take on mentoring roles in an informal context.*

ICT Experts

The Technology Together facilitator and/or companion mentors are not necessarily your school's ICT experts. In fact, there can be benefits in keeping these roles separate.

ICT experts play very important roles within a school. However, they are not always the best people to mentor other adults, particularly those who are less confident with technology. ICT experts may take for granted the learning strategies that they (often innately) employ. They do not necessarily realize that these strategies do not come easily for everyone. Often, without realizing it, ICT experts showcase their skills with every task they perform. They seem to make a technology-based skill look effortless, even when they have spent many hours and much heartache learning to do it themselves. Additionally, ICT experts are often the busiest people in the school. They frequently play the role of problem solver and fix-it person on top of all their other responsibilities.

ICT experts may also not see benefits in the metacognitive process. As they do not often experience technology anxiety themselves, they may have trouble understanding the relevance of focusing on others' feelings, attitudes, and beliefs. They may not be "affective domain" people; in other words, they may not be focused on, or alert to, people's feelings, attitudes, and beliefs. Also, some ICT experts have preconceptions about directive-skills training, seeing it as the only way to pass on their knowledge to others.

> *I consulted the computer coordinator for help. He went so quickly with his explanation and then proceeded to do it himself while I watched. I knew he wouldn't be the ideal mentor for me.*

ICT experts play invaluable roles in schools and hence are critical to the success of Technology Together. However, the roles they play might vary depending on their personal characteristics, their interest in supporting other teachers, and their level of commitment toward the metacognitive approach. In any case, ICT experts will play an important role in the following ways:

- Making suggestions on hardware and software purchases that will benefit the whole-school community;
- Providing technical support for initiatives implemented by teachers;
- Advising on which ICT implementation goals are and are not possible (without discouraging teachers from ambitious or innovative goals); and
- Supporting and assisting when problems arise but carefully balancing solving problems for teachers with allowing them to learn to solve their own problems.

External Partners

Although Technology Together must be owned and driven by school staff, the process can, at times, benefit from the involvement of an outside, or external, partner. This partner might be from a university, another school, an educational district office, or an outside organization. The Technology Together external partner can

- Bring a fresh perspective and share ideas between schools;
- Act as a "critical friend" as you implement the project;
- Collaboratively conduct the initial school analysis, providing a more objective perspective and asking some of the more difficult questions;
- Visit your school to plan and discuss your initiatives and strategies;
- Revitalize and challenge your school community with new ideas; and
- Provide support to facilitators and companion mentors in their implementation of the metacognitive approach.

As previously mentioned, some school executives view relationships with external partners as beneficial in providing an increased level of accountability, emphasizing that the partner expects to see learning results. For example, identifying Technology Together as part of a university research project provided instant credibility and accountability in some schools that participated in the process of developing Technology Together. This credibility ensured that teachers' professionalism came to the forefront and all were more willing to participate to the best of their ability.

At other schools, however, such an emphasis may be met with resentment and resistance. Only you can best judge whether having an external partner for Technology Together is the best choice for your school and, if so, what role that partner will play.

Deciding to Play a Leading Role

There are many benefits for teachers who decide to play a specific role in Technology Together. Acting as a companion mentor or facilitator constitutes excellent leadership development and provides invaluable experience in managing and leading change, working with and coordinating staff, facilitating professional development, and leading short- and long-term planning within a school. Such experiences are highly valuable for accreditation and career progression and are likely to benefit those seeking future promotion.

In addition, playing a leading role in Technology Together can provide personal satisfaction, a sense of accomplishment, and pride from helping others. You are likely to gain professional invigoration from sharing ideas with others and building collegiality and friendships. Do not be concerned if you are not highly confident with your technology skills. Position yourself as a co-learner who is willing to analyze and reflect on your classroom practice and to try new things:

> *Don't be scared. You are never the expert with computers. Somebody always seems to know more, and that is OK. Use this knowledge to enhance your own understandings, and take it and share with others.*

However, potential challenges do arise for those teachers playing the role of companion mentor. These challenges include staff conflict, competitiveness, time demands, and concerns about perceptions if a protégé is not "successful." We provide some tips and advice in avoiding and overcoming these challenges and other issues in Chapter 7.

Working Together as a Coordinating Team

It is critical to the Technology Together process that school executives, companion mentors, facilitators, and ICT experts establish a good working relationship and function well together as a team. Regular staff meetings are essential, and it is important to talk both informally and formally about issues and progress. Be specific about meeting times and commit to them (e.g., weekly or biweekly Wednesday afternoons or the first Wednesday of each month). Ideally, meeting times will take into account school schedules.

> *As companion mentors, we met and talked regularly about the pros and cons of the program and ways we could support colleagues who were struggling. We also met quite regularly with the principal and ICT coordinator, and in clarifying the process and progress for them, we provided ourselves with valuable insights and directions.*

If you know of other schools that are implementing Technology Together, you might also create opportunities to share experiences with them. An external partner who is involved in working across multiple schools can help share ideas and experiences between project teams. The Technology Together website also provides an opportunity for this sharing (in the Community section).

Step 5
Conducting a School Analysis

In Chapter 1, we discussed the idea that ICT learning is influenced by a complex interplay of factors including school history, culture, and context, and individual teachers' values, attitudes, and beliefs toward change. Consider, for example, the impact of the following factors on your school's receptivity to ICT professional learning:

- Socioeconomic background of students and their level and type of ICT use in the home,
- Availability of technology resources,
- Location of technology and how it is managed,
- Attitude toward embracing change,
- How teachers approach their own learning and how they view professional development,
- Whether all teachers take responsibility for ICT integration,
- Teachers' motivation and commitment to integrating ICT,
- Teachers' willingness to take risks and try new things,
- Which pedagogical approaches are most widely employed in a school,
- Whether teachers regularly engage in productive professional discussion,
- Whether achievements are shared and showcased,
- Whether the school feels like a "learning community," and
- Whether there is an overall vision of what future education might be like.

Why Conduct a School Analysis?

The school analysis is important for the Technology Together process because it provides a systematic means of identifying what already works well in a school and a structure for identifying areas that need attention or improvement. An analysis stimulates staff discussion about the need for change and enables you to customize the Technology Together process to fit your school's culture and context.

In Chapter 2, we touched on the notion of self-efficacy—individuals' beliefs about their capacity to perform a certain task. Recent research has also begun to discuss collective efficacy (Goddard, Hoy, & Hoy, 2004)—a recognition that groups of people or communities can collectively develop a sense of efficacy. We believe that whole schools can develop a collective belief about their ability to use technology and our aim is to develop a collective, positive self-efficacy about technology across your whole school. To do that, we need to have a reasonably objective picture of what has influenced, and is continuing to influence, ICT learning in your school.

The school analysis is not only a process of collecting information. It should be approached as an opportunity to engage staff, and potentially also students, in reflecting critically on what is happening with ICT in your school. The analysis is an opportunity to begin what will be a continuing dialogue about strengths that can be built upon and issues or problems that might be addressed.

The School Analysis: Who, When, and How

Although it is entirely possible for the principal, assistant principal, and/or key teachers within a school to conduct the school analysis without outside assistance, the analysis can be more beneficial and rigorous when an outside, critical friend is involved. Someone who is less familiar with your school context can often see things that may not be evident to those within the school culture. A critical friend can ask the more difficult questions—those we may choose to shy away from ourselves. A critical friend may also know less about the background history and politics within a school and ask questions that help identify connections to culture and contexts that previously went unnoticed. Earlier in this chapter we discussed the value of having an external partner, such as someone from a university or a teacher from a neighboring school. If you decide to seek out such a partner, the school analysis is an important opportunity for this outside critical friend to get to know your school.

Ideally, the school analysis happens at the beginning of the implementation process and forms the basis for introducing the process to your school. The school analysis needs to be collaborative and consultative. It should not result in staff feeling threatened or under scrutiny; instead, it can be approached as a means of identifying the focus for ongoing support and additional resourcing.

If an external partner facilitates your school analysis, then allow it to take at least two full days, which should include a staff meeting. Two days will allow the external partner time to observe and absorb what takes place across the school and get to know staff a little better. The partner could organize a series of individual or small group meetings with key staff and possibly a random sample of other staff from across the school. These meetings will involve talking through relevant questions from the school analysis scaffold (**Resource 2** | **Table 3.1**). If you conduct the school analysis yourself, then you can either gather a small group of teachers together as a focus group to discuss the questions, or you can take the questions to a whole-school staff meeting for broader input. A combination of these approaches may also be beneficial. Overall, it is important to keep a record of the group discussions, including any contextual information, such as who was or was not available to contribute to the discussion.

Collecting Information

The type of information you collect as part of the school analysis will depend on your school context. The scaffold we provide (**Resource 2** | Table 3.1) can either be used as is or adapted as you see fit. Broadly, the scaffold is structured to collect the following information:

- General school demographics (this is particularly important if you have an external partner who is less familiar with your school);
- ICT context—past, present, and future;
- School culture—past and present;
- School leadership—past and present;
- Students' technology use and confidence; and
- Individual teachers' values, attitudes, beliefs, and skills.

Again, because the school analysis is not only about collecting data, but also about reflecting on your school's current context, it is important that the information is not purely descriptive but also engages staff in critical thinking and open and honest dialogue. The kind of information important for the school analysis is outlined in the following table.

Resource 2 | Table 3.1 School analysis scaffold

Part 1 – General school demographics

Students: Indicate number of students and whether this is growing, decreasing, or stable. What is influencing growth or decline? How many classes are there per year or semester?

Teachers: Provide a list of teachers, the grade/KLA they are allocated to, and any other special roles they play. Include part-time staff, indicating the number of days they work. Include administrative staff and other nonteaching staff, such as teacher's aides or assistants. Clarify whether there is a separate teacher librarian or any staff with specific ICT responsibilities.

Community context: Provide the size of the town/suburb/district and the demographic characteristics affecting the local community (e.g., rural, tourist input, high level of retirees). Consider the nature of parent groups.

School history: Indicate how long the school has existed, particular characteristics of the school, governance structures, history of school reviews, and the physical nature of school buildings.

Key project participants (once identified): For each key project participant (including the principal, assistant principal, facilitators, companion mentors, and ICT experts) document the following: how long they have been at the school and/or in their current role; the nature of their role in relation to ICT; their confidence and experience with ICT; their professional development experience/background; their interest in participating in Technology Together; and their vision for ICT in the school [see Step 3].

(Continued)

Resource 2 | Table 3.1   *(Continued)*

Part 2 – ICT context

Hardware infrastructure: Include the nature of infrastructure (e.g., desktops, laptops, tablets); where hardware is located (e.g., labs, classrooms); how long hardware has been in this configuration; quality of Internet access; staff facilities; access to scanners, printers, projectors, cameras, and other peripherals; booking systems; and so forth.

Software infrastructure: List what software is used in the school, including application suites (e.g., Microsoft Office, OpenOffice, cloud computing) and other educational software; any subscriptions to online resources; and how often software is purchased and who makes decisions.

Patterns and culture of ICT use: Include whether there is any core expectation on teachers' ICT use; whether some teachers have greater involvement in ICT integration; culture and patterns of collaboration and support; what computer time is used for; use of scope and sequence; patterns of electronic communication by teachers, parents and students; any past history of ICT issues (e.g., bullying, accessing inappropriate resources); and past or current ICT initiatives or focused activities (e.g., online projects).

ICT support: Indicate who is responsible for ICT support (both inside and outside school); the sort of support they provide; whether there is an overreliance on this support; and who people turn to most for help and whether these people are overloaded.

History of ICT professional development: Include the types of professional development undertaken by individuals (past and present); any professional development undertaken by the whole school; what has worked and what has not and why; and the level of support, interaction, sharing, and discussion among staff.

Future agendas: Indicate whether the school has an ICT vision; whether the school has any specific priorities or goals in relation to ICT; whether there are immediate perceived issues or staff development needs; and how to foster ownership of any school-wide initiatives.

Part 3 – School culture

Teacher culture: Include whether the school has a relaxed or formal atmosphere; reaction of staff to visitors or outsiders (e.g., whether hesitant, welcoming); teachers' relationships with students; teachers' relationships with each other and social networks; general level of motivation and receptivity to ICT learning and change; and the attitude of staff toward engaging with educational theory.

Pedagogical culture: Indicate classroom arrangement and management style; for example, how classrooms are arranged or the balance of collaborative versus individual learning; balance of constructivist and directive-style teaching approach; other teaching approaches in use, for example, Bloom's Taxonomy or Gardner's multiple intelligences; and the degree of risk taking and experimentation with teaching methods.

Culture of learning and openness to change: Indicate the attitudes toward learning among staff; teachers' approaches to trying new things; who are seen as leaders; who are seen as change agents; cultures of collaboration; and any history of mentoring.

Resource 2 | **Table 3.1**   *(Continued)*

Culture of meetings and discussion: Indicate the frequency and nature of school meetings; what is covered at meetings; level of engagement and commitment to meeting agendas; potential for integrating Technology Together discussion; receptivity to collegial discussion; and receptivity to reflection.

Part 4 – School and ICT leadership

Leadership and management: Include who the main ICT leaders in the school are; what management structures are in place (e.g., IT committee); the level of input classroom teachers have in the school's ICT decisions; and whether teachers feel that they can take risks with what they try in their classrooms.

Financial issues: Indicate how finances are managed in relation to technology; how hardware and software is purchased; and whether there is a plan for replacement.

Policy: Include what ICT-related policies or other related documents are in place; what policies have been in place in the past; what new policies might be needed; and who might be involved in policy development and review.

Vision: Ask does the school have an ICT vision? Is this a shared vision? How can ownership of any school-wide initiatives be fostered?

Part 5 – Students' technology use

Teachers' perceptions of students' knowledge and skills: Include the types of ICT activities students are currently performing in classrooms; what ICT activities students have done in past; teachers' perceptions of students' ICT abilities; and how much teachers know about students' recreational use of technology.

Students' perspectives and vision: Schools can consider to what degree they will involve students in the school analysis. This could vary from a simple survey on home computer access and use to a much deeper engagement around what they like about technology use in the school, what they do not like, and what suggestions and visions they have for change (see **Resource 3** | **Form 3.1** and other student surveys in Appendix B and on the Technology Together website).

Part 6 – Teachers' values, attitudes, beliefs, and skills

See the teacher survey in Appendix B or on the Technology Together website.

A version of **Resource 2** school analysis scaffold is provided on the Technology Together website.

Incorporating Students' Perspectives and Vision

In recent years there has been a growing recognition of the importance and value of providing students and young people with a voice concerning what happens in schools. In our initial research and development of Technology Together, we were focused primarily on teachers' learning. However, we now recognize the importance and potential for engaging students more actively in aspects of the process. To do so is consistent with the collaborative and participatory action-learning foundations of Technology Together. Not only will this engagement enable richer and deeper teacher learning as staff come to understand their students better, but it will also help students to better understand their teachers and feel more active in shaping their learning experience.

As part of the initial school analysis, schools should consider to what extent to involve students directly (versus indirectly) in Technology Together. For example, at a basic level, it can be beneficial to have a good understanding of the degree to which students have access to technology in their home environments, what this technology is, and what they use it for. Such data can be enlightening for teachers, as it raises their awareness of students' existing skills, knowledge, and interests, and the possibilities for synergies between home computer use and classroom learning. As one teacher in Technology Together commented:

> *The surveys completed by the children had a big impact when the data was presented to staff. Almost all of the children at our school had a computer at home; some had multiple computers. The conversation was significant as many staff were amazed at the level of computer ownership, and possibly they realized that teachers can't be left behind.*

It can be beneficial to seek students' views on what they like and do not like about ICT and whether and how it supports their learning. Such a proactive approach is more respectful of the experience, needs, and preferences of students and more likely to result in improved "buy in" with their learning.

At a much more engaged level, students can be made aware of their teachers' focus on new ICT learning goals and be invited to participate and collaborate throughout the year as the teacher experiments with new strategies and skills. Many of the activities suggested in Chapter 5 involve teachers engaging with their students as they put metacognition into practice in the classroom. While not essential, these activities will make much more sense if students are aware of the Technology Together project and what it entails. Further, the ideas in Chapter 5 about learning with and from students will be most effective when students are explicitly part of the process.

Again, the nature and extent of student involvement will depend very much on each school's existing culture and practices. If teachers are not accustomed to consulting students on matters related to their learning and students are not used to participating in decisions about pedagogy, there will be limitations on what a more collaborative approach can achieve. Further, if teachers do not have a relationship of collegiality and trust with students, teachers may not feel as willing to open up and admit that they are learners, too. Participatory approaches, which actively engage students in co-constructing the learning experience, potentially invert conventional power relations in classrooms—students' experiences are acknowledged and actively sought by teachers. However, not every teacher is comfortable with, or accustomed to, such an approach. Of course, once teachers start to engage with the Technology Together process, the goal is for this process to build their confidence with involving students in gradual ways. So, even if students' perspectives and visions are not sought at the start of the Technology Together implementation, a more participatory approach might be something that teachers experiment with through the development of their goals and strategies.

The Technology Together website provides a variety of student surveys that are categorized into three different levels—early primary, middle years, and upper secondary. A simple but indicative example follows (**Resource 3** | **Form 3.1**). Note that there are several formats to choose from when conducting a survey:

- Verbal discussion in the classroom,
- Print-based survey completed by students either at school or at home (which can be part of building parental involvement with the school's priority to increase ICT integration), or
- Online survey accessible via the Technology Together website or one of the many freely available online survey tools that you can set up yourself.

Be aware that access to technology and technology competency can be sensitive issues for students. Some students may feel peer pressure to indicate particular responses to avoid appearing "nerdy" or as disadvantaged if they do not have similar access or skills as their peers. Sensitivity is required, and the online option may be an advantage in this sense.

Additional surveys appear in Appendix B. These surveys are also available online at the Technology Together website.

Student Survey 1
SUITABLE FOR MOST AGES

Resource 3 | **Form 3.1**   Simple student survey

Do you have access to a computer at home?	☐ Yes ☐ No
How often do you use the computer at home?	☐ Every day … How many hours a day? _____ ☐ Two or three times a week ☐ Once every couple of weeks ☐ Never
Do you have access to the Internet at home?	☐ Yes ☐ No
Are you allowed to go on the Internet?	☐ Yes, anytime I like ☐ Yes, but with restrictions. Please explain. _____ _____ ☐ No
What do you use your computer at home for? (Mark all that apply.)	☐ Playing educational games (e.g., math or science) ☐ Using social networking sites such as Facebook ☐ Playing noneducational games ☐ Digital photos ☐ Listening to music ☐ Writing stories ☐ Researching information ☐ Using email ☐ Other (please give examples)
Which of these technologies do you have regular access to? (Mark all that apply.)	☐ Mobile/cell phone ☐ iPad or similar ☐ MP3 player ☐ Wii, Nintendo, or similar ☐ Digital camera ☐ Smartphone with Internet access ☐ Digital video camera

	1 = Not much **5** = Lots
How much do you like using computers?	1 2 3 4 5
Do you think using computers helps you to learn?	1 2 3 4 5
How much would you like to use computers in class?	1 2 3 4 5
What do you like **most** about using technology at school?	
What do you like **least** about using technology at school?	
What would you like to see done differently with technology at school?	

The Teacher Survey

A key component of the school analysis is the teacher survey, the purpose of which is threefold:

- To collect base-level data on individual teachers' values, attitudes, and beliefs about ICT, so that schools and teachers themselves can see whether and how these change after involvement with Technology Together;
- To provide companion mentors and facilitators with an understanding of general levels of ICT confidence and skills within the school; and
- To begin to engage teachers in the metacognitive aspects of the process by reflecting on what influences their relationship to technology.

The teacher survey collects data on many metacognitive elements that we discussed in Chapter 2, including support and encouragement, attitude, perceived usefulness, reflective approaches, learning confidence, pedagogical orientation, and ICT skills.

The teacher survey is provided in Appendix B and also as an online survey, accessible through the Technology Together website. Once your school is registered on the site, teachers will be provided with access to the survey, and a report that collates the data will be emailed to your school. This report serves as a valuable resource for your school and assists the school management team and mentors in understanding the diversity of teachers' learning readiness, hence informing implementation planning of the metacognitive approach. The teacher survey is conducted anonymously so that teachers feel confident to respond honestly and openly. Although anonymity prevents mentors and school executives from identifying the specific individuals with ICT concerns, it is more important that the survey generates an overall picture.

Step 6
Facilitating Goal Setting

The metacognitive approach is founded on teachers setting their own learning goals within a scaffolded and supported environment. An issue with setting personal goals, however, is that teachers "don't always know what they don't know." For this reason, Technology Together provides lots of stimuli and ideas to assist teachers with setting learning goals.

It is important to emphasize that Technology Together is not about achieving a set of skills or a specific benchmark, but more about everyone moving forward:

> *When I am in charge of my own learning, my goals continually change. As I move forward with my use of computers, I find that I am continually wanting to do more and new things with them—each possibility opens up another, and I seek the learning which enables me to attain my new goal.... I continue to explore, accomplish new skills, transfer learning, take short cuts, and do what I need in order to reach my goals.*

It is important that all staff, no matter what their current level of knowledge or skill, set goals. *All* staff includes ICT experts, companion mentors, facilitators, and school executives, including the school principal.

We acknowledge that each learner is starting from a different place on the technology learning ladder and encourage each of them to take small steps up, one rung at a time. The program encourages everyone to be ambitious and challenge themselves. Some teachers will find the goal-setting process daunting, but they can be encouraged to start small and grow toward more ambitious goals as their confidence develops:

> *Not everyone is ready for whiz-bang IT lessons. There are still many members of staff who need to feel more capable with smaller tasks before moving on. Don't overwhelm everyone!*

Many teachers think of ICT goals as only related to skills. However, in the metacognitive approach, we focus on goal setting in five areas:

- Skills goals,
- Integration goals,
- Recreational goals,
- Metacognitive goals, and
- Leadership goals.

We refer both to "big-picture" goals and immediate, short-term goals (often skills) that might contribute toward the achievement of big-picture goals.

We talk more about goal setting in Chapter 4 and devote the whole of Chapter 6 to facilitating goal setting. However, what needs to be thought through at the initial planning phase are the strategies that will be used to engage teachers in setting at least their first Technology Together goals. We provide guidance on how to go about doing this in Chapter 6.

Step 7
Planning Your Mentoring Strategies

A key purpose of planning is to talk through the approaches your school will use for supporting teacher learning. In particular, your school needs to plan who will mentor which teachers as well as whether mentoring will occur individually or in small groups, be formal or informal, and will occur in a regular or irregular time frame.

Remember, Technology Together focuses on developing and implementing the strategies most appropriate for your school's culture. However, some key principles that underpin Technology Together might influence the planning of your mentoring strategies, namely:

- Mentoring is not always best done by the most ICT-experienced people in the school;
- Mentors should not be perceived as primarily for teaching technology skills—rather, their main role is to support, encourage, motivate, and provide ideas;
- Mentors and mentees should not always meet at a computer;
- Mentoring does not always have to happen between one or two identified mentors. Rather, schools may develop structures whereby everyone mentors and supports everyone else;
- Mentoring might occur in informal ways rather than at structured times, for example, through conversations in the staff room; and
- Mentoring might happen through side-by-side team teaching in the classroom.

Resource 4 | **Table 3.2** provides a range of suggested mentoring strategies that have been implemented in Technology Together schools. The first three approaches address the interpersonal partnerships—the "who" of mentoring strategies. The remaining approaches address the "how" of mentoring strategies. There is no one "best fit" approach, and it may be necessary to experiment with several approaches to discover what works and what does not. Other structures that we have not identified here may be more effective within your school. Remaining open to change if things don't work as planned is important (see Chapter 7).

Resource 4 | Table 3.2 Possible mentoring strategies

"Who" Approach 1 — One ICT expert mentor

- School identifies one person to be the mentor for all teachers.

Potential strengths	Potential problems	Tips or advice
Selection can be based on level of expertise and ability to work effectively with a range of teachers. One person can build a good picture of overall school development needs, identify individual strengths, and find ways to share this expertise. One person can focus on the immediate needs of individual learners. One person can focus on helping teachers develop appropriate learning strategies.	Much relies on the personal qualities and mentoring capabilities of the individual. Selected individual may not be open to mentoring within the metacognitive process. Interpersonal tensions or frictions within the school can be exacerbated. Responsibility and ownership of the process is not shared. If the selected individual becomes unavailable, Technology Together might not progress effectively. Risk of dependency	Carefully consider and plan the role of the ICT experts in your school (see Step 4).

"Who" Approach 2 — Several mentors (expert and nonexpert)

- School selects a small group to be mentors for the rest of the teachers.
- Selection can be on the basis of ICT expertise, but some mentors may bring other qualities to the role.

Potential strengths	Potential problems	Tips or advice
Nonexpert mentors can help engage all teachers. Teachers can select preferred relationships. Responsibility is dispersed. Activities do not rely on the availability of one person. Group problem-solving and planning can draw on collective wisdom.	Some mentors may not feel confident with their ICT skills (although this can also be an advantage). Coordination and group communication needs to be considered.	Be aware that mentors who are most accessible are likely to be the ones most relied upon. Balance experts with nonexperts who bring other interpersonal qualities to the role. Place emphasis on co-learning.

Resource 4 | **Table 3.2** *(Continued)*

"Who" Approach 3 — Like-to-like (nonexpert) mentoring

- Every teacher is paired with another, with teachers generally choosing their own partners.
- Both are mentors, and both are learners.
- Both can be released from their classrooms (e.g., relieved by a substitute) at the same time.
- Both embrace common goals.
- Both seek extra assistance when needed.

Potential strengths	Potential problems	Tips or advice
Active involvement of every teacher Less threatening for staff intimidated by more confident users Builds a culture of support and collegiality. Promotes learning together Teachers have ownership and are self-directed. Fosters a focus on learning strategies, particularly exploratory learning Overcomes nonavailability of specified mentors	Difficult to monitor effectiveness as no one person works with all staff Unmotivated teachers might select each other and make little progress. Some teachers might give unhelpful assistance or feedback. Support may be more competency focused rather than capability focused. Some staff may not be skilled at giving appropriate feedback and support to other adults.	It is essential to explicitly discuss mentoring approaches. Be aware of the metacognitive approach, particularly the notion of capability.

(Continued)

Resource 4 | **Table 3.2** *(Continued)*

"How" Approach 1 — Group skills input session

- Can be a full or half day or an after-school session
- Can form part of regular or extended staff meeting time, for example, after-school "coffee-and-pizza afternoons"

Potential strengths	Potential problems	Tips or advice
Provides opportunities for short, focused learning	Difficult to meet the needs of all individuals in a group	Choose the tutor(s) carefully.
Can be scheduled weekly or biweekly to build momentum	Difficult to go at a pace that is appropriate for all	Ensure that the group dynamics are nonthreatening.
Provides a rapid way of addressing skills goals	Can carry the negative implications of a formal training model	Approach either as a training session or an opportunity for collaborative learning and help seeking (the latter is preferable).
Can be useful if staff have identified a common need	If teachers don't follow up, learning is lost and self-efficacy may be decreased.	
Builds a sense of collegiality and encourages teachers to support one anothers' ongoing ICT use	If not compulsory, unlikely to coax the less motivated staff to participate; if compulsory, teachers may feel resentful.	Emphasize the importance of building follow-up practice and implementation into the process.
Can emphasize exploratory learning and play, for example, after-school playtime sessions		Alternate meeting days so all teachers are able to attend.

"How" Approach 2 — Structured mentoring time

- Regular scheduled release time for each teacher
- Typically this time is spent side-by-side with a mentor.

Potential strengths	Potential problems	Tips or advice
Keeps the learning process regularly on the agenda	Time available is often not very long.	Aim to balance structured and nonstructured opportunities.
Formalizes learning and goal achievement	Teachers are not always prepared or focused on their goal.	Place emphasis on checking goals, problem solving, and so on, with an expectation that learning happens outside structured times.
	Easy for teachers to get distracted	
	Can build expectation that learning only happens at an allocated time	

Resource 4 | **Table 3.2** *(Continued)*

"How" Approach 3 — Visits to other classrooms

- Can involve either observation or co-teaching

Potential strengths	Potential problems	Tips or advice
Opportunity to see ICT integration in practice Immediate outcomes for students Can build teachers' confidence to try new things and take risks	Can become negative if viewed in a comparative sense Can reinforce a "guru mentality" or dependency on ICT experts	Choose partners carefully. Maintain focus on exploratory learning (for teachers and students) rather than demonstration.

"How" Approach 4 — Grade-level–based meetings

Potential strengths	Potential problems	Tips or advice
Can focus specifically on curriculum needs and integration in the classroom Great for planning integration goals	ICT experts can dominate.	Meet regularly (e.g., weekly or biweekly). Include informal discussions. Do not always meet at a computer.

"How" Approach 5 — Just-in-time learning

Potential strengths	Potential problems	Tips or advice
Can address immediate needs, thus reducing frustration Can promote teacher-directed, goal-focused learning Can happen through incidental and informal discussions	Can put added stress on skilled teachers if they are viewed as the only source of support Can promote either appropriate or inappropriate help seeking, depending on the individuals' approach	Explicitly discuss help-seeking and problem-solving strategies. Encourage mentors and ICT experts to provide tips or guidance, rather than solving problems for teachers

Step 8
Managing Release Time

Allocating teacher release time is important to the success of Technology Together, not only in its own right, but in terms of the commitment it represents. Providing some release time indicates that professional learning is valued. However, Technology Together makes the most of whatever release time is available. It is not dependent upon any particular level of release and focuses more on the processes by which release time is perceived, allocated, used, and managed within a school.

Teachers' attitudes toward time can affect their ICT learning (discussed further in Chapter 4) and become an excuse for not engaging with ICT or an attribution for lack of success. The process of planning and managing release time, therefore, should go hand-in-hand with understanding these potential pitfalls from a metacognitive perspective.

One strategy that proved to be very successful in several schools was that of only allocating release time on the basis of expressed need, as explained by one assistant principal:

> *Staff were not informed about the amount of time available. This was a deliberate tactic.... From previous experience, it was thought that as soon as the amount of time was disclosed, teachers would immediately work out how much time they should be allocated and would restrict their efforts to that time and, therefore, severely restrict the scope of the project. When the question of time was raised, staff were informed that time was available.... The success of this approach lies in the fact that time can't be seen as an excuse! Whenever someone says, "I haven't got time to learn/do that," the companion mentor says, "Yes, you do!" Teachers value the release more and perceived that they are being personally rewarded for their efforts.*

In our experience, the following advice should be considered when planning and managing the use of release time:

- Avoid associating the Technology Together process with release time;
- Avoid establishing a perception that learning will only occur if release time is provided;
- Take care when scheduling regular, short periods of release for all teachers—technology learning takes time, and having only a short amount of time can lead to frustrations and not be conducive to problem solving;
- Consider using release time as an incentive for more ambitious goal setting; if teachers come up with good ideas, time can be allocated for them to achieve that;

- Provide opportunities for just-in-time learning, which are important, but much more difficult to plan; keep some time in reserve to meet these needs;
- Make sharing of learning a condition for taking release time; teachers will be held accountable for their learning, and everyone in the school benefits;
- Consider allocating release time on the basis of "equity versus equality" to avoid unequal time distribution among all staff;
- Value time spent discussing and reflecting as much as time actually "doing"; some of the best use of release time is spent in activities such as goal setting and discussion of learning strategies; and
- Recognize that facilitators and companion mentors need time to plan and reflect as well as to work with staff.

Resource 5 | **Table 3.3** summarizes some of the potential approaches to allocation and management of release time.

Resource 5 | **Table 3.3** Potential approaches to allocation of release time

Approach	Strengths and weaknesses
Releasing a whole grade's teachers at the same time to set collaborative goals, plan, and/or prepare initiatives. May include demonstrations of particular technologies	The approach relies on availability of multiple casual staff.
	Great for enhancing professional dialogue, support, and collegiality
	Can have immediate benefits in terms of classroom integration initiatives
Mentor has regular release time (e.g., Wednesday afternoons), and the assistant principal relieves for any other teacher who wants or needs support on that afternoon.	Flexibility of the approach enables any staff member with needs on that day to have access to mentoring, that is, just-in-time learning.
	Accommodates both long and shorter release sessions
	Requires a booking system
	May require some negotiations if multiple teachers need support

(Continued)

Resource 5 | **Table 3.3** *(Continued)*

Approach	Strengths and weaknesses
Structured regular release time for each teacher in rotation	One teacher is brought in each week to release all staff in rotation (with or without the mentor also being released).
	Teachers may then have a regular allotment of time (say, a half hour each month) to work on their goals, although such an approach carries the same issues as regular release time (as above)
If someone sets an ambitious goal, time is allocated to achieve it. Used to support goal achievement	More flexibility is required in allocating and staffing release.
	Very positive in encouraging goal-focused learning and teachers feel supported
	It is important to ensure all staff are encouraged to use the time to meet goals.

Step 9
Embedding Strategies for Reflection and Discussion

A key strategy employed by Technology Together is to facilitate reflection and discussion among staff and between teachers and students. Reflection and discussion are important aspects of fostering a school culture that is collaborative, collegial, and promotes lifelong technology learning. In this section, we suggest potential strategies for facilitating reflection and discussion.

Teachers can benefit greatly from investing time to debrief, throw around ideas, affirm achievements, unpack problems and difficulties, and share ideas for solutions. Reflection can be a key tool to support teacher professional learning, and it can also provide a valuable means for gathering data on what works and what does not work in your school. However, teachers are very busy people who like to be hands-on and active. Teachers rarely provide themselves with "time out" or permission to engage in professional dialogue and reflection. Some teachers are resistant to reflective learning at first, although most who do give it a go find they benefit immensely.

> *[There was] some initial resistance, particularly in relation to owning up to things they can't do. Now teachers are MUCH more comfortable with this because they realize that no one is being judgmental. They have realized that the journal works to support their learning.*

Reflection and discussion can be formal or informal, verbal or written, regular and planned, or more spontaneous. It is important that the strategies adopted are appropriate within your school culture. Some schools are more open and willing to engage in discussion and reflection than others. Some present a more verbal culture, where group discussion will be more successful. In other schools, written reflection might be more practical. In our experience, it is beneficial to experiment with a range of strategies and see what works best.

Seven strategies for reflection and discussion have been trialed as part of Technology Together: embedding discussion in staff meetings, reflection sheets and scaffolds, reflective journals, e-portfolios, visual displays and graffiti boards, informal and incidental discussions, and video reflecting. In this section, we consider the strengths and weaknesses of each strategy.

Embedding Discussion in Staff Meetings

Staff meetings are generally busy with a lot to cover. However, allocating regular time at staff meetings will send a clear message that Technology Together is important and valued. It gives the process status and ensures that ICT learning remains at the forefront of teachers' attention. Staff meeting discussion can also keep up the momentum in teacher learning and provide an opportunity for showcasing and celebrating achievements. Discussion can encourage reluctant teachers to follow the lead and actively seek additional support. The key advice from participants in our research was to give Technology Together a permanent place on the staff meeting agenda:

> *Our major strategy for supporting staff was during staff meetings where time was allocated to discuss strategies to support teachers and to gauge how teachers were going with their planned goals. Initially we used staff meetings to attempt to incite passion and commitment for the project by brainstorming potential ICT applications … [and] to highlight the importance of metacognitive reflection when using computers.*

Devoting significant time on a regular basis for discussion is not always easy or even possible. However, any time, no matter how small, can be valuable. Five minutes at the beginning of a meeting, as teachers are coming in and settling down, can be used for writing reflections in journals or displaying a pertinent quote or visual stimulus with a data projector. Ten minutes is sufficient to prompt two or three teachers to share some experiences from the week. Fifteen or twenty minutes can open up discussion around the purpose, value, or possibilities of a metacognitive approach. In Chapters 4 and 5, we provide ideas for 5-, 10-, 15- or 20-minute time slots in staff meetings, and we provide resources on the Technology Together website to support these activities.

As a final note, if your staff meetings are filled with announcements and reminders, consider transitioning to an electronic approach for these communications. Email alerts, a school blog, or a wiki can manage such messages while also forming a whole-school focus for technology learning.

Reflection Sheets and Scaffolds

A second strategy for engaging teachers in reflection is to use sheets or scaffolds that prompt them to write their experiences and reflect on the meanings they draw from these experiences. For example, a scaffold can guide teachers to reflect on a problem they had with ICT, noting what they did, what happened, what they learned from the experience, and what they would try next time (see, for example, **Resource 6** | **Reflection 3.1**). Another approach is to use a "PMI" process, whereby teachers think about the *pluses*, *minuses*, and *interesting points* about an ICT experience. Combining reflective scaffolds with a follow-up discussion can be most beneficial.

The success of these scaffolds will vary from school to school. Some schools have found it difficult to encourage teachers to fill them in, even when time was allowed at staff meetings. Making the scaffolds compulsory may be counterproductive. In any event, scaffolds may work best when used occasionally or irregularly rather than repetitively. Most mentors involved in Technology Together reflected that in hindsight they wished they had made a greater effort to encourage teachers to engage in this form of reflection.

Resource 6 | **Reflection 3.1**   Example of a reflection scaffold

Scaffold for Reflection		Name: Jane Tippentry
		Date: 31st March 2011
What did you do/try?	Two parents asked whether notes could be emailed home as their children kept losing them.	
	Asked Terry if it was possible to send one email to multiple parents	
What happened?	Terry said the address book function allowed this and that he'd show me how next Monday.	
	Initially frustrated because wanted to email class note tomorrow	
	Thought I'd try myself. Clicked on address book icon and saw a button to create a new group	
	Realized that the screens guided me through the process	
	Managed to send out one email to all parents in class	
What insights did you gain about yourself as a computer learner?	Felt great to know I could do it myself!	
	Sometimes I only need some "tips" to get me going in the right direction.	
	I think I'll remember how to do this better than if Terry had done it for me.	
	Have more confidence in my ability to try things myself	
What else would/could you try?	Ask for "tips" from Terry next time I need help	
	Get my class to try setting up their own email list of friends	

Reflective Journals

Journals (and e-portfolios, which are discussed in the following section) are a valuable means for teachers to look back and see how much they have learned and achieved—something that can greatly enhance their self-efficacy. For some teachers, their journal becomes an ICT learning companion:

> *Progression over time became apparent through the journaling that took place. This enabled people to write, reflect and discuss, and especially to share their "aha" experiences.*

Journals can either be unstructured or structured. Unstructured journals (such as a blank exercise book) provide teachers with a place to spontaneously write free-form and random thoughts, insights, and reflections, as well as computer tips, instructions, and steps. Structured journals, in contrast, provide a series of prompts or stimuli to guide teachers' reflections. Structured journals can also be a means of embedding some of the metacognitive ideas into teachers' reflective processes. As part of our research, we developed and trialed this form of structured journal; examples are provided on the Technology Together website.

Some schools chose to leave the journals with teachers to write in at any time, while other schools handed journals out at the beginning of staff meetings and collected them at the end, ensuring teachers had them at the meeting and conveying an expectation that teachers needed to complete entries within an allocated time.

> *Providing teachers with a weekly journal encouraged accountability and "stickability." Teachers felt obliged to keep up with their journal writing in order to fill in each week's page.*

Some teachers and school cultures find extra paperwork to be a burden. In this case, it can help to stress that journals are valuable as a learning support—not for accountability.

Choosing whether to use a journal and, if so, whether to use a structured or unstructured one, will vary among schools. However, if you are implementing Technology Together over an extended period of time (which we recommend), then you may choose to use both types of journal at different times to add variety. As with the scaffold sheets, reflective journals can be used as prompts for discussion at staff meetings.

E-portfolios

An e-portfolio is a structured collection of work, created across time that evidences continual growth and development, as well as the current competencies of the learner. An e-portfolio is not only a tool to support teachers' own professional development, but it is also a valuable approach to learning and assessment that teachers can employ with students in their classrooms. Developing a technology-based e-portfolio combines developing technical skills with reflection and documentation of learning.

There are two types of e-portfolios: working portfolios and showcase portfolios. A working portfolio contains a wide range of good and not-so-good samples that demonstrate growth over time. It emphasizes learning processes and the construction of knowledge. A showcase portfolio, on the other hand, is more selective and emphasizes demonstrated outcomes. Both types of portfolio can be produced as hard copy as well as in digital (e-portfolio) format.

Obviously, when our goal is to be supporting teachers' (and students') ICT learning, a digital portfolio makes a lot of sense. This format involves an electronic collection of work samples linked together by hyperlinks in a word-processed document, PowerPoint (or similar) presentation, wiki, or blog. There is also a variety of software products designed specifically for e-portfolio development (such as the open source Mahara at https://mahara.org).

E-portfolios most effectively support teacher and student learning that emphasize reflecting on what has been learned. Including only work samples is not generally considered sufficient. Rather, the e-portfolio should also include annotations on learning. Such annotations include

- What was new (what you learned, how you met your learning goals, etc.);
- How you went about your learning (strategies employed, challenges faced, how you dealt with these challenges, problem solving, help seeking, etc.);
- Relevance of your learning in the school or classroom; and
- Ongoing goals.

Teachers can be encouraged to compile an e-portfolio themselves during the year or to engage their students in creating one. A progressively compiled staff or student e-portfolio provides an excellent way of showcasing work and achievements at the end of the year. Schools can also consider compiling a whole-school e-portfolio.

Visual Displays and Graffiti Boards

Sometimes a visual display, pinned up on the staff room bulletin board or near a high-use area, such as by a photocopier, refrigerator, or sink, can be a good prompt for reflection and discussion. The display might range from sharing a quote (many are provided throughout this book) to a poster that invites contribution. In Chapters 4 and 5 (and on the Technology Together website), we provide examples of visual displays that can be used to support teachers' reflection. Thought-bubble displays, for example, succinctly convey the essence of many of the elements of the metacognitive approach and encourage teachers to consider how these ideas apply to them.

Alternatively, you might choose to construct a graffiti board somewhere near the staff computers or in the general staff room. Graffiti boards can be either unstructured (simply a large empty space for people to write ideas) or structured (with a framework to scaffold reflection). If structured, it is best if the board addresses a different issue or theme every two weeks to keep people's attention. One Technology Together school used its graffiti board for staff to record problems that they encountered. Other staff would then add comments, either helping to solve problems or acknowledging the successes of the people involved:

> *The ICT graffiti board gave staff an outlet to vent their frustrations (of which there were plenty), ask questions, and share successes and useful websites. It also heightened whole-school awareness of what was happening with ICT in other classrooms and stage groups (grades). This was a useful reflection tool because it was generally affirming, producing healthy discussion and promoting collegiality.*

Informal and Incidental Discussions

Informal discussions among companion mentors, facilitators, school executives, and teachers, or among teachers themselves, need to be embraced by schools as valid sources of reflection and learning in their own right. Much happens in a school's corridors or in the staff room over a cup of tea. Informal discussions can be critical times for staff to identify and share *aha* moments and also frustrations.

The difficulty with informal and incidental discussion and reflection is that it is not well captured and, therefore, more difficult to monitor and evaluate. In Technology Together, the key is to acknowledge and encourage this discussion, but also to try to make it more explicitly part of the learning process. More formal discussion points, such as time in staff meetings, can be used to prompt teachers to remember and consider the value of these passing conversations. Teachers can help each other to report back on these discussions.

Video Reflecting

A good way of capturing teachers' reflections, particularly at summative stages, is to conduct video interviews. In these interviews, teachers and/or students are invited to talk to the camera about their learning achievements and experiences. Video reflecting provides an excellent way of celebrating the outcomes of Technology Together and sharing these achievements with others, which leads us to Step 10, the final step of our implementation planning process.

Step 10
Planning to Showcase and Celebrate Achievements

An important aspect of a metacognitive approach is encouraging technology learners to affirm their accomplishments. So, a key part of the planning process is to discuss how you will create opportunities for teachers to share their achievements and discoveries. This may sound straightforward, but teachers often need support to identify that they have something worth sharing. Creating a school culture that encourages sharing and intentionally providing opportunities for showcasing and celebration is important:

> *Much ado was made of people's achievements purely by word of mouth. Simple achievements were met with positive reinforcement and encouragement to stretch even further. Enthusiasm bubbled among staff members, and several participants were happy to try and stretch further next time. Some classes chose to use ICT in whole-school assemblies, which showcased achievements in the wider school community.*

One way of celebrating teachers' achievements is to showcase and display students' work. Displaying student work reflects what teachers have been doing in their classrooms, indirectly celebrating teachers' learning as well. Displaying student work also provides teachers from different classes and grades the opportunity to realize what students are capable of and provides ideas for personal goals. We provide ideas for celebrating achievements in Chapter 6.

It is important that your school builds a dynamic not focused only on what goes well. Sharing experiences that are less successful or did not go to plan is just as important. Such experiences should also be celebrated because the learning that occurs in these situations will benefit the whole-school community. Establishing an environment where teachers feel confident to speak of their less positive experiences will convey the message that risk taking and "failure" is an important part of technology learning.

Again, there are lots of ways you can showcase and celebrate achievements. **Resource 7 | Table 3.4** suggests some strategies you might plan to use.

Checklist for Implementation Planning

In summary, then, this chapter has outlined what we see as the 10 important steps which schools should take when planning to implement Technology Together.

We conclude with a planning checklist, **Resource 8 | Form 3.2**, that will assist in ensuring you have considered all the necessary implementation issues.

Resource 7 | **Table 3.4** Strategies for showcasing and celebrating success

Potential strengths	Potential weaknesses
Strategy: Regular time set aside in staff meetings for show and tell	
Motivates teachers to try similar things Can encourage non–ICT experts to present their achievements (no matter how small) to show that all learning is significant	Less confident technology users may feel intimidated by more experienced teachers. Teachers may not like to draw attention to their achievements in a whole-school context.
Strategy: Individual teachers encouraged to record their achievements (e.g., using a simple scaffold or via a journal)	
Can capture moments of small, but significant, learning Is more immediate, so achievements are not lost Useful as a basis for regular whole-school sharing	Teachers may not allocate time and effort unless regularly prompted and reminded.
Strategy: Formal or informal small group meetings where teachers come together regularly (say, once a month) and share what they have been doing	
Can encourage acknowledgment of achievements, no matter how big or small Builds collegiality Provides support and reassurance regarding problems Keeps ICT on the agenda if done regularly	Requires a time commitment Teachers may not view it as "hands on."
Strategy: Showcasing students' work at assemblies or presentation ceremonies	
Provides positive outcomes for students and teachers Can excite and motivate other teachers Can profile ICT agenda to parent groups	Requires encouragement to get teachers to plan for tangible and shareable products resulting from ICT learning experiences
Strategy: Digital display of student work via a school or class website	
Provides a tangible and permanent product for teachers and students alike Students can show it off to parents, friends, and other relatives. Teachers can show it off to colleagues and friends.	Takes effort and time to compile and produce

Resource 8 | **Form 3.2** Checklist for implementation planning

- [ ] Is ICT identified as a priority in your school's annual plan?
- [ ] Is the 12–18 month period you have identified for implementing Technology Together relatively free from major disruptive events or agendas?
- In introducing Technology Together to your school, have you:
  - [ ] Positioned it as a school priority?
  - [ ] Emphasized that it will meet all individuals at their own level and provide lots of practical ideas and support?
  - [ ] Conveyed enthusiasm but also a degree of expectation and accountability?
  - [ ] Considered how explicit to be (at least initially) about the metacognitive approach?
- Will all staff be encouraged to be directly involved (preferable), or will you initially focus on a smaller group? Will you include teacher aides and administrative staff?
- When will you facilitate a discussion around your ICT future "vision"?
- Will your school have an external partner?
  - [ ] If yes, will the partner conduct the school analysis?
  - [ ] If no, who will coordinate the school analysis?
- Who will participate in the school analysis discussion? When will this occur?
- Have you registered your school on the Technology Together website so you can access the online teacher survey? When will teachers complete this?
- Which version of the student survey will you use? How will you implement it?
- What are the key findings from your school analysis, and what aspects of the school culture will you need to take into account in your planning?
- Are all school administrative leaders on board?
- Who will be your Technology Together facilitator?
- Who will be your companion mentor(s)?
- What roles will your ICT experts play?
- Is everyone aware of their roles?
- How will you meet and work together as a team?
- How and when will the initial goal-setting process take place? Who will play what roles?
- What mentoring strategies will you initially trial?
- How will you manage staff release time?
- Which reflection and discussion strategies will you plan to try?
- How and when will you showcase and celebrate teachers' and students' achievements?

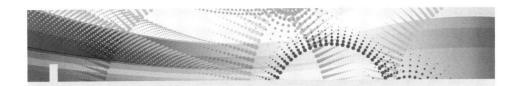

CHAPTER **4**

Mentoring within a Metacognitive Framework

In Chapter 2, we introduced the three dimensions of the metacognitive approach: affects, motivation, and strategies. We also explored how this approach encourages reflection on a range of related elements and how these elements are likely to influence past, present, and future learning. In this chapter, we explore in closer detail the particular metacognitive model employed by Technology Together and consider what each element means for mentors and mentees when put into practice. In particular, the approaches to mentoring that we suggest here are consistent with fostering capability rather than only competency.

Why Technology Together Mentoring Is Different

Traditionally, mentoring involves a more experienced or senior person, the mentor, helping a less experienced or junior person, the mentee or protégé. However, contemporary definitions of mentoring propose that mentors might also be of equal or similar standing to their protégés. These definitions focus on psychosocial aspects of mentoring, such as providing support, building self-confidence, and improving working relationships. In particular, ICT mentoring is likely to differ from traditional mentoring models in that it is not uncommon for a younger or less experienced person to mentor an older and more experienced professional.

Mentoring in Technology Together is not only about providing technical guidance or assisting with skills. Although this type of training is at times important, a mentor's role also includes the following aspects:

- Helping colleagues make a mental shift in how they view ICT;
- Helping teachers to set goals and prompting them to be ambitious;
- Discussing and suggesting learning strategies that foster capability;
- Listening when the mentee has a problem;
- Providing side-by-side support;
- Providing feedback on what you hear your colleagues say and confronting negative thoughts, intentions, or behaviors; and
- Encouraging teachers to document, share, and celebrate achievements.

Thus, the main role of mentors includes supporting, encouraging, motivating, and providing ideas to those teachers with whom they work—helping mentees to become skillful and independent learners:

> *We spent much time rephrasing and challenging negative and self-derogatory comments about ICT. Whilst these comments were often said in a humorous manner, we felt the underlying message reinforced a negative attitude to ICT.*

There are no approaches that work with all teachers in all school contexts. However, the research that informs Technology Together provides insights into the strengths, weaknesses, and potential outcomes of particular strategies. In this section, we share some of this learning.

Mentoring to Develop Capability

In Chapter 1, we discussed very explicitly how Technology Together helps teachers become capable technology users, rather than simply competent ones. As we noted, competency is an ingredient of capability; however, capable people are also those who can operate in unknown contexts and with new problems. We focus on capability because it is a much stronger characteristic than competency in contexts of rapid change, as is the case with ICT.

The ideas of competency and capability weave through all three dimensions of the metacognitive approach. In fact, simply becoming aware of the competency/capability distinction can prompt changes in both confidence and practice, as illustrated in these two teacher quotes:

> *I appreciate the difference between being capable and being competent. This is clear when asking for help at work. Many can tell me what to do only if they have done it themselves. A select few are able to help solve problems unfamiliar to them.... Now, I think I am more willing to become capable and hence more willing to tackle unfamiliar problems.*

> *By working and concentrating on the processes involved, teachers are becoming more capable. They realize that although a program or application may be slightly different, the process that they need to follow will be very similar.*

Mentoring to develop capability rather than competency involves different considerations. Most important, it requires that mentors recognize and understand the difference between the two and realize how that difference will affect their relationships and interactions with mentees.

Teachers who approach their learning from a competency-based perspective have a very different view about the type of strategies they use and the support they need compared with teachers who approach learning from a capability-based perspective. Teachers focused on competency perceive ICT as a defined body of knowledge and an identifiable set of skills. They believe that competency can be passed from expert to novice and are likely to view the proper place for learning as a structured, planned, and professionally delivered training course. Typically, teachers focused on competency feel overwhelmed by the range of skills to learn.

Teachers who focus on capability, in contrast, see ICT as an ongoing learning journey with no beginning and no end. They perceive ICT knowledge as fluid, flexible, and multifaceted, and they recognize there is much to learn from others, but that no one person has all the answers. Capable technology users understand that they can discover answers and solve problems by using good learning strategies. They also recognize that motivation, enthusiasm, confidence, and investment of time are the main requirements for becoming a proficient technology user.

The thought-bubble display (**Resource 9 | Thought bubble 4.1**) helps to capture the competency/capability distinction visually. A full-color version of **Resource 9 | Thought bubble 4.1** is available for download at the Technology Together website .

Resource 9 | Thought bubble 4.1   Competency/capability thought-bubble display

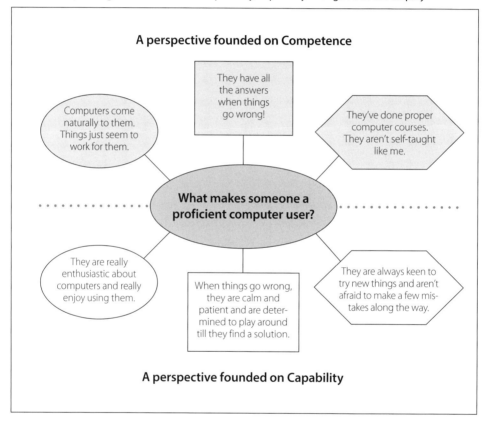

Once you start to understand the distinction between competency and capability and identify its manifestations for yourself and your colleagues, it can help you to understand the technology learning process in a different way.

We created a model to provide a visual representation of learning for competency and capability based on ideas from complexity science (discussed in Chapter 1). The competency/capability model, **Resource 10 | Figure 4.1**, can be seen in color on the

Technology Together website (http://technologytogether.scu.edu.au). It can also be downloaded.

The competency/capability model (**Resource 10** | **Figure 4.1**) can be helpful when describing to teachers what Technology Together aims to achieve in terms of teachers' learning. The model will also help you to compare and contrast the two different approaches.

Eight Key Points of the Competency/Capability Model

1. Both the competency and capability approaches to technology learning require some basic skills and knowledge;
2. Both forms of learning take time;
3. Competency-based learning can progress learners quickly but with limited outcomes;
4. Capability-based learning may take a little longer, but the potential outcomes are far greater;
5. Competency-based learning requires outside input—training by another person, usually in the form of directive-style training;
6. Capability-based learning relies on dialogue and conversation—a two-way interaction between people;
7. People can "go backward" in terms of both their competence and capability;
8. People can have *aha* moments that send them in a new learning direction, usually (although not always) from competency to capability. These *aha* moments are what the metacognitive approach tries to promote.

What, then, are the implications of all this for mentors? To foster capability, mentors should explicitly discuss these ideas with staff. The concept of capability is so critical to Technology Together that it warrants a longer session at a staff meeting. Resources to facilitate such a discussion are provided on the Technology Together website.

Some specific strategies that mentors can use to foster capability include the following:

- Focusing on learning strategies rather than specific skills or outcomes;
- Encouraging teachers to explore software they haven't seen before;
- Emphasizing general principles, or the "big ideas" of learning, rather than specific steps;
- Pointing out the similarities between different software applications;

- Using opportunities (such as transitioning to a newer version of software, or from one brand of hardware or software to an alternative) to emphasize the importance of lifelong learning and capability; and
- Emphasizing that capability does not exclude competency.

Resource 11 | Table 4.1 (and the associated **Resource 12** | Table 4.2) provide some suggestions for how you might engage teachers with these ideas. The website provides a PowerPoint presentation.

Resource 11 | Table 4.1   Competency/capability: Ideas for engagement

Prompts for teacher reflection, discussion, and action	
15 min	Discuss the concepts listed in the competency/capability comparison table (**Resource 12** | Table 4.2).
20 min	Follow instructions in the 15-min prompt, but also discuss the visual model (**Resource 10** | Figure 4.1); distribute copies together with the eight key points on what the diagram illustrates (page 91).
Wall display	Pin up the competency/capability thought-bubble display (**Resource 9** | Thought bubble 4.1).
Weekly challenge	Challenge teachers to reflect on whether their goal in teaching is to support students to be competent or capable. What in their teaching contributes to each of these?
Metacognition in the classroom	
Challenge teachers to try something new with ICT in their classroom and to notice examples of ICT competency/capability among their students.	

Resource 12 | Table 4.2   Competence and capability in a school context: A comparison

The competent computer-using teacher …	The capable computer-using teacher …
… has been shown how to use certain features of Microsoft Word such as cut, copy, paste, changing fonts, using WordArt, and inserting a table. He uses these functions well and frequently in preparing his lesson resources, but when he needed to format a bullet list so that it displayed with checkmark boxes, he asked the ICT coordinator to show him how do it.	… has been shown how to use basic features of Microsoft Word such as cut, copy, paste, changing fonts, using WordArt, and inserting a table, but in creating her lesson resources, she encountered a need to draw a diagram, so she explored the menus and toolbars and found the Insert shapes feature and gave it a try herself.

Resource 12 | **Table 4.2** *(Continued)*

The competent computer-using teacher …	The capable computer-using teacher …
… went to a workshop on using Microsoft PowerPoint. She has used it since to present at school assemblies, but she is not yet confident enough to set up the data projector without assistance.	… went to a workshop on using Microsoft PowerPoint. He has used it since to present at school assemblies. He tried setting up the data projector to give a presentation in his classroom and has since engaged his class in creating self-running storybooks based on a theme he is covering in class. His students took the projector and presented these stories to the Kindergarten students.
… went to a two-hour Microsoft Excel training session after school. Under the guidance of the trainer, he created an excellent spreadsheet with a graph. When he returned to his own computer, he couldn't find how to open Excel and became discouraged. A year later he still has not tried using Excel again.	… realized that the new syllabus requires her to teach spreadsheet concepts to her class. Never having used a spreadsheet, she asks a friend to help get her going. After a half hour of being shown the basics, she sets herself the goal of creating a spreadsheet based on growth rates of a seed relative to light and temperature. After playing with setting up this spreadsheet, she decides to give it a try with her class.
… heard about another teacher who was creating quizzes, crossword puzzles, and cloze passage activities for his class using software called Hot Potatoes. She thought, "I better ask John to show me how he does this."	… heard about another teacher who was creating quizzes, crossword puzzles, and cloze passage activities for his class using software called Hot Potatoes. He did a web search, located and downloaded the software, and played around, creating some resources for his own class.
… is told that the school has bought a new digital video camera and waits for someone to give him at least one (probably more) lessons on how to use it.	… is told that the school has bought a new digital video camera and quickly finds out where it is and how she can borrow it. She learns the features one weekend while videoing her kids playing sports. The following week she plans a lesson with students videoing science experiments.

Mentoring with Mindfulness toward Affects

Figure 4.2 focuses on affects. In Chapter 2, we introduced affects as one of the three dimensions of the metacognitive approach and discussed various affective elements that impact on technology learning (see **Resource 1** | **Figure 2.1**). In this section, we consider each of these affective elements—their significance to technology learners and how you can use this understanding as part of the mentoring process.

Figure 4.2   The visual model of the metacognitive approach to technology learning, focused on affects

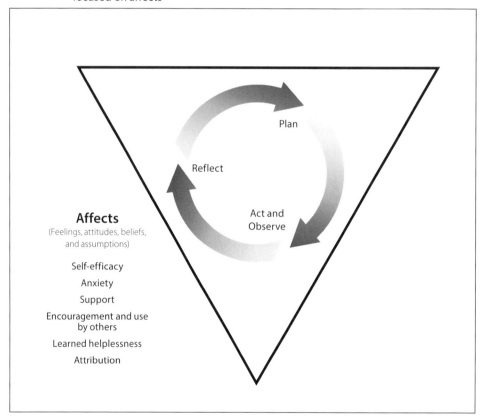

Mentoring to Build Self-Efficacy

Previously, we defined computer self-efficacy as individuals' beliefs and judgments about what they are capable of doing as opposed to what they can actually do. In other words, self-efficacy is not about skills. Rather it is about the judgments you make about your knowledge and skills. From this definition, you will probably begin to recognize the connection between self-efficacy and capability. As Ertmer, Conklin, Lewandowski, Osika, Selo, and Wignall (2003) argue, "teachers who have high levels of efficacy regarding teaching with technology are more likely to participate more eagerly, expend more effort and persist longer on technology-related tasks than teachers who have low levels of efficacy" (p. 97). Put simply, if teachers believe that they cannot use technology, then they will not be motivated to try, and hence may never build skills or confidence.

The concept of self-efficacy helps mentors understand that for some people it is not only lack of computer skills that hinders their technology use. All the training in the world may not change their self-efficacy.

You may be thinking, "But don't the skills come first, and self-efficacy follows?" Well, not always. In fact, many people with well-developed skills do not have high computer self-efficacy. Although they may use computers frequently, they may be held back by their beliefs that they either aren't doing things adequately or properly or that they simply do not know enough to be confident.

Furthermore, for teachers with low computer self-efficacy, skills training can actually be detrimental. Teachers who do not believe in their ability to learn will often create barriers within the training context and not employ appropriate strategies to reinforce their learning. For these teachers, training is ineffective, reinforcing their beliefs that they cannot use technology and cannot learn.

Similarly, there are many individuals (usually those who become capable technology users) who start out with very few computer skills but high computer self-efficacy. In some instances, they make progress with their technology use very rapidly and often end up with broader skills than training itself would facilitate. Our visual model of computer capability (see **Figure 4.1** on the website) helps illustrate why this is the case.

The metacognitive approach proposes that it is not sufficient for mentors only to be conscious of self-efficacy. Those teachers (and students) with whom you work also need to recognize and reflect on the important role that self-efficacy plays in influencing their use of technology:

> *By enhancing my understanding of self-efficacy and its effects on one's computer abilities, I can stop the chain reaction before it begins and influence the success of my own learning.*

To help build self-efficacy, mentors can

- Help teachers become aware of their self-efficacy and the factors that have influenced it (the other components of the metacognitive approach will also help);
- Discuss the relationship between self-efficacy and technology skills and confidence;
- Prompt teachers to vocalize how they would like to feel about their technology use in the future;
- Focus on building capability rather than competency;
- Encourage teachers to take on small, achievable goals;
- Help teachers acknowledge and celebrate their successes, no matter how small or insignificant these might seem.

Table 4.3 (below) shows more ideas to engage mentees. **Resource 13**, available on the website, provides additional engagement ideas. The color wall display for **Resource 13—Resource 14 | Thought bubble 4.2**—is also available on the Technology Together website (http://technologytogether.scu.edu.au) as is a PowerPoint presentation.

Resource 13 | Table 4.3   Self-efficacy: Ideas for engagement

Prompts for teacher reflection, discussion, and action	
5 min	Ask teachers to list three to five things that they think they do well with technology but *not* to compare themselves to anyone else—just focus on achievements they are proud of. Teachers do not need to share this list with anyone else unless they choose to.
20 min	Explain the concept of self-efficacy using the resources on the Technology Together website and facilitate a brief discussion where teachers share their responses if they feel comfortable doing so.
Wall display	Pin up the self-efficacy thought bubble display **Resource 14	Thought bubble 4.2** (available from the Technology Together website).
Weekly challenge	Challenge everyone to identify one happening during the week that raises their computer self-efficacy—no matter how big or small.
Metacognition in the classroom	
Encourage teachers to notice indications of high and low self-efficacy among their students. These indications need not be solely related to computer self-efficacy. Teachers may look for them in other areas, such as sports or language learning.	

Mentoring to Decrease Computer Anxiety

Most of us can readily relate to the concept of computer anxiety. Whether we conceive of ourselves as technophrenics or technophobics, many people have at some stage experienced a level of anxiety related to their computer use and learning.

There are two types of anxieties: trait-based anxiety and state-based anxiety. Trait-based anxiety occurs when individuals are generally anxious in their personality. State-based anxiety, on the other hand, is related to specific situations. For most people, anxiety with technology is state-based, but occasionally we encounter someone who has a more generally anxious disposition; these people get concerned about all sorts of things.

For some teachers, computer anxiety is related to the more general fear that technology use will conflict with their capacity to teach in the way they feel most comfortable or familiar. Some teachers fear that technology will restrict their interpersonal contact with students and, in turn, expose students to inaccurate and unverifiable information. Other teachers are concerned about social and ethical issues in relation to ICT, such as students accessing inappropriate material on the Internet or not getting enough physical activity. A major source of anxiety for many teachers is change itself. All of us can get comfortable doing things a certain way, and technology, in particular, challenges us to change at an often uncomfortable rate.

Although these concerns are relevant, for some teachers they become excuses that prevent them from learning enough about technology to determine whether their concerns are even valid.

> *I used to scoff at the push for everyday use of computers in the class—but I see that my reluctance was more to do with my fear of technology rather than my perception of its usefulness and place in the classroom.*

To use these concepts in our interactions with our colleagues, mentors can

- Recognize the symptoms of anxiety in the teachers with whom they work;
- Help teachers to recognize their own anxieties and what has contributed to them;
- Focus on strategies rather than on specific skills only; and
- Involve more confident computer users in discussing how they overcome problems and how they perceive the value of technology in the classroom.

Resource 15 | **Table 4.4** Anxiety: Ideas for engagement

Prompts for teacher reflection, discussion, and action	
5 min	Have teachers fill out the simple confronting anxieties scaffold (**Resource 16** | **Form 4.1**).
10 min	Target one or two teachers in your school who might share a story of overcoming anxiety and giving technology a try.
Weekly challenge	Challenge everyone to identify one point during the week when they start to become anxious about their technology use and reflect on (and preferably record) what contributed to the anxiety and what they could do to minimize it.
Metacognition in the classroom	
Suggest teachers talk to students about what, if anything, makes them anxious about using or learning to use technology. Or, more specifically, suggest teachers ask students their views on things they think teachers may be anxious about, for example, access to inappropriate material.	

Resource 16 | **Form 4.1** Confronting anxieties scaffold

Computer anxieties	Steps to alleviating anxieties
Something that concerns me about technology is …	Something positive that I can do about this is …

The Role of Support, Encouragement, and Technology Use by Others

Conventional wisdom suggests that being in an environment where others are using technology is generally positive for fostering learning. Support, encouragement, and technology use by those around you (teachers, students, family members, and/or friends) can be a positive influence on computer self-efficacy. However, for some technology learners, seeing others who have well-developed technology skills can also diminish their own self-efficacy. Interacting with others you perceive as more capable may feel intimidating, and admitting that you do not know how to do something may feel embarrassing. Some teachers may rail against a perceived social pressure to "keep up." Other teachers may do things for you rather than teaching you how to do things, and because others volunteer to do computer tasks, there is little need to learn yourself. Further, teachers may feel threatened by ICT-capable students because this challenges traditional knowledge and power balances between teacher and student:

> *Just when I think I know enough about IT to get by, another person does or says something that makes me feel incompetent.*

So how can we use these concepts in our work as mentors? A metacognitive approach helps create a school culture and climate where the type of support, encouragement, and technology use by others is more positive. As a mentor you can do the following:

- Keep your hands off the mouse when helping others (as much as possible);
- Encourage teachers to recognize the impact of different forms of support, including the potentially negative impact of too much support;
- Help teachers understand which learning strategies are most effective for them in building capability—and empower teachers to be explicit in asking for this type of support;
- Let teachers have some say as to who provides them with support and assistance;
- Work with the school's ICT experts so that they are aware of the differences between supporting teachers to develop capability as opposed to solely competency; and
- Embed reflection and discussion into staff meetings and encourage sharing of problems by all—even the most experienced.

Resource 17 | **Table 4.5** Support and encouragement: Ideas for engagement

Prompts for teacher reflection, discussion, and action	
10 min	Talk to staff explicitly about the positive and negative potential of support, encouragement, and technology use by others. Use the resources on the Technology Together website (http://technologytogether.scu.edu.au).
20 min	Follow instructions as in the 10-min prompt, but have one or two teachers share their experiences of support and encouragement—some may reflect on support they receive from their own children at home. Explore how this support might build or diminish capability but also what you can do, that is, take back the mouse or ask to be shown a different way.
Weekly challenge	Ask teachers to be more conscious during the week of the support and encouragement they offer others and what impact this might have on them.

Metacognition in the classroom
Suggest to teachers that they seek out at least one opportunity during the week to ask a student to show them a technology skill. Ask teachers to critically reflect on whether their help was positive or not so positive and in what way.

Recognizing Patterns of Learned Helplessness and Attribution

In Chapter 2, we discussed the concept of learned helplessness and its relevance to technology learning contexts. It is not uncommon to encounter individuals who, when faced with technology challenges or difficulties, avoid any personal responsibility and resist efforts to problem solve. Some individuals also employ self-handicapping tactics, such as procrastination and blaming others. Such individuals are "failure accepting"—they come to expect technology problems will happen to them, so it is natural and normal when things do not go to plan. They fail to help themselves in order to avoid any implication of their own low ability.

Learned helplessness often relates to attribution. Attribution theory is concerned with individuals' judgments about their successes and failures. When individuals comment about a problem they have experienced and indicate that the task was too difficult, that they lacked training, or they didn't have enough time, they are making attributions. When individuals experience success and claim it is due to luck, ability, effort, help from others, or hard work, they are also making attributions.

Attribution can get in the way of good learning and can become a major contributor to learned helplessness. Therefore, understanding attribution theory can help mentors and mentees become more effective ICT learners.

There are four dimensions that come into play when we talk about attribution:

- **Locus of control.** Individuals are said to have *internal attribution* when they predominantly believe that the reason for success or failure resides within themselves. They have *external attribution* when they predominantly believe that the reason for their success or failure is due to influences outside themselves;
- **Stability.** The degree to which individuals believe that the cause of their success or failure will change over time;
- **Controllability.** Whether individuals feel they have control over the determinants of their successes and failures; and
- **Globality.** Whether individuals believe success or failure will occur in all similar situations.

Attribution theory generally assumes that internal attribution is a positive thing—that it encourages you to take responsibility for your own actions and your own learning. In many respects, this assumption is correct. However, people with internal attribution are also more likely to blame themselves when things not within their control go wrong, even technical faults with hardware, networks, or other equipment.

"Appropriate attribution" (in other words, the willingness and ability to determine whether the cause of success or lack of success is external or internal—due to yourself or to factors outside your control) is a central component of a metacognitive approach. Appropriate attribution is also very important for teachers to model and to explicitly discuss with their students:

> *Reflecting on attribution theory … has made me aware of my own change of attitude in relation to success and failure when using computers. Originally, I had an ongoing tendency to blame myself when I was unable to complete tasks.… However, after working in a classroom that housed extremely old and often faulty computers, I have been able to accept that some factors are completely out of my control.*

Metacognition can be powerful in avoiding and overcoming learned helplessness. It can support and motivate teachers and students to actively and consciously adopt appropriate help-seeking strategies. It can convince teachers and students that effort is a learning investment more than a risk for self-esteem. Metacognition can also reinforce the idea that lack of success does not imply low ability but, rather, is part of the normal process of learning.

Mentors can support teachers to become more conscious of the attributions that they make. This support can be most easily performed by noticing attributional comments made by your colleagues and gently pointing them out. However, only learners themselves can really be aware of their attributional thought processes, so explicitly discussing attribution with staff can help them self-regulate their own responses. Mentors can also

- Be aware of teachers with a tendency toward learned helplessness,
- Help teachers understand the concept of attribution,
- Gently point out when you hear teachers making inappropriate attributions for either successes or frustrations,
- Encourage teachers to become aware of their students' attributions, and
- Encourage reflection and discussion about learned helplessness and attribution.

The color wall display for **Resource 19 | Thought bubble 4.3** is available on the Technology Together website (http://technologytogether.scu.edu.au).

Resource 18 | Table 4.6 Learned helplessness and attribution: Ideas for engagement

Prompts for teacher reflection, discussion, and action	
10 min	Explain the concept of attribution and the consequences of "inappropriate" attribution, using the resources on the Technology Together website (http://technologytogether.scu.edu.au).
Wall display	Pin up the attribution thought-bubble display (**Resource 19 | Thought bubble 4.3**).
Weekly challenge	Have teachers become more aware of the attributional comments their students make (in all learning contexts—not only technology).
Metacognition in the classroom	
Encourage teachers to explicitly discuss the concept of attribution with their students.	

Mentoring to Foster Motivation

In this section, we unpack the three elements of the metacognitive framework related to motivation: perceived usefulness, pedagogical orientation, and goal orientation. **Figure 4.3** focuses on motivation and its three elements.

Figure 4.3 The visual model of the metacognitive approach to computer learning, focused on motivation

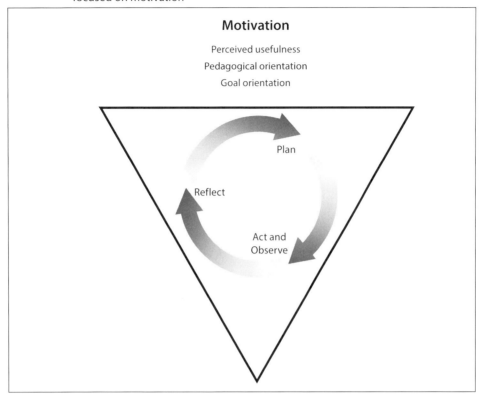

Fostering Perceived Usefulness

In Chapter 2, we identified perceived usefulness as one of the most important elements of a metacognitive approach. We emphasized the enormous influence it has on teachers' motivation to engage in technology learning as well as the amount they retain from their learning experience. For many people (although not all) if a computer skill does not have immediate application, they will not be interested in it, as the following quote illustrates:

> At the time I grasped all that was involved, but I could see no use for PowerPoint at that stage, and my skills became redundant. Then many months later, when I was about to work on a presentation, I needed to be shown again—it was relevant, I had a need to learn, and I was more determined to retain my new skills. When I think back to how my computer skills have increased and diversified, it has only been successful when I've pursued something for my own interest.

Things can be a little more complicated than what this quote illustrates. Some people simply are not interested in new hardware, software, or in searching for new resources. They wait for someone to point out what might be of use. Capable computer users, however, will always be on the lookout for something new and will investigate hardware and software before making a judgment about its relevance in their own context. Only when a school has enough people who are motivated to explore and discover ICT's usefulness will that school begin to become a capable ICT-using community. Now let us consider the two types of perceived usefulness: personal and pedagogical.

Personal perceived usefulness, that is, the usefulness of technology to individuals in their own personal or recreational lives, is often overlooked when schools are implementing teachers' professional development.

Teachers often voice concern (understandably so) about the many impositions and demands made on them. Having to use computers as part of mainstream teaching and learning is just one more of these agendas imposed on teachers by someone else—another pressure on top of an already crowded curriculum.

However, sometimes these teachers can be prompted to see personal and recreational ICT benefits that interest and motivate them far more than any professional application. Once teachers start using technology in their personal lives, using it with their students becomes far less daunting. For example, a teacher might be encouraged to book flights online for a family holiday, use PowerPoint to create a birthday presentation for a relative, borrow a school video camera to film a newborn baby, use Skype to chat with a son or daughter who is overseas, or sign up as someone's Facebook friend.

Pedagogical perceived usefulness, on the other hand, refers to teachers' beliefs regarding the usefulness of technology in the classroom. You may have heard the saying that "we tend to teach the way we were taught." Many teachers have difficulty recognizing the creative and innovative ways to use technology to enhance their students' learning, mainly because they have never had the opportunity to experience learning using ICT themselves.

Teachers tend to either see ICT as a set of skills to be taught to students or as a tool to enhance and enrich learning and teaching practice. It is not only individual teachers who hold these beliefs. School cultures can reinforce and perpetuate these views, too. Consider the comparisons between the two beliefs in **Resource 20** | Table 4.7 and the ideas for engagement in **Resource 21** | Table 4.8. We pick up on these further in Chapter 5, Strategy 4.

Resource 20 | **Table 4.7** Comparison of ICT as a set of skills to be taught or a tool to enhance learning

ICT as a set of skills to be taught	ICT as a tool to enhance and enrich learning and teaching
Often influenced by teachers' own personal focus on ICT competence	Tends to be informed by a capability-based approach
Assumes that students need to be taught computer skills	Assumes that students will pick up these skills as a result of using technology as a normal part of their learning
Assumes the teacher needs to teach the skills	Realizes that students can learn skills independently and help and support each others' learning
Assumes there is a logical order in which skills need to be taught	Recognizes that computer skills can develop in an emergent way
Leads to teaching ICT as a separate subject at a designated separate time of the week	Leads to including ICT as an integrated part of the whole curriculum

Resource 21 | **Table 4.8** Perceived usefulness: Ideas for engagement

Prompts for teacher reflection, discussion, and action	
5 min	Ask teachers to write on a piece of paper one to three things that they use technology for in their recreational/personal life. Pin them up on a central display board.
10 min	Follow the instructions for the 5-min prompt, but also ask teachers to volunteer to share one ICT integration idea that they think has been particularly beneficial for students' learning.
Wall display	Pin up the comparison chart (**Resource 20** | Table 4.7).
Weekly challenge	Ask teachers to find one new technology-based resource that might relate to an interest or hobby and is either fun or personally useful. These resources might include a website or a game they download. Set up a wall chart for teachers to share their finds during the week.

Metacognition in the classroom

Encourage teachers to talk to students about whether there are technologies that they use recreationally that they would consider useful to support their learning in the classroom.

Identifying Pedagogical Orientation

Another element that affects teachers' perceived usefulness of technology in the classroom relates to pedagogical orientation—whether, in their teaching, teachers predominantly adopt one of the following:

- Objectivist (or directed) approaches—beliefs that learning is about transmitting knowledge from one person to another; or
- Constructivist approaches—beliefs that learning is about individuals constructing their own understandings.

These approaches are not discrete or distinct beliefs, and teachers tend to fall somewhere along this continuum.

Teachers who are more constructivist are strongly represented among ICT-using teachers. This fact raises a "chicken and egg" question of whether constructivist teachers perceive the usefulness of ICT and thus embrace it more readily than objectivist teachers *or* whether ICT use leads teachers to become more constructivist. Some research claims that teachers who hold the transmission view of teaching will not adapt to technology use in the classroom because the power it gives directly to students threatens their identity as teacher (Lloyd & Yelland, 2003). Although research is inconclusive on these issues, pedagogical orientation unquestionably needs to be taken into account as a part of ICT professional development.

A metacognitive approach aims to engage teachers in reflecting on their own pedagogical orientation. It encourages whole schools to engage in dialogue about pedagogical practice and prompts school executives to encourage and support teachers to take risks with their pedagogical practice. Teachers who begin to recognize that their students generally enjoy learning in the different ways that ICT enables will often gain "pedagogical perceived usefulness."

Chapter 5 is specifically devoted to pedagogical orientation and covers a range of suggestions for engaging teachers around these ideas.

Modeling Goal Orientation

Another key element of motivation is goal orientation. As we indicated in Chapter 2, many new technology users fail to grow and develop simply because they do not strive to pursue new knowledge and skills. When they see someone do something they cannot do, they lack the impetus to give it a try. A key feature of the metacognitive approach is that participants are encouraged to identify, articulate, and pursue personally relevant goals. Again, Technology Together is about believing "I can–You can."

Everyone, no matter how skilled they are at using technology, will be able to identify new goals. Modeling goal setting for novice technology users can be a positive way of showing how all (or most) learning begins with intent and commitment to achieving something. Goal setting is part of building a whole-school culture of ICT learning:

> *During the year, many staff noted that they felt less intimidated and more supported because there was no expectation that they would all reach the same level of competence or capability.*

In Chapter 3, we introduced the goal-setting structure that identifies goals as related to skills, integration, recreation, metacognition, or leadership. We also talked about big-picture goals and immediate, short-term goals (often skills) that might contribute toward achieving big picture goals. We suggested that when teachers are resentful of an ICT agenda at school, they can be prompted to discover personal and recreational benefits of ICT use that interest and motivate them far more than professional ones. Once teachers start using technology in their personal lives, using it with students becomes far less daunting:

> *A reluctant ICT user and a teacher who would normally restrict all their learning to the allocated time had recently purchased a new video camera. During the holidays this teacher spent time learning how to download and edit video and discovered many applications for the classroom. Since then, this teacher has regularly asked when we are getting software on the server for the students to use.*

It is very important, even critical, that goals remain flexible and changeable. Some learners find that their initial goals are too ambitious, and goals that cannot be achieved in the short term become long-term goals. For other learners, particularly those who are less confident, the goals they set might be easily achieved, and so they quickly find themselves setting new goals. Situations also often arise that lead a teacher to want to change direction, abandon initial ideas, and take on new goals. Having the flexibility to change goals is positive, but teachers need to be aware of the reasons when they make the change. It is not positive, for example, to give up on a goal simply because an obstacle is met at the first attempt. That said, setting ambitious goals should not be discouraged as they can be really motivating—achieving these goals can influence self-efficacy tremendously.

The main problem with goal setting is that learners don't always know what they don't know. They are able to get by using the skills they have learned, and they see no need to develop new skills. These learners do not see the value in further learning. While there is no point learning how to do things that you don't believe you will ever need to know (perceived usefulness), often when you see how such skills or knowledge can be valuable, you will wonder how you ever got by without them.

A key strategy of Technology Together is to provide lots of stimulation and ideas and encourage learners to take on challenges. It is, however, important that teachers themselves own their goals. Chapter 6 is specifically focused on scaffolding goal setting.

Mentoring to Develop Appropriate Strategies

A central part of the metacognitive approach is supporting teachers to adopt beneficial and productive learning strategies—those that build capability rather than only competency. **Figure 4.4** focuses on strategies.

Figure 4.4 The visual model of the metacognitive approach to technology learning, focused on strategies

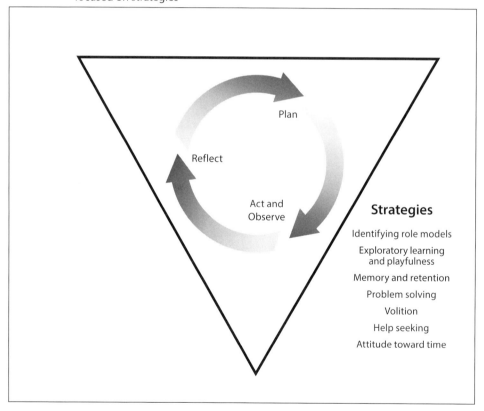

In this section, we discuss how mentors can support teachers to reflect critically on the learning approaches they employ and encourage them to develop into capable, lifelong computer learners. We begin with an exploration of the value of identifying role models for learning and consider the advantages and disadvantages of some commonly used pathways to learning. We then consider the following elements of the metacognitive model: playfulness, memory and retention, problem solving, volition, help seeking, and attitudes toward time.

The traditional view of a role model is of someone in an influential position, such as a parent, teacher, supervisor, or mentor—someone who provides an example for individuals to imitate. However, a role model can be anyone who provides us with stimulus for reflecting on what we would like, or perhaps not like, to be (negative role model). We can look toward role models to help us actively construct our ideal or "possible" selves, based on our needs and goals (Gibson, 2002).

When learners are asked to reflect on the characteristics of someone they see as a proficient technology learner, they often respond with a surprising degree of consistency. Proficient technology learners are generally described as confident in their own skills and abilities yet patient, persistent, determined, and calm when things do not go to plan. They are risk takers with the courage to experiment and try new things and are not afraid to make mistakes. Typically, proficient technology users are seen as methodical/logical thinkers but also enthusiastic and motivated with a positive attitude and love of learning. They constantly use technology, but most importantly they recognize their abilities to problem solve. All of these characteristics are indicative of the concept of technology capability, and all are influenced by attitudes, motivation, or strategies.

When teachers are asked to reflect on how these role models learn, they almost always cite such approaches as self-directed learning, experimentation, trial and error, exploring, and "playing around." In reflecting in a deep way about the characteristics of role models, many less confident technology users come to realize that proficient technology users do not actually know everything there is to know, but rather have employed good learning strategies to get them where they are:

> *At the beginning ... I had to identify what characteristics make up a proficient and capable IT user and I wrote "someone who knows everything." This is clearly not the case. It is more the ability to apply that knowledge across all situations ... the willingness to try is clearly what makes an expert because as one takes on the challenges of trying, one does become familiar with technology and hence becomes an expert. This will clearly be my goal.*

In Chapter 2, we emphasized that although all learning strategies play an important role in technology learning, a metacognitive approach focuses on those strategies that promote capability rather than only competency. Technology Together encourages teachers to reflect on the strengths and weaknesses of various pathways to learning, including group instruction, individual instruction, self-directed learning, and peer-group learning.

Teachers' understandings and insights into each of these pathways and their expectations about their ability to learn in each context can significantly influence their confidence with technology. We have already discussed how some learners believe the only real way to learn a new technology skill is through formal training or by being shown, and hence they do not give themselves permission to try learning it on their own. Other learners believe that self-directed, exploratory approaches are somehow inferior. The realization that most proficient technology users do a good deal of their learning in the same ways can be a big breakthrough and *aha* moment:

> *The main thing that I have learned about my own learning is that I haven't been doing it wrong for all these years.*

Some of the advantages and disadvantages of these learning pathways are summarized in **Resource 23** | **Table 4.10**. However, it may be beneficial to involve school staff in reflecting on the advantages and disadvantages of each of the pathways themselves in light of their own role models. Reflecting on the pathways can

- Challenge learners' assumptions about the most effective approach to technology learning;
- Enable technology learners to better understand their own reactions, successes, or non-successes within these learning pathways;
- Prompt technology learners to try strategies that they might not otherwise have tried;
- Reinforce that there is no one right way of learning;
- Be an important prompt for technology learners to understand how they best learn; and
- Provide confidence with technology.

Resource 22 | **Table 4.9**   Pathways to learning: Ideas for engagement

Prompts for teacher reflection, discussion, and action	
2 min	Have staff think about someone (or more than one person) who they consider to be a proficient technology user. Have them write the characteristics of the technology user on note paper or sticky notes. Collect the notes and pin them to a display wall.
5 min	Introduce the pathways to learning (i.e., the first column of **Resource 23** | **Table 4.10**) and have three or four teachers share their thoughts about the strengths and weaknesses of each.
15 min	Have staff reflect on and discuss the pathways to learning they have used in the past few weeks and the strengths and weaknesses of these pathways. Plan to celebrate examples of teachers taking risks and choosing to be more self-directed or exploratory.
Wall display	Pin up the various pathways to learning table (**Resource 23** | **Table 4.10**).
Weekly challenge	Challenge teachers to try using one of the pathways to learning that they might not normally employ and, as they do so, be mindful of the advantages and disadvantages of the pathway.

Metacognition in the classroom
Encourage teachers to run a lesson (or set a challenge) that explicitly requires students to use self-directed, exploratory learning strategies.

Resource 23 | **Table 4.10** Advantages and disadvantages of various pathways to learning

Pathway to learning	Advantages	Disadvantages
Group instruction (e.g., a workshop in a computer lab) Focuses on a particular skill or piece of software Usually there is one computer per person (or pair). Teaching typically follows a directive approach. Instructor either demonstrates steps on a screen or verbally talks participants through the process. Tends to be competency-based	Can follow a logical sequence Efficient for training large groups of people Participants usually feel supported. Participants can maintain a sense of anonymity, which some feel more comfortable with. Good for getting an overview of a software program's features Participants feel they are learning a lot in a short period of time.	Driven by the instructor Difficult to respond to individuals Hard to set a pace right for everyone Learners can feel intimidated by others. Learners can be nervous about asking for help. Can reinforce learner dependency Minimal opportunity to explore and experiment Usually not meeting an immediate real need Generally poor retention of learning Learning can become dated.
Individual instruction: A more experienced person teaching a less experienced person one-on-one Usually both learner and instructor work at the same computer. Can be either competency- or capability-based	Instructor can work at learner's preferred pace and, in some cases, cover more content more quickly. Instructor can respond to an individual's learning needs. Participants usually feel supported. The degree to which the process is driven by the instructor versus the learner can vary. Can lead to incidental learning Can model effective learning strategies Can encourage engaging in dialogue and address feelings, attitudes, beliefs Generally tailored to meet an immediate real need	Some learners can feel inhibited and don't like to show their lack of knowledge. Can lead to "proximity paralysis" Can reinforce learner dependency The instructor significantly influences success. The strategies for individual instruction influence long-term learning outcomes.

Resource 23 | **Table 4.10** *(Continued)*

Pathway to learning	Advantages	Disadvantages
Self-directed exploratory learning: Individuals identify a need to learn and try things for themselves, usually through exploration Individuals seek help if and when, it is required. Help is drawn from a variety of sources: manuals and documentation, on-screen tutorials and online help, and approaching others for specific assistance. Tends to be capability-based	Individuals maintain responsibility for learning and drive the learning process. Learning usually takes place in authentic real-need contexts (i.e., as need arises). Individuals can work at a time, place, and pace appropriate for them. Leads to higher retention of learning Can increase confidence and self-efficacy and provide a sense of achievement Sometimes it becomes a necessity if other forms of learning aren't possible. Generally the preferred approach of most proficient computer users	Not everyone is confident with this form of learning. Can lead to frustrations and problems for which the individual can't find a solution, particularly if reassurance and support aren't readily available Can be more time-consuming; however, if learning focuses on authentic need, it can be more efficient than training before starting a real project. Requires a level of "readiness"
Peer-group learning: A group of people, perhaps with similar skill levels, work together to learn a new technology Often the group members use similar self-directed learning approaches, but they are collaborative. The group members need not be learning at the same place at the same time; learning can take place asynchronously. Tends to be capability-based	A good response to new technology or problems when no one knows a solution Learners sharing learning can be efficient. Draws on strengths of individuals and compensates for weaknesses (e.g., reading manuals or exploring) Can lead to incidental learning Learners can pick up each others' learning strategies. Learners can build collegiality and friendships.	Individuals aren't always available or willing to invest time in learning the same thing (i.e., issue of sharing goals). Some individuals may feel intimidated by others or left behind.

Encouraging Exploratory Learning and Playfulness

It is understandable that technology learners want quick fixes and ready answers, and most will be delighted if their mentor tells them directly how to do something or, better still, does it for them! However, this is not always the best approach to supporting learning.

In Chapter 2, we introduced the concepts of exploratory learning and playfulness. By playfulness we don't only mean playing computer games. Rather, playfulness is the tendency of an individual to interact spontaneously, inventively, and imaginatively with computers (Webster & Martocchio, 1995). Children tend to naturally adopt exploratory, playful learning strategies (sometimes called active experimentation) particularly with regard to technology. Adults, through a variety of life experiences, tend to decrease in their tendency to learn in these ways. A metacognitive approach aims to rekindle teachers' willingness and ability to learn through exploration, play, and experimentation.

If you reflect on the staff in your school, you will no doubt be able to think of some who are playful in their technology use—perhaps this is you! You will also be able to identify many less confident technology users who feel anxious about exploring. This anxiety is something that can significantly limit ongoing learning:

> *One aspect that was common to all staff was that they were all afraid that they might break something. They all seemed to be reluctant to try new things without being shown the correct way to do something. This is probably indicative of many school environments where ICT budgets are tight and personnel with the technical ability to fix problems are rare. Teachers do not want to be responsible for crashing the lab and, therefore, restricting the use of computers for the whole school.*

An important point to make here is that exploratory learning can be both fostered and taught, and it can also be explicitly adopted as a strategy and practiced by teachers:

> *So much on the computer is interrelated and interconnected, and the knowledge gained doing one task can often enable you to work out how to do another task, so the knowledge and skills can be transferred to other activities. You get a good feeling when you try something new based on previous knowledge, and it works!*

Technology Together aims to engage a whole-school community—teachers and students—in recognizing and embracing exploratory learning and realizing that it can be done without irreversibly breaking things!

> *Teachers are recognizing that to be an effective ICT user, one does not have to, and indeed cannot, know it all. However, the key to success in this arena is the willingness to experiment, problem solve, and "have a go."*

Of course, encouraging exploratory learning and playfulness brings with it an element of risk. Leadership plays a critical role here. Teachers need to be prepared to take risks with their own learning and feel supported to do so. Promoting risk taking is most effective when it comes from, or is strongly reinforced by, the school principal. Modeling by school executives and mentors is also valuable in ensuring exploratory learning is not just given "lip service" but carried through in practice. Consciously encouraging ICT experts and novices to bring learning successes and failures to staff meetings will encourage teachers to realize that their experimentation is supported.

Although all teachers will not prefer or find comfort with an exploratory learning approach, it is certainly positive to encourage them to have a go (give it a try), even in small ways. To foster exploratory learning strategies, mentors need to

- Continue to emphasize that exploratory learning is one of the most important ways of becoming a capable, lifelong technology learner;
- Point out that proficient technology users generally employ these strategies;
- Draw parallels with how students learn computer skills and emphasize that teachers can do this too;
- Reinforce that very little can go wrong when exploring software or a computer's features, providing you use a little common sense;
- Explicitly discuss the tips for exploratory learning (see **Resource 25** | Box 4.1);
- Model exploratory learning yourself and explicitly discuss it during mentoring sessions (e.g., through the think-out-loud strategy discussed later in this chapter);
- Encourage a school culture that embraces mistakes as learning opportunities; and
- Prompt teachers to foster exploratory learning in their classrooms.

Resource 24 | **Table 4.11** Exploratory learning: Ideas for engagement

Prompts for teacher reflection, discussion, and action	
5 min	Hand out the tips for exploratory learning (**Resource 25** | Box 4.1).
10 min	Follow the instructions for the 5-min prompt, but also ask teachers to share their past experiences of using exploratory learning.
20 min	Follow the instructions for the 10-min prompt, but connect discussion to consideration of how students learn (see Chapter 5, Strategy 3).
Wall display	Pin up the tips for exploratory learning (**Resource 25** | Box 4.1) near all staff computers.
Weekly challenge	Set teachers the challenge to solve one problem during the week using the exploratory learning tips.
Metacognition in the classroom	
Have teachers run a lesson that explicitly involves students exploring or playing to work out a solution (it need not necessarily be related to technology).	

Resource 25 | **Box 4.1**   Tips for exploratory learning

- ✓ **Know how to control windows:** Almost every window on a Windows PC has controls in the top right (minimize, full screen, and close). Click them to see what happens. When you minimize a window, look at the bottom of the screen. Also, make sure you know how to move a window around the screen to see where it has gone. Dragging on the top bar of a window will move it. Dragging on the edges or corners of a window will resize it. Resizing is very useful when you want to look at two documents at once (e.g., to view a Help document while following the directions).

- ✓ **Try right-clicking** on icons or on the desktop. Right-clicking will usually bring up a menu with all sorts of options related to the item that you right-click on. Give it a try at the desktop level, as well as within programs while you are working.

- ✓ **Try dragging and dropping:** Clicking on something and holding down the mouse button while dragging will enable you to move items around in many instances. Dragging and dropping is valuable for moving files and folders, editing work, backing up, or filing email.

- ✓ **Explore the menus** within any software program that you use. Exploring the menus and seeing what the functions are available is an important way to learn.

- ✓ **Use shortcuts:** Many software programs provide keyboard shortcuts to enable you to do certain functions from your keyboard without using menus. The most common shortcuts (for Windows) are Ctrl-C to Copy; Ctrl-V to Paste and Ctrl-S to Save. However, there are many more shortcuts, and they are usually consistent among software programs. Most program menus list shortcuts next to their corresponding functions.

- ✓ **Learn to use Help:** Most software programs have several different types of help available. The three most common are the following:
  - Help contents is similar to a book table of contents, with chapters on each topic—you use contents when you want to read a comprehensive guide on how to do a particular task;
  - Help index is similar to a book index, and you use it for looking up specific pieces of information—sometimes you need to try a couple of terms before finding what you are after (just as in a book index); and
  - Natural language searching lets you type a question when you do not know exactly what to look up.

Now try these tips with one or more of the following challenges:

- ✓ Find one new feature of a commonly used program (try exploring the menus or browsing the Help files).
- ✓ Learn one new shortcut (see above).
- ✓ Explore one program on your computer that you have not used before.
- ✓ Explore the Control Panel and find the settings for one thing that you did not previously know about—this is an area that requires a little common sense, so if you change something, it is good to remember how to change it back!

Reconsidering Memory and Retention

Many less confident computer users approach technology learning from a perspective of needing to memorize things. While memory undoubtedly plays a role, technology learners often struggle when they focus on memorization as a learning strategy.

Writing or reading through steps can be valuable but often gets in the way of really looking at what is being shown and seeing patterns, or getting in and giving things a try yourself. For most people, the best way of remembering is through doing, as this teacher realized:

> *I wrote down everything that would help me remember the steps.... It occurred to me however, that this was a waste of time and really not practical. Sure, I could write down some things, but to write absolutely everything was silly, especially when the computer has the "help" function. This was an eye-opening experience.*

In Chapter 2, we mentioned that learning is best retained when it involves a degree of difficulty. As explained by Bjork (1994), rapid progress in training may be reassuring to a learner, however little learning may actually have taken place, and learners may be fooled by their successes. Although struggling and making errors can be distressing, causing novices to underestimate their own comprehension, Bjork (1994) points out that substantial learning may, in fact, be taking place:

> We should probably find the absence, not the presence, of errors, mistakes and difficulties to be distressing—a sign that we are not exposing ourselves to the kinds of conditions that most facilitate our learning, and our self-assessment of that learning. (p. 201)

Contrary to conventional training methods, this perspective advocates introducing difficulties and challenges, such as variation or unpredictability. Bjork (1994) notes that responding to difficulties and challenges forces learners into more elaborate encoding and more substantial and varied retrieval processes, hence their memory is enhanced.

To support learners who tend to focus on memorization, then, mentors need to

- De-emphasize the importance of terminology and jargon;
- Not focus as much on steps, but rather emphasize learning strategies when demonstrating or assisting mentees;
- Point out patterns and commonalities between programs and processes;
- Reinforce that the best way of remembering is through doing;

- Encourage mentees to write general processes or key points rather than each specific, discrete step, if mentees feel they need to write down steps;
- Encourage teachers to gradually move away from writing down steps to repeating tasks a few times;
- Point out where staff can find the steps if they do forget (e.g., in Help). If mentees need steps, encourage them to print the help screen;
- Emphasize that learning involving a degree of difficulty leads to much better long-term learning outcomes; and
- Be confident in yourself as a mentor. Realize that making learning too easy may make your mentees happy and make you feel liked, wanted, and needed, but you might not be doing mentees a favor in the long term.

Resource 26 | **Table 4.12** Memory and retention: Ideas for engagement

Prompts for teacher reflection, discussion, and action	
5 min	Brainstorm processes that staff have found are common across most computer software programs (e.g., save, cut and paste, shortcuts).
10 min	Explicitly discuss memory and retention, drawing on resources from the Technology Together website.
Weekly challenge	Have all teachers access the Help section of a software program they use and look up and/or print the directions on how to do one new thing. You can also encourage teachers to search for answers to their questions or computer problems on the web.

Metacognition in the classroom

Have teachers reflect during the week on whether they try to make their students' learning easy and comfortable. How do they respond when students encounter difficulties?

Fostering Problem Solving and Volition

Problem solving may be the most important opportunity for learning about technology, but it can also be something that many novice technology users try to avoid. If you are a confident and capable technology user, you will no doubt confess that problems happen to you all the time. Less confident technology users, however, often think that problems only happen to them. Helping less confident technology users to understand that hiccups are a normal part of technology use and encouraging them to persevere when they encounter problems is a key part of Technology Together.

Problem solving requires both motivation and volition. Volition refers to willfulness or dogged perseverance in pursuit of difficult goals—the tendency to maintain focus and effort despite potential distractions. Thus, whereas motivation refers more to commitment, volition denotes follow-through. The metacognitive approach views problem solving and volition as strategies but also as attitudes—it takes the right attitude *and* the right strategies to give things a try, and it is only through engaging both that you gain confidence in your own ability to work through problems:

> *I had a bit of trouble with my home email. In all my playing around, I must have changed the makeup of the tool bar and added a filter. I tried to change it back with no success. I am getting too tired, but I didn't get stressed or anxious, just thought I'll look again when I don't feel so tired—a quantum leap in my attitude to computers. I didn't really think I couldn't fix it, just that I'd do it later.*

Assisting technology users to develop problem-solving abilities is not, however, easy. Simply teaching strategies does not guarantee that learners will continue to use them, nor that they will use the appropriate strategies in the appropriate contexts. However, it is very easy, as a mentor, to diminish learners' problem-solving abilities. Support that is too readily available can detract from a teacher's willingness to problem solve, as explained earlier. That said, it is important that learners don't get too frustrated. As a mentor you need to balance providing support with providing opportunities (and the necessity) for your mentees to give things a try on their own:

> *Some teachers want the end result of someone else's learning … and miss the little bits of learning in between. They don't become competent and capable, lack the motivation to put themselves "on the line," and consequently perpetuate their lack of belief in themselves.*

Mentors need to

- Emphasize that problems happen, even to the most experienced technology users;
- Explicitly discuss the need to balance help seeking with problem solving;
- Emphasize that while problem solving takes time, experience, patience, and perseverance, most of all it takes the right attitude;
- Realize that if they provide assistance too readily they can detract from a mentee's ability to learn to problem solve;
- Reassure mentees that confidence will come from success, but to experience success, you need to give things a try;

- Emphasize strategies rather than only solutions;
- Recognize the frustration tolerance level of mentees and ensure that they recognize this point themselves; and
- Advocate that, while volition is important, sometimes we all just need to walk away for a while, give things some thought, and come back to a problem with a fresh view.

Resource 27 | Table 4.13   Problem solving and volition: Ideas for engagement

Prompts for teacher reflection, discussion, and action	
5–10 min	Have one or two teachers share a story of their problem-solving experiences. Encourage ICT experts in particular to vocalize that problems do happen for them, and to share their strategies.
20 min	Follow the instructions for the 5–10-min prompt, and then use the following as a discussion starter: *If a computer user encounters a computer problem and takes 5–6 hours to solve it but sticks with it and succeeds, is this computer user a "capable" computer user? What if the computer user tries for that long and does not succeed?*
Wall displays	Create a graffiti board for teachers to share problems and tips for solutions.
Weekly challenge	Ask teachers to be mindful this week of their approach to any ICT problems they encounter and to debrief with a colleague to reflect on their volition in this context.
Metacognition in the classroom	
Suggest to teachers that they take the opportunity to talk to their students about problem solving and the concept of volition.	

Balancing Help Seeking

Many teachers find it uncomfortable seeking help for all kinds of reasons. Some resist doing so altogether. Teachers' hesitancies can stem from many reasons: embarrassment, pride, a perception that no one is available to help, not wanting to place demands on already busy colleagues, or even dogged determination and independence. Yet help seeking can be a very appropriate strategy to deal with problems, and help seeking is always preferable to getting frustrated and giving up. The approach that teachers take to their help seeking is critical in influencing long-term outcomes. Some technology learners try to get immediate answers, while others seek tips on how to move their own learning forward. Effective help seeking is purposeful and aims toward building long-term autonomy.

We have emphasized that the metacognitive approach promotes self-directed and independent computer learners. Some people misinterpret self-directed learning as meaning that they have to do everything themselves without seeking any assistance. Self-direction, however, does not mean learning in isolation. Rather, it is the ability to make conscious and informed choices about sources and strategies for support.

Another aspect of help seeking relates to teachers' willingness to learn with and from their own students, something we deal with further in Chapter 5.

Resource 28 | **Table 4.14** Help seeking: Ideas for engagement

Prompts for teacher reflection, discussion, and action	
10 min	Discuss the pros and cons of help being readily available versus working things out yourself first.
Wall displays	Pin up the help-seeking thought-bubble display available on the Technology Together website (**Resource 29** | **Thought bubble 4.4**).
Weekly challenge	Make a conscious effort to determine when the time is appropriate to seek help on ICT problems.
Metacognition in the classroom	
Explicitly discuss with students the benefits of giving things a go first before asking for help.	
Suggest teachers introduce an "explore first, ask three (other students), and then ask me" policy in their classrooms.	

The color wall display for **Resource 28—Resource 29** | **Thought bubble 4.4**—is available on the Technology Together website (http://technologytogether.scu.edu.au).

Considering Attitudes toward Time

Time is frequently mentioned as the biggest influence on teachers' technology learning. However, time in itself is not a simple consideration. Time is usually associated with priority and motivation. School culture can also exert a big influence on teachers' attitude toward time, particularly whether time spent learning ICT is perceived as an investment or a waste.

Consider the following ways that teachers' beliefs about time can influence their computer use:

- **Amount of time.** *How much time spent on the computer is too much time?* One teacher might view spending 10 minutes on a task or skill as too much, while another teacher might happily work on the same thing for a whole hour.

- **Time as investment.** *Is computer learning viewed as a waste of time or as an investment (either for themselves or students)?* One teacher might "stick with what I know," whereas another might aim to learn new features of the software in case they can utilize these or pass skills on to their students.

- **Rate or speed of change.** *How fast should new technologies or teaching approaches be incorporated into practice?* For one teacher, it might be important to be on the "cutting edge" of new developments and ideas, whereas another teacher might resist trying new things in case they quickly become obsolete or redundant.

- **Time on/time off.** *When can teachers relax and disengage?* For some teachers, computers are only work related—they only see a use for them at school, and learning about computers should only be done during work time. For other teachers, learning about technology has personal and recreational benefits, and they invest time in learning both during and outside of school hours.

- **Sequence of events over time.** *What should be done in what order? Does computer learning take a lower priority compared to other things?* Some teachers see ICT learning as something to begin today, while others always find other things that are more important.

The color wall display for **Resource 30—Resource 31 | Thought bubble 4.5**—is available on the Technology Together website (http://technologytogether.scu.edu.au).

Resource 30 | Table 4.15   Confronting the time issue: Ideas for engagement

Prompts for teacher reflection, discussion, and action	
10 min	Use the preceding five questions about time as the basis for discussion.
Wall display	Pin up the approaches toward time thought-bubble display (**Resource 31 | Thought bubble 4.5**)
Weekly challenge	Notice whenever you think or say "no time." Consider if you can make time or change priorities.
Metacognition in the classroom	
Set aside some specific time for students to explore and play with a new computer resource or program with you.	

General Advice for Mentors

Now that we have unpacked the various elements of a metacognitive approach, we hope you can better engage yourself and the teachers you work with in thinking about their thinking and learning about their learning! As a reminder, as companion mentors we cannot hope to fully understand or capture the influence of these elements on each of our colleagues. No one knows the complex interplay of factors that affect an individual or the significance of any one factor beyond the individuals themselves. This is not to assume for a moment that individual learners are fully aware of all these factors but rather that they are in a better position to understand them than anyone else. The metacognitive approach focuses on engaging teachers to reflect on these factors on their own. Through guided reflection, individuals are prompted to recognize at a deeper level the influence of past experiences (initial conditions) on their current learning contexts.

Thinking Aloud Strategies

Although teachers need to come to their own understanding of their thinking processes, one approach that mentors can use to model and engage teachers in thinking processes is a "thinking aloud" strategy. Thinking aloud (sometimes referred to as cognitive modeling) occurs when mentors verbally explain the thought processes that they go through as they work through a task or problem. These thought processes are likely to relate to all three metacognitive dimensions: affects, motivation, and strategies. Thinking aloud strategies are particularly valuable when assisting a mentee with technology because these strategies emphasize that computer learning is a process of constant mental activity—of actively juggling emotions, being positive, and intentionally thinking about appropriate strategies.

This approach can be a little difficult to do until you get used to it, but here are some strategies from our experience:

- Draw on exploratory learning strategies—vocalize these strategies as you put them into practice;
- Sometimes it is useful to pretend that you are less certain about how to do something than you might actually be;
- Do not take the little things that you think and do for granted;
- Build in such skills as remembering to save; and
- Encourage mentees to vocalize their own thinking processes as they interact with technology—get them to think aloud and share with you how they are approaching their learning or problem solving.

Tips

Before concluding this chapter, we thought it would be helpful to provide a checklist of some general tips and advice that previous companion mentors have passed on to future companion mentors. This list summarizes some of the general points from this chapter. In Chapter 7, we provide further advice on dealing with problems that might arise, including sustaining the Technology Together approach.

- Don't overestimate the abilities of your colleagues.
- Be enthusiastic and use lots of positive talk but also lots of listening.
- Take care not to establish any expectation that you will have all the answers. Actively present yourself as a fellow learner.
- Be prepared to discuss your own past and present feelings and experiences.
- Be nonjudgmental and establish a nonthreatening environment so people feel that they can "ask dumb questions."
- Share the fact that you are working toward your own goals and model risk taking.
- Try to have regular contact with mentees, even if it is an informal chat in passing.
- Try to establish a relationship where you feel comfortable to challenge and question what mentees are doing, not just provide support.
- Ensure that any learning sessions are followed up and more practice time negotiated if necessary. Encourage mentees to request extra time.
- Promote thinking aloud sessions.
- Don't be afraid—no one is ever an expert! Use this knowledge to enhance your own mentoring confidence.
- Avoid becoming overwhelmed by mentee problems and don't expect to have all the answers.
- Don't do for mentees what they can do for themselves.
- Be a guide from the side of room—or even from across the room—prompting with tips rather than doing things for mentees.
- Model problem-solving strategies.
- Try not to always be available to mentees when they need assistance, as this is when they may just work things out for themselves!

CHAPTER **5**

Supporting Teachers' Teaching

One factor that significantly influences resistance to change in schools is the resilience of established roles, in particular, roles of students and roles of teachers (Carroll, 2000; Davidson, 2003).

In earlier chapters, we discussed how Technology Together encourages teachers to reflect on and challenge the culture of teaching and learning that exists within their classrooms and schools. We mentioned pedagogical perceived usefulness and the relationship between constructivist teaching approaches and ICT use, noting the chicken-and-egg arguments and tensions.

It takes time for individuals and whole schools to change deeply ingrained beliefs about teaching and learning. However, becoming aware of the impact of school culture and opening up discussion about its implications is an important first step in leading informed change. Indeed, simply changing the school culture to be one that actively discusses technology and pedagogy can lead to significant transformation in teaching and learning practices.

This chapter is brief but important as it builds on our discussions about motivation from Chapter 4. We begin by considering six strategies for supporting teachers to reflect on and challenge their pedagogy. We then move to discussing a central Technology Together strategy—one of supporting teachers to learn with and from their students.

Six Strategies to Challenge Pedagogy

Much of the current research on exemplary technology-using teachers suggests that teachers who achieve meaningful technology use do so in learner-centered, constructivist environments (Ertmer, Ottenbreit-Leftwich, & York, 2006–07). An integral part of Technology Together is to encourage teachers to talk more about how they implement ICT in their classrooms and to challenge them to move toward more constructivist teaching approaches.

All the evidence (and common sense) emphasizes that pedagogy should be the first priority—start with the pedagogies, not the technologies (Moyle, 2006). Technology Together supports this notion, while emphasizing that pedagogy is as much about teachers' beliefs and values as about specific teaching strategies.

Our experience has also highlighted a readiness issue when exposing teachers to new pedagogical possibilities. Teachers have strongly emphasized to us that, at first, some teachers just are not ready to have their classroom practices challenged. In other words, without basic technology skills and confidence, teachers do not want to think about wider change. Thus, while a focus on pedagogy is important, schools themselves need to judge the readiness of staff to engage in such discussions.

In this section, we present six strategies that can be tried with staff at appropriate times. You may favor those strategies that are less (or more) theoretical, depending on your school culture.

1. Reflecting on objectivism, constructivism, and connectivism
2. Reflecting on authenticity in teaching and learning
3. Reflecting on students as digital natives

4. Reflecting on whether students need to be taught ICT skills
5. Reflecting on how ICT can transform teaching
6. Developing students' metacognition

Strategy 1
Reflecting on Objectivism, Constructivism, and Connectivism

In Chapter 4, we considered the role of pedagogical orientation and discussed the distinction between constructivist and objectivist (also called behaviorist) teaching approaches. If your school staff may not be conversant with these ideas, then they may warrant some discussion. Raising awareness of these underlying theories can assist teachers to identify and more accurately name and reflect on their own approaches. Of course, as previously noted, teachers rarely identify clearly with one approach or the other. Rather, each teacher's practice will sit somewhere along a continuum.

Although objectivism and constructivism have been the focus of much educational research and practice over many years, a more recent concept to gain attention is that of "connectivism." Connectivism was first described by Siemens (2005) as a powerful theory for learning, consistent with the needs of the 21st century, one that takes into account trends in learning, the use of technology and networks, and the diminishing half-life of knowledge. Many writers have since adopted Siemens's ideas and, while not yet widely discussed or implemented in schools or classrooms, connectivism provides much potential for educators to reflect on and challenge their existing practice. Interestingly, Siemens's work is influenced by complexity science, which we discussed in Chapter 1.

The following table (**Resource 32** | **Table 5.1**) is derived from Roblyer (2004), but we have modified it to include the dimension of connectivism. It summarizes the differences among directed, constructivist, and connectivist models of teaching and can be helpful to form the basis of a staff discussion.

Resource 32 | **Table 5.1** Contrasting directed, constructivist, and connectivist teaching approaches

	Directed	Constructivist	Connectivist
Teacher roles	Transmitter of knowledge; expert source; director of skill/concept development through structured experiences	Guide and facilitator as students generate their own knowledge; collaborative resource and assistant as students explore topics	Breaking down of distinctions between the roles of teachers and learners; in a learning organization everyone collaborates and learns together; learning is not viewed as occurring only within an individual but also within and among networks of people
Student roles	Receive information; demonstrate competence; all students learn the same material.	Collaborate with others; develop competency; students may learn different material.	
Curriculum characteristics	Based on skills and knowledge hierarchies; skills taught one after the other in a set sequence	Based on projects that foster both higher-level and lower-level skills concurrently	Learning is nonlinear and "messy"; greater emphasis on informal learning that occurs through communities of practice, personal networks, and work-related tasks
Learning goals	Stated in terms of mastery learning and behavioral competence in a scope and sequence	Stated in terms of growth from where student began and increased ability to work independently and with others	Learning is viewed as a continual process lasting a lifetime; there is less distinction among learning, work, and recreation.
Types of activities	Lecture, demonstration, discussions, student practice, seatwork, testing	Group projects, hands-on exploration, product development	Emphasis is on exposing learners to networks and exploring diverse opinions; technology plays a major role (e.g., contributions to wikis or blogs).
Assessment strategies	Written tests and development of products matched to objectives; all tests and products match set criteria; same measures for all students	Performance tests and products such as portfolios; quality measured by rubrics and checklists; measures may differ among students.	Emphasis on the capacity to find out, rather than what is currently known; the ability to form connections between sources of information and to apply information to authentic problems

The color wall display **Resource 33** | **Thought bubble 5.1**, Constructivism thought-bubble display, is available on the Technology Together website (http://technologytogether.scu.edu.au).

Resource 34 | Table 5.2 Considering constructivism and connectivism: Ideas for engagement

Prompts for teacher reflection, discussion, and action	
10 min	Provide time for staff to read through the table (**Resource 32** | **Table 5.1**) then mark on a continuum (e.g., a line) where they see their teaching practices falling and whether they would like to move toward a different point. Note that different lessons may be more or less constructivist. Annotate these examples on the continuum.
20 min	Talk through the "chicken and egg" dilemma of which comes first—being a constructivist teacher or being an ICT integrating teacher.
Wall display	Display **Resource 32**	**Table 5.1** and/or **Resource 33**	**Thought bubble 5.1** (available on the Technology Together website).
Weekly challenge	Have teachers be conscious of which pedagogical orientations each of their lessons reflects. Suggest teachers read Siemens's seminal article on connectivism (this may not be for everyone but could result in an *aha* moment for those more interested in theory).
Metacognition in the classroom	
Ask teachers to discuss with their students how they view their role as student and how they view the role of teacher. This discussion is likely to reflect what students are used to. Are students' views consistent with teachers' views? (See also our discussion on Strategy 3.)	

Strategy 2

Reflecting on Authenticity in Teaching and Learning

One strategy for encouraging teachers to reflect on the teaching and learning culture in their classrooms is to stimulate discussion around how *authentic* learning activities are and how problems are conceptualized and practiced.

Authentic learning involves solving real-world problems—learning by doing rather than only listening, reading, and memorizing. Authentic learning is inherently multidisciplinary, in that learning experiences are not constructed to teach a specific disciplinary topic, such as geometry, physics, or algebra but rather are about investigating or solving problems that have meaning to learners. Much has been written on authentic learning approaches (for example, Lombardi, 2007), and we do not provide a major overview here. We recommend further reading in this area if you are not familiar with the principles.

It is important to convey to school staff that technology creates exciting opportunities to enhance learning authenticity in primary and secondary school classrooms. Some technology-based resources are designed specifically to facilitate such experiences (such as simulation software and the many global projects outlined in Chapter 6). The web provides an authentic source of information to inform problem solving and inquiry-based learning. It also provides multimedia resources that can bring ideas and information to life. Communication tools, such as email, blogs, wikis, and synchronous chat, provide opportunities to establish real-learning communities with students and teachers in one classroom networked with those from across the country or the globe. Learning to work in collaboration with others to solve problems of mutual concern and importance brings learning alive and makes it meaningful to students' futures.

Access to resources alone, however, is not enough. Teachers scaffold the learning experiences for their students, and any resources can be used both authentically or otherwise. Although authentic learning has been a focus of good pedagogy for many years, it is still underutilized in many schools and classrooms. Many exciting opportunities that technology opens up are not put to use even by the more technology-savvy teachers. Why? Again, we believe the reason has much to do with teachers' values, attitudes, and beliefs—about themselves, their role as teacher, and the roles of their students.

One reason authentic learning is not more common is that students often prefer traditional, more passive, forms of instruction (Lombardi, 2007). Older students in particular have often become acculturated to passivity, seeking right answers and black-and-white mental models. Just as the metacognitive approach in Technology Together challenges teachers to move outside their comfort zones and take a more active role in their own learning, so teachers can be prompted to recognize the benefits of confronting students with uncertainty, ambiguity, and conflicting perspectives through authentic learning experiences.

One strategy, then, is to challenge teachers to reconsider how their classroom relationships and dynamics function and to encourage them to move from teacher-directed dynamics to collaborative-learning models.

The following figure (**Resource 35** | **Figure 5.1**) is derived from Carroll (2000). The three cultures illustrated are reflective of those described in **Resource 32** | **Table 5.1:** Culture 1 is directed, Culture 2 is constructivist, and Culture 3 is connectivist.

Resource 35 | **Figure 5.1** Cultures of teaching and learning

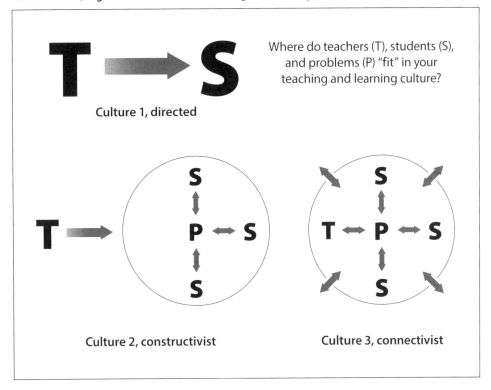

Remember that, as we signaled earlier, students do not always take to nonteacher-directed learning straight away, particularly older students. Similar to adults, students need support and encouragement:

> *Since starting ... I have significantly more student-centered work, and students now use help, reference material, and peers for the majority of their problems. Not only are the students benefiting from this approach, but I am getting more and more time to spend with students in a small group or one to one. Initially students reacted with typical outbursts that I was not helping and that I must have better things to do. I am now finding that students are wanting to discuss possible solutions rather than be shown how to do things.*

Resource 36 | **Table 5.3** Cultures of teaching and learning: Ideas for engagement

Prompts for teacher reflection, discussion, and action	
10 min	Use the three images in **Resource 35**	**Figure 5.1** to prompt discussion on the role of teachers, students, and problems in teachers' classroom practice.
15 min	Follow the instructions for the 10-min prompt, but have teachers share examples of lessons that might "fit" within Culture 3.
20 min	Follow the instructions for the 10-min prompt, but add some discussion of how students in your school respond when given more responsibility for their learning.
Weekly challenge	Have teachers reflect on their lessons for a week and how they "fit" with these cultures. Encourage them to write their thoughts in their journal.
Metacognition in the classroom	
Challenge teachers to try using a WebQuest, global project, or other problem-based learning experience with their students (see Chapter 6).	

Strategy 3
Reflecting on Students as Digital Natives

Numerous writers have talked about the Net generation—sometimes referred to as Millennials or digital natives (for example, Lee, 2001; Prensky, 2001; Tapscott, 1998). The notion of generational difference in relation to technology has been much emphasized in the media. Young people are portrayed as a multitasking generation and simultaneously discussed as both autonomous (personal music, YouTube, Facebook) and collaborative in their technology use (file-sharing, texting, chatting, online gaming). Some writers imply that young people think and process information in fundamentally different ways from their predecessors. Others emphasize a generation of youth at risk of everything—from sexual predators, inappropriate content, and declining literacy levels to obesity.

Hawkes (2006) compiled the following table (**Resource 37** | **Table 5.4**) to highlight how different generations have been influenced by different factors, leading to different preferred teaching and learning styles.

Resource 37 | **Table 5.4** Hawkes' generational comparison

	Matures 1900–1945	Baby Boomers 1946–1964	Generation X 1965–1981	Net-Geners and Millennials 1982–Present
Influenced by	War and recession	Post-war optimism	Workaholic parents	Technology
Typical technology	Vacuum tube radio; Dial telephone; 78 rpm records	Transistor radios; Mainframe computers; 33 and 45 rpm records	CDs; Emails; Personal computers	MP3s; Mobile phones; Personal digital assistants
Typical characteristics	Conservative; Respect authority; Self-sacrificing; Community minded	Optimistic; High energy; Enjoy a challenge; Driven to succeed; Want to stay young	Free and independent; Balanced in life; Skeptical of inherited values; Laid-back	Like technology; Optimistic; Connected; Experiential; Want immediate gratification
Preferred teaching and learning styles	Emphasis on teaching by transmission; Students are passive recipients. Teachers are commanders and controllers. Accent on memorization and repetition; Individual learning		Emphasis on constructivist paradigm; Students are active partners. Teachers are facilitators and mentors. Accent on discovery learning; Collaborative learning	

Source: Hawkes, T. F. (2006, November). *Teaching the Millennial Boy*. Used with permission.

Of course these comparisons are broad generalizations and only useful to a certain point. That said, many people do acknowledge from their own observations and experience that young people, in general, learn rapidly when it comes to new technology. Adults who watch a child use a new software program or computer game for the first time will no doubt note the ease with which children adapt. They tend to adopt exploratory and playful approaches to learning—something we have already identified as different from the approaches adopted by many adults. Young people are curious and motivated and learn through play and discovery, employing trial and error. This reflection is useful for teachers as it helps them to think about how they can transform their own learning approaches:

> *Unlike the students, I tend to only experiment with the computer when I am pressed for time to complete a task. Students experiment constantly and thus learn far more quickly and effectively. They are prepared to make mistakes and have things go wrong.*

However, the problem with this kind of thinking is that it can create an "us and them" mentality—a dichotomy that suggests that adults just don't fit with the "technology generation"—an assumption that is misleading. After all, it is adults who have originally invented most of the technologies that the young now use—not the other way around.

A further major problem with this thinking is that it assumes that all young people are the same. This assumption also is simply not the case. As Selwyn (2009) emphasizes:

> Whilst often compelling and persuasive, the overall tenor of these discursive constructions of young people and technology tends towards exaggeration and inconsistency. The digital native discourse as articulated currently cannot be said to provide an especially accurate or objective account of young people and technology. (p. 370)

Many young people like technology, but others do not. Furthermore, access to technology is highly influenced by socioeconomic and cultural factors. Surveys of young people also suggest that their actual uses of digital technologies remain more limited in scope than the digital native rhetoric would suggest, with a predominance of game playing, text messaging, retrieval of online content, and less active and creative engagement than might be assumed (Selwyn, 2009).

It is interesting for teachers to reflect critically on their assumptions and beliefs about generational differences in technology use. Such reflections can be productive if teachers use them to proactively change learning approaches and opportunities, not only for their students but for themselves as well. These ideas can prompt some teachers to recognize how critical it is to embrace change—this can provide many *aha* moments as they recognize that students are not that different from them. Teachers may realize that, as adults, they can emulate their students' learning strategies and, importantly, they do have a major role to play—to diversify and provide equity in their students' technology learning.

Resource 38 | **Table 5.5** Students as digital natives: Ideas for engagement

Prompts for teacher reflection, discussion, and action	
10 min at staff meeting	Use Hawkes' (2006) generational comparison (**Resource 37** | **Table 5.4**) to engage teachers in discussion—but encourage them to remain critical!
Weekly challenge	Have teachers either read the article by Selwyn (2009) or watch a YouTube video on the issue of digital natives, for example, the 2007 video podcast Pay Attention (available on TeacherTube or http://t4.jordandistrict.org/payattention). Have teachers reflect critically in their journals or come back to a staff meeting to discuss.
Metacognition in the classroom	
Encourage teachers to have a conversation with their students about what sorts of things they do with technology in their recreational lives.	

Strategy 4
Reflecting on Whether Students Need to Be Taught ICT Skills

As previously discussed, some research views technology as challenging traditional teacher–student relationships in classrooms, particularly concerning control of information and what constitutes effective learning strategies for technology use. Despite this, some teachers still persist with a very directive style of teaching when engaging students in learning technology skills. These teachers see it as critical to teach skills before students can engage in activities that use those skills. This perception can be shaped by teachers' focus on competency over capability, and perhaps their belief that they need to maintain authority and be seen as the one with the knowledge to pass on to students. Some teachers have a concern about their ability to manage or control students' behavior if they are not directing what their students have to do. Other teachers, though, simply lack the awareness that most young people can and will learn technology skills independently and from each other while they engage in tasks. The introduction of laptop computers and mobile devices into many classrooms in developed and developing countries is bringing to the forefront teachers' concerns about the behavior of students who wish to use the technology independent of any "lock-step" instructions from the teacher.

A very interesting research project that can challenge teachers to think critically on their approach to developing students' technology skills is the "hole in the wall" research by Sugata Mitra and colleagues (Mitra et al., 2005). This ongoing project places unsupervised computer terminals in rural villages in India where children have never before had access to such technology. When children are later tested, they have been able to successfully complete a computer exam:

> Even in the absence of any direct input, mere curiosity led groups of children to explore, which resulted in learning. This, coupled with minimal input from peers, or from anyone familiar with computers, helped the children learn more. This leads us to believe that any learning environment that provides an adequate level of curiosity can cause learning in groups of children. Children's desire to learn, along with their curiosity and peer interaction, drives them to explore the environment in order to satisfy their inquisitiveness. (p. 409)

If you aren't aware of Mitra's work, visit the Hole-in-the-Wall website (www.hole-in-the-wall.com) or view the video presentations by Sugata Mitra on TED (www.ted.com).

Resource 39 | **Table 5.6** Do students need to be taught technology skills? Ideas for engagement

Prompts for teacher reflection, discussion, and action	
10 min	Discuss what approaches are being employed in the school for teaching computer skills. Are these appropriate and necessary?
Weekly challenge	Have teachers visit the Hole-in-the-Wall website, read an article on this project, or view the TED video (www.hole-in-the-wall.com or www.ted.com).
Metacognition in the classroom	
Have teachers try an ICT lesson where students may not yet know all the skills but are encouraged to explore and help each other.	

Strategy 5
Reflecting on How ICT Can Transform Teaching

ICT can open up new opportunities and contexts for teaching and learning. Many of the practical integration initiatives suggested in Chapter 6 illustrate this. As a key part of the metacognitive approach, we aim to challenge teachers to reflect on their values, attitudes, and beliefs about the pedagogical potential of ICT and to form new visions of how ICT might transform their own teaching practice.

Resource 40 | **Table 5.7** The pedagogical potential of ICT: Ideas for engagement

Prompts for teacher reflection, discussion, and action	
10 min	Use Norton and Wiburg's framework (**Resource 41** | Box 5.1) or Richardson's 10 big shifts (**Resource 42** | Box 5.2) as a discussion starter. Have teachers read through these ahead of the meeting then discuss teachers' responses.
20 min	Follow the instructions for the 10-min prompt, but also swap ideas for classroom management in the transformed (nontraditional) ICT-enriched classroom.
Visual display	Use Norton and Wiburg's framework (**Resource 41** | Box 5.1) or Richardson's 10 big shifts (**Resource 42** | Box 5.2) as the basis of a graffiti board, so teachers can write comments around each point.

Norton and Wiburg (2003) provide eight key points that they claim represent the potential of ICT in transforming teaching practice. Richardson (2010) also provides a stimulating framework for considering changing pedagogy through his discussion of technologies such as blogs and wikis (which he terms the "Read/Write Web"). Both of these frameworks provide excellent discussion stimuli for staff. We have summarized these two frameworks (see **Resource 41** | Box 5.1 and **Resource 42** | Box 5.2) so they may be easily shared with teachers.

Resource 41 | **Box 5.1** Norton and Wiburg's framework

Note: The following discussion starters are summarized from *Teaching with Technology: Designing Opportunities to Learn* (Norton & Wiburg, 2003).

From linear to hypermedia learning. Traditional approaches to learning are linear and reflect the structure of books as the central learning tool. Most textbooks are written to be read from beginning to end. N[et]-Geners' access to information is more interactive and nonsequential. They navigate back and forth between TV, books, video games, and the Internet. They typically participate in several activities at once.

From instruction to construction and discovery. As Papert (1996) states, "The scandal of education is that every time you teach something, you deprive a child of the pleasure and benefit of discovery" (p. 68). Today's learners seek a shift away from teaching toward learning partnerships and learning cultures. They want to learn by doing, experiencing, inventing, and creating rather than consuming prepackaged instruction.

From teacher-centered to learner-centered. The new media support shifting learning to the learner and away from the transmitter. This does not suggest, however, that teachers suddenly play lesser roles. Teachers remain critical and valued and are essential to the creation and structuring of the learning experience. N-Geners are challenged by teachers who engage them in discussing, debating, researching, and collaborating on projects instead of by teachers who seek to "pass along" information.

From absorbing material to learning how to navigate and how to learn. N-Geners assess and analyze. More importantly, they synthesize. They engage information sources and people to build or construct higher-level structures and mental images.

From school to lifelong learning. Previous generations divided life into the school years and the work years. Today's learners understand that in a world of constant and rapid change, with knowledge doubling annually, learning is a lifelong process. They are not motivated by the prospect of "finishing" school. Rather, they are motivated by a challenge to master or a problem to solve.

Resource 41 | **Box 5.1** *(Continued)*

> **From one-size-fits-all to customized learning.** Mass education was a product of the industrial economy. In an industrialized society, it made sense to assume that a large proportion of students at any given grade level would "tune in" and be able to absorb the information. Today's students expect to be treated as individuals—to have highly customized learning experiences based on their backgrounds, talents, and cognitive and interpersonal styles. After all, that is the way they structure their nonschool learning experiences.
>
> **From learning as torture to learning as fun.** One of the goals of redesigned schools should be to make learning fun. Entertainment has always been a profound part of the learning process, and teachers have, throughout history, been asked to convince their students to entertain ideas. From this perspective, the best teachers are entertainers. Entertainment builds enjoyment, motivation, and responsibility for learning.
>
> **From teacher as transmitter to teacher as facilitator.** As N-Geners assume more and more responsibility for their own learning, understand learning to be a social act, and use the new technologies available to them, they need teachers who can act as a resource and consultant to their learning. They seek teachers who can support their emerging competence as collaborators, researchers, analyzers, presenters, and resource users.

Resource 42 | **Box 5.2**   Richardson's "10 big shifts" in understanding how best to teach

Note: The following discussion starters are summarized with some modifications from *Blogs, Wikis, Podcasts, and Other Powerful Web Tools for Classrooms* (Richardson, 2010, pp. 149–155).

Big Shift #1: Open content. It used to be that teachers "owned" the content they taught, most stemming from textbooks, and students had limited access to additional information. Today the breadth and depth of available content is staggering, rendering many textbooks passé. In open-source classrooms, everyone can contribute to the curriculum.

Big Shift #2: Many, many teachers and 24/7 learning. The web allows us to connect with many teachers, not just those from schools but scientists, historians, librarians, actors, and artists. These people are willing to share ideas and experiences, bringing diverse cultures, geographies, and experiences into the classroom. Unlike traditional student-teacher relationships, students no longer just consume content but can be part of broader conversations.

Big Shift #3: The social, collaborative construction of meaningful knowledge. For generations it was expected that students work independently and produce work for a limited audience—usually the teacher and perhaps parents or other students. Once finished, work was just that—finished. Today students can produce work collaboratively for large audiences. Work can have a real purpose and does not need to be "finished" but continually added to and refined.

Big Shift #4: Teaching is conversation, not lecture. By being able to publish to a wider audience, students learn that their voice matters. Educators can present ideas as a starting point for dialogue, not the end point, and invite students to be active in designing their own learning.

Big Shift #5: Know "where" learning. In technology-rich classrooms it is not as essential to know the answer is as it is to know where to find it—factual answers are only a few clicks away. It isn't enough simply to find resources; we must identify which are worthy of our attention.

Resource 42 | **Box 5.2** *(Continued)*

Big Shift #6: Readers are no longer just readers. Today, readers cannot assume that what they are reading has been reviewed by someone else with an eye to truth and accuracy, so they must learn to be critical consumers of information themselves. Readers must also be writers, able to engage in conversations with the sources in debate and discussion with others.

Big Shift #7: The web as notebook. The web renders paper less and less effective as a way to capture information we find relevant. Blogs and wikis allow us to save and organize digital ideas so that we can annotate and easily return to them. We can collect links, audio, video, and photographs in web notebooks and share these easily with others.

Big Shift #8: Writing is no longer limited to text. As we move away from plain text to multimedia, we move to a new definition of what it means to write. Blogs and wikis allow us to write in different genres, including audio and video, music, and photography.

Big Shift #9: Mastery is the product, not the test. In the past, mastery was generally exhibited by passing a test. Today, however, students can display mastery in countless ways by creating digital content, and the concept of an electronic online portfolio is coming to fruition.

Big Shift #10: Contribution, not completion, as the ultimate goal. Instead of handing in countless assignments to teachers to be read, graded, handed back, and most likely thrown away, students' work can now be seen as meant for the world, not to be discarded or stored away but to be added to the conversation and potentially used to teach others.

Strategy 6
Developing Students' Metacognition

Teachers who experience the benefits of metacognitive approaches to learning may pursue strategies for using metacognition in their own classroom. Throughout the previous chapters we have suggested a range of ways in which teachers' thinking about their own thinking might then be transferred to the classroom.

Resource 43 | **Table 5.8**   Developing students' metacognition: Ideas for engagement

Prompts for teacher reflection, discussion, and action	
10 min	Ask teachers whether they see themselves as using metacognitive strategies in their teaching and to share some of these with others.
20 min	Use Papaleontiou-Louca's strategies (**Resource 44**) as a discussion starter.
Visual display	Display the suggested strategies.
Weekly challenge	Teachers try one or two strategies in their classrooms.

Papaleontiou-Louca (2003) provides an excellent overview of a wide range of ways that metacognition can be fostered in classrooms. We have summarized these in **Resource 44** | Box 5.3, for teachers to refer to.

Resource 44 | **Box 5.3**   Strategies to develop students' metacognition in practice

> *Note:* The following strategies were summarized from *The Concept and Instruction of Metacognition* (Papaleontiou-Louca, 2003).
>
> **Identifying "what you know" and "what you don't know":** At the beginning of a research activity, children need to establish what they already know and verify, clarify, expand, or replace this with more accurate information by researching the topic.
>
> **Planning and organizing strategy:** It is important for children to assume increasing responsibility for planning and regulating their learning, as it is difficult to become self-directed when learning is planned and monitored by someone else.

Resource 44 | Box 5.3   *(Continued)*

> **Generating questions:** Learner-generated questions involve a high degree of metacognitive involvement, as learners are independently monitoring and regulating their own comprehension, enabling them to become more self-aware and take control of learning.
>
> **Choosing consistency:** Helping students explore the consequences of decisions and providing nonjudgemental feedback about effects of behaviors and decisions may assist students to perceive the relationships between their choices, actions, and results.
>
> **Setting and pursuing goals:** Metacognitive assistance may be provided by helping students define personal goals and justifying reasons for decisions, highlighting relevant perceptual or conceptual facts, and arranging the environment so each step of the problem can be dealt with separately.
>
> **Evaluating the way of thinking and acting:** Independent reflection and evaluation may be assisted with the development of criteria that enable students to think and ask questions of themselves during a learning activity, such as identifying and self-correcting errors and distinguishing what was helpful or hindering.
>
> **Identifying the difficulty:** Instead of giving excuses, students can be encouraged to identify their difficulties in order to develop attitudes and enhanced abilities to implement appropriate strategies.
>
> **Paraphrasing and elaborating students' ideas:** Helping students organize their thoughts and communicate effectively may be assisted by teachers' paraphrasing what is said, extending ideas, putting thoughts in order, and clarifying questions.
>
> **Labeling students' behavior:** Labeling students' cognitive processes helps students become conscious of their own actions (e.g., highlighting when a student makes a plan of action or is experimenting).
>
> **Debriefing the thinking process:** Closure activities focus student discussion on the thinking process and develop awareness of strategies that can be applied to other learning situations.

(Continued)

Resource 44 | Box 5.3   *(Continued)*

> **Problem solving and research activities:** Focusing student attention on how tasks are accomplished with problem-solving and research activities can provide opportunities for developing metacognitive strategies.
>
> **Role playing:** Role playing and dramatization help students understand how other people think, feel, and act in a particular situation, thus helping to reduce egocentric perceptions.
>
> **Thinking aloud:** Thinking aloud, especially during problem-solving processes, helps students organize and enhance their thoughts and assists with developing deliberate planning and transferring strategies to similar situations.
>
> **Interactive multimedia learning environments:** Student thinking, information processing, and self-monitoring of the learning process can be enhanced with the use of computers, which support reflective thinking by enabling students to compose new knowledge by adding new representations, modifying old ones, and comparing the two.
>
> **Keeping a thinking journal:** With the use of a journal or learning log, students can reflect on their thinking, make a note of their awareness of ambiguities and inconsistencies, and comment on how they dealt with difficulties.
>
> **Children teaching children/cooperative learning:** Along with the fostering of collaboration, cooperative learning (including peer tutoring) allows students to become more aware of their thinking and the thinking of others.
>
> **Modeling:** Of all the instructional techniques suggested, the one that probably influences most students is that of teacher modeling. As students learn best by imitating the adults around them, the teacher who publicly demonstrates metacognition will probably produce students who are metacognitive.

Source: Reprinted by permission of Taylor & Francis Ltd. (www.tandfonline.com), on behalf of Teacher Development.

Learning *with* and *from* Students

In many respects, teachers are very isolated in their own classrooms. However, in relation to technology learning, most teachers have many co-learners and assistants readily available to them throughout the day—their students.

Some teachers, however, are more willing to learn with and from their students than others. As previous Technology Together schools have observed, some teachers feel they need to become the expert before introducing new technologies into the class. Other teachers need only a small introduction to a new initiative before joining with the class as a co-learner. Some let students jump in and find their way around new software even when they, the teachers, have not used it themselves. Risk taking is also an element here in terms of teachers being prepared for students to see their lack of ICT knowledge, skills, or confidence.

In those schools where Technology Together was most successfully implemented, the notion of learning with and from students became a significant theme. In many instances, this theme was explicitly discussed with the whole-school community, and teachers were encouraged to come to staff meetings ready to share their experiences of trying new things with their class. Not only is this strategy of learning with and from students effective, efficient, and rewarding for many teachers, but it is also consistent with constructivism and connectivism *and* the more student-centered teaching approaches:

> *Staff members recognize that students are often highly skilled in ICT practice and keen to share their knowledge with teachers. This is a highly significant shift in the perception of good teaching practice at our school. No longer is the teacher seen as the receptacle of all ICT knowledge.*

With encouragement, teachers come to see that they do not need to have all the knowledge before trying something new with their class. For this approach to work, teachers need to perceive their role as one of facilitator of learning rather than the source of all knowledge.

Resource 45 | Table 5.9   Learning with and from students: Ideas for engagement

Prompts for teacher reflection, discussion, and action	
5 min	Share the journal excerpts (**Resource 46** | Reflection 5.1).
20 min	Explicitly discuss the benefits of learning with and from students and have teachers share experiences, including the benefits for students.
	School executives need to explicitly be supportive of teachers taking risks and moving outside their comfort zones.
Wall display	Pin up the journal excerpts (**Resource 46** | Reflection 5.1).
Weekly challenge	Encourage all teachers to learn three ICT facts or skills from their students.

Resource 46 | **Reflection 5.1**   Learning with and from students—journal excerpts

Journal excerpt 1

The teacher next door to me sent in a message that he was having difficulty with the data projector and could I come to help. I sent a child from my class in, who I knew would be successful. The child returned one minute later with the message, "Thanks very much, I will use one of my own children." He discovered the children from his own class were an invaluable resource.

Journal excerpt 2

A teacher was attempting to use the videoing function on a digital camera and having major difficulty. He asked his class, "Does anyone know how to do this?" and received the reply, "I'm not sure, but I think I can work it out." A short time later, the student taught the teacher how to use the function.

Journal excerpt 3

I told my students I had no idea how to do PowerPoint; no use lying to them. "No worries sir" was their reply. They walked me through the process. It was one of the best units of study I have done with this class. Interaction/learning was occurring in a two-way process. I can say with little or no hesitation that I, too, can now do PowerPoint presentations. I can also see how computers in class can become addictive…. There was no need to be ashamed. The students really enjoyed showing me their skills. A very enjoyable unit.

Journal excerpt 4

My class project gave me the greatest joy! After searching for a program that I was not familiar with, I finally decided upon "Kid Pix." Neither the children nor I had used the program before, so I thought it would be fitting that we all started at the same point.

The first session was to explore the program and view the movie explaining how the program worked. This was the only input the children had. From this they were able to play and discover the functions of the program. The children were set 10 tasks using the different functions of the program. At no stage over the 12-week period did any student stop discovering.

From the work samples they provided, it was evident that the children were self-motivated and able to adapt their skills and apply them to the new program. This was then taken further in the last term, where they have now progressed to PowerPoint with little or no instruction on how the program functions.

It has become evident that the children were more willing to explore, play, and adapt than the adults. They took greater risks within a shorter time frame and thus were able to achieve their learning goals at a quicker rate. The information that they had attained was also then transferable to other new experiences and [software] programs.

CHAPTER **6**

Goals and Initiatives

This chapter provides ideas for working with teachers as they set their own learning goals. The ideas we discuss serve as stimuli to move teachers outside their comfort zones and embrace ICT initiatives that they previously might not have considered.

This chapter does not attempt to duplicate the wealth of other existing resources that are available to teachers. Many other excellent published texts (including those from ISTE) and other online resources provide specific suggestions about techniques and teaching ideas for various curriculum areas. We suggest you encourage teachers to access these. Rather, this chapter provides more general guidance to help teachers identify what they do not yet know but would like to be able to do. It does so according to the goal-setting structure (see Chapter 3), although for presentation purposes we cover the goals in a slightly different order: recreational goals, metacognitive goals, leadership goals, skills goals, and integration goals. First, however, we provide some broad guidance on helping teachers set goals, including how best to use the material provided in this chapter.

Helping Teachers Set Goals

We have previously emphasized that Technology Together is about working with teachers to set goals and that no matter what their current level of knowledge or skill, all school staff, including ICT experts, companion mentors, facilitators, and school executives, can take on new challenges.

As a mentor, your role is to emphasize to confident technology users that there is always something to learn about technology. For teachers overwhelmed by the amount that they don't know, your role is to focus them on taking small steps on the ladder of learning—one rung at a time. Explicitly discussing the fact that ICT learning is a lifelong process and that there is no expectation that they "know everything" is critical.

> *At no time were teachers given standardized benchmarks to achieve. Rather, all participants were encouraged to identify their current level of skill in, and attitude towards, ICT and to move onward from there. Teachers who were highly skilled were encouraged to venture into unknown territory. Those at the other end of the scale were more closely supported and guided but also set and worked towards their own goals.*

It is very important that staff own their goals. Companion mentors can encourage, stimulate, and provide ideas; however, ultimately individuals must have the motivation to achieve their own goals. As one assistant principal described:

> *Teachers were provided with resources, opportunities, and ideas, but at no time was this mandated. The clear message was "Start from where you are comfortable and enjoy the ride."*

For some teachers, goal setting leads to tangible outcomes (e.g., digital stories showcased at book week, digital artwork sold at the school fund-raiser, or movies or presentations shown to parents). For other teachers, goals are less visually spectacular but significant for the individual (e.g., learning to manage files or discovering a previously unknown feature of a software program). While it is easy to consider the former as more notable outcomes of Technology Together, the latter, in many instances, may have a more profound impact on the individuals involved.

Remember that goal setting should not be perceived as a rigid or linear process. Keeping goals flexible is important because some learners find their initial goals are too ambitious and the goals they hoped to achieve in the short term become long-term goals. Situations often arise that lead a teacher to change direction or abandon initial goals and take on others.

In these cases, it is important that variations in goal setting are conscious decisions. For example, deciding to adopt another goal because it is more relevant is preferable to abandoning a goal too early without giving it much thought.

Most importantly, goal setting needs to occur alongside discussion of strategies. Staff should be encouraged to use appropriate learning strategies and to explore, play, and learn collaboratively with others. While it is critical that Technology Together results in practical technical learning for teachers, the most profound outcomes will be in relation to teachers' capacity to continue employing self-directed learning strategies to achieve future goals.

The Goal-Setting Structure

In Chapter 3, we introduced the goal-setting structure of Technology Together, specifically, that goals can focus on skills, pedagogy, recreation, metacognition, or leadership. Staff may identify big-picture goals or immediate subgoals.

One way of introducing this structure to teachers is through the following goal-setting pie chart (**Resource 47** | Figure 6.1), which can prompt staff to identify goals in each segment.

Resource 47 | Figure 6.1   Goal-setting pie chart

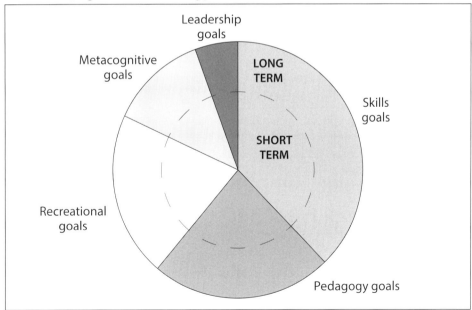

Another method of introducing teachers to the goal-setting structure is through a simple matrix. For instance, you might present teachers with the following (or similar) completed matrix (**Resource 48** | Table 6.1) and then give them a blank matrix to fill in for themselves. These templates are provided on the Technology Together website.

Resource 48 | Table 6.1   The goal-setting matrix

	Examples of long-term goals	**Examples of short-term goals**
Skills goals	Learn to compose digital music Learn to use a video camera	Figure out why the projector cord doesn't fit in my laptop Insert sound in my PowerPoint presentation
Pedagogy goals	Integrate ICT in my creative and performing arts teaching Use more constructivist approaches to ICT integration Use the interactive whiteboard (IWB) for small group rotation	Take my class on a virtual tour of the Louvre
Recreational goals	Start using my home computer more Talk to my own children more about how they use ICT	Book my next flight online
Metacognitive goals	Become more confident in my computer use Not ask for help as soon as something goes wrong	Ensure I keep control of the mouse when my mentor helps me
Leadership goals	Encourage other teachers in my grade to integrate ICT more	Share my unit on art appreciation with my teaching colleagues

Whole-School Goal Setting

Some schools choose to set whole-school goals and encourage teachers to take on individually relevant subgoals, depending on their existing knowledge and skill level. The advantage of a whole-school focus is the sharing of enthusiasm, ideas, and learning—teachers who might otherwise be hesitant or fearful can feel a sense of collegiality.

Ideally, whole-school goals will be suitably broad so as to enable staff to use a diversity of approaches. It is also important that whole-school goals allow for teachers' subgoals to be both relevant and achievable while also challenging. Examples of whole-school goals might include

- Increasing teachers' use of interactive whiteboards;
- Increasing use and integration of spreadsheets;
- Focusing on ways of enhancing literacy learning through the use of ICT;
- Selling students' ICT creations at a school fund-raiser;
- Aligning current teaching theories with ICT integration (e.g., Bloom's Taxonomy or Gardner's Multiple Intelligences).

There are, however, some risks in adopting defined whole-school goals where all staff focus on achieving the same result. For example, one Technology Together companion mentor reflected:

> *Although it was positive for the staff to all work on the same goal, to produce a class web page, there was not the scope or diversity for people within this goal.... People felt they had to do a web page because they saw what others were doing. On reflection, this was a negative for some teachers. The peer pressure of seeing what others were producing made some feel inferior and that they weren't achieving a certain level. On reflection, individual goal setting and working privately with their mentor would have encouraged people to work at their own level.*

We suggest that it is preferable for whole-school goals to be overarching and not too ambitious, and for the focus to remain on individual and/or small-group goal setting.

Whole-school goals do not necessarily need to be in place at the beginning of the implementation process. In some circumstances, whole-school goals can emerge as the process evolves. One school, for example, decided during the year that all classes and students would do digital photo artwork and create a portrait gallery to display and sell at the school fund-raiser. This collaborative whole-school project enhanced professional support, conversation, and sharing, and provided a firm time frame and visual way of showcasing learning achievements.

How to Use This Chapter

This chapter provides lists of learning possibilities and integration ideas as prompts for goal setting. These prompts enable teachers to identify gaps in their knowledge and skills, alerting them to possibilities and helping them identify what they would like to know.

We do not attempt to provide step-by-step instructions on how to perform particular tasks or skills. Many other resources provide this type of support, including books, websites, and the online help features of software programs. Technology Together takes the approach that it is more beneficial to give teachers the confidence to locate and use these resources when and where they need them. We believe it is important to excite teachers about wanting to learn something and then help them do this learning by adopting effective strategies and accessing authentic sources of support.

Ideally, goal setting will occur at the beginning of each term or half semester; however, goals should continue to be revisited as the term or semester progresses. Some schools will choose to use a goal-setting scaffold (as in **Resource 49** | **Form 6.1**) that is completed each term, semester, or half semester and regularly revisited. This scaffold can be pasted inside teachers' journals. Such templates are available on the Technology Together website.

Resource 49 | **Form 6.1**   Goal-setting scaffold

	Specific goal	How did it go?
Skills goals (Developing your own skills or those of students)		
Pedagogy goals (Doing things in your classroom)		
Personal/ Recreational goals (Doing things you want to do for fun)		
Metacognitive goals (Thinking about your thinking)		
Leadership goals (Helping and encouraging others)		

The ideas set out here can be used in a range of ways to support the goal-setting process within your school. We summarize the advantages and disadvantages of some of these approaches in the following table (**Resource 50** | **Table 6.2**). Again, it is important to choose an approach based on knowledge of your school culture and individual teachers. Remember that some staff can become overwhelmed at the prospect of setting individual goals and that providing them with too many options can be intimidating. You will need to make some judgments about what might work best for individual teachers, and you may need a different approach for different groups.

Resource 50 | **Table 6.2** General goal-setting approaches

Goal-setting approach	Advantages	Disadvantages
Individual—independent Staff choose a broad area of interest and then are given a copy of the relevant page from this chapter (e.g., spreadsheets) to identify subgoals. More confident teachers might browse the full chapter.	Time efficient	Some teachers may not know where to start or feel overwhelmed.
Individual with mentor Mentor sits with each staff member (individually or as a pair) and talks through the goal-setting process using the relevant page from this chapter.	A great way to establish the mentoring relationship Teachers will feel less overwhelmed and can be efficiently guided to some relevant goals.	Need to ensure mentors don't inappropriately influence mentees and that mentees retain ownership
Whole grade or faculty/department All teachers from the same grade or department work together to set goals.	Can strongly focus teachers on classroom application and curriculum Can build collegiality	Requires whole-grade teacher release time Some teachers may not want to expose their limitations to peers. Some individuals may not extend themselves. Strong ICT teachers may drive and dominate the process. Less suitable for individual skill, recreational, metacognitive, or leadership goal setting

(Continued)

Resource 50 | **Table 6.2**   *(Continued)*

Goal-setting approach	Advantages	Disadvantages
Whole school All staff are required to have embraced some goals before they leave a staff meeting (individual, mentor, and whole-grade approaches can also be drawn on). A data projector can be used to share a range of ideas from this chapter.	Time efficient Can build networks between teachers (e.g., pairing like-to-like)	Staff may feel pressured or influenced by peers. May lead to conformity in goals
Demonstration Someone demonstrates hardware, software, or integration ideas at a staff meeting as stimulus Peers demonstrate to each other and focus on showcasing each other's learning achievements and encouraging others to embrace the goals.	Can produce the "wow factor" and inspire teachers with a range of ideas Can bring new ideas into a school so teaching practices don't get stale	Teachers can feel overwhelmed. It is difficult to target everyone's level of readiness. Can reinforce the expert–novice divide

Metacognitive Goals

Metacognitive goals are goals related to attitudes, beliefs, or confidence. **Resource 51** | Goals list 6.1 shows some metacognitive goals that teachers might set.

Resource 51 | **Goals list 6.1**   Examples of metacognitive goals

- To attempt solving technology problems before seeking assistance
- To not be concerned about making mistakes
- To be prepared to learn with and from my students
- To try using exploratory learning skills
- To introduce an "explore first, ask three (other students), and then ask me" policy in my classroom
- To be more conscious of what I attribute my successes and nonsuccesses to—no more seeing them as only luck!
- To become more capable

Leadership Goals

The following leadership goals don't just relate to school executive leaders. All teachers can set leadership goals. **Resource 52** | **Goals list 6.2** provides some broad ideas.

Resource 52 | **Goals list 6.2** Examples of leadership goals

- To model appropriate technology learning strategies for my colleagues
- To encourage my colleagues to utilize ICT
- To create one place (a web page or wiki) where all teachers in our department can share links to web-based resources
- To share my interactive whiteboard lessons with others in my grade or department
- To discuss my learning experiences with others and encourage them to give them a try

Recreational Goals

As outlined in Chapter 4, it can be just as important to support teachers to strive toward and achieve recreational goals as professional ones. Achieving recreational goals can help teachers develop their sense of perceived usefulness, increasing their skills and confidence and allowing them to transfer their achievements to their school and classroom environments.

It is worth mentioning to teachers that they need to be aware of some basic cybersafety issues, such as ensuring they have virus protection software installed, take care when providing personal information online, and only use secure sites for credit card payments. Learning about cybersafety can become a foundational computer skills goal.

Some ways teachers can embrace technology recreationally are shown in
Resource 53 | **Goals list 6.3**.

Resource 53 | **Goals list 6.3**   Examples of recreational goals

- Email family photos to a relative
- Book flights for a family vacation online
- Create a birthday presentation for a relative
- Borrow a school video camera to film the kids playing sports
- Install Skype on my home computer to chat with my son or daughter overseas
- Organize my music collection using a media player (e.g., iTunes, Windows Media Player)
- Find out how to copy music to my MP3 player
- Access my favorite radio shows via podcast
- Sign up for and learn to use online banking
- Set up a Facebook or Twitter account
- Order tickets online for a football match
- Find a good website or software program to record my local rainfall data electronically so I can see totals, averages, and graphs

Skills-Based Goals

Perhaps the most obvious area for setting goals is in relation to technology skills. Broadly speaking, skills-based goals can be considered as falling into three broad areas:

- Foundational computer skills—these skills relate to general computer use or knowledge that carries across multiple software programs and operating systems;
- Skills in using a range of hardware;
- Skills in using core software applications, including word processors, spreadsheets, communication applications (both asynchronous and synchronous), World Wide Web, databases, multimedia, presentation software, interactive whiteboard flipchart software, and mobile apps.

In the following sections we provide resources to guide staff in embracing goals in one or more of these areas. We create an arbitrary distinction between "core" and "extensional" skills and also suggest ways that teachers might implement and integrate their skills in the classroom.

Foundational Computer Skills

For many teachers in schools who have had good technology infrastructure in place for some time, some of the following foundational skills may seem rudimentary. However, we begin at this basic level for two reasons. First, some teachers, particularly those in developing countries, have had very little, if any, exposure to technology, and this might be their starting point. And second, even in more technologically advanced schools, some teachers find it affirming to have their basic achievements acknowledged.

Resource 54 | **Table 6.3** Foundational computer skills goal-setting scaffold

Core skills	Taking it further
Locate and open software programs and files.	Download and install some online software (e.g., Hot Potatoes for creating quizzes or jMemorize for creating flashcards).
Create, name, and rename folders.	
Understand and use the various drives, such as the C:, D:, and/or E: drives (Windows).	Use Help to find information on any software program or for the computer generally.
Close a file and exit a program (and know the difference between the two).	Set up a computer and peripheral devices (i.e., know where to attach all the cords).
Understand the importance of backing up.	Print a document so that two pages display side-by-side on the sheet.
Minimize, move, resize (maximize /minimize), and close windows; view two windows at once.	Check that your virus protection software is up to date.
Move and copy files and folders, including backing up to a removable disk.	Try both Mac and Windows platforms.
	Create a PDF file.
Delete a file (intentionally).	Know how to add items to the Start menu (Windows) or Apple Menu (Mac).
Print a document.	
Rename a file.	Create shortcuts (Windows and Mac) or aliases (Mac).
Run two or more programs simultaneously.	
Understand about compressed files (e.g., .zip or .rar) and how to decompress them.	Create a read-only file.
	Burn a CD or DVD.
Read about cybersafety issues, including using virus protection and malware, protecting your identity online, and credit card security.	Explore the control panel, including functions such as changing the date and time, changing the desktop appearance or screensaver, screen resolution, and/or mouse or keyboard functionality.
Investigate cloud file storage systems (e.g., Dropbox).	

(Continued)

Resource 54 | **Table 6.3** *(Continued)*

Implementing and integrating	
Your skills	**Students' skills**
Organize (spring clean) your computer files; create a logical folder structure and move your files into the folders.	Have students set up several folders to organize their work by subject (or into folders for homework and fun).
Buy an external drive (e.g., USB drive) and learn how to back up your files to it.	Discuss with students the importance of backing up and have them share and show each other different ways to do it.
Install some recreational software at home.	
Put a fun or appealing image on the background of your computer desktop.	Have students look up the solutions to problems using online help.
Make a student worksheet into a read-only document and save it on the school server to be used as a template for students.	Create a digital resource showcasing and celebrating students' work.
	Allow students to disassemble and reassemble a disused computer.
Create shortcuts on the classroom computer desktops that lead to frequently used software or websites (tip: to create a shortcut to a website, try dragging a browser bookmark or favorite to the desktop).	Have students print their work two-to-a-page to save paper.
	Set a student-created image as the class computer's desktop image.

Hardware Skills

The hardware goals that schools or individual teachers take on will be entirely dependent on the resources available to them. Schools with limited resources might set hardware goals that focus on increased or more effective use of existing resources—for example, you might explore using more unfamiliar or advanced features of existing hardware. If your school is better resourced, Technology Together might provide the impetus to purchase some new technologies.

Here we provide a general list of types of hardware that may (or may not yet) have found their way into your school. For each type of hardware, teachers might set out to do the following: learn to use it for the first time, learn to use it more effectively, explore more advanced features, teach others to use it, or integrate it into their teaching in more creative ways.

Resource 55 | **Form 6.2**   Hardware skills goal-setting scaffold

Hardware	Use for first time	Use more effectively	Teach others	Integrate more creatively
Data projector				
Digital stills camera				
Digital video camera				
Interactive whiteboard				
Personal response system (for voting)				
Digital voice recorder				
MP3 player or iPod				
Tablet or slate				
Digital TV recorder				
Digital music keyboard				
Data loggers				
Mobile (cell) phones				
Mobile devices (e.g., smartphones, tablets)				
Video game devices/consoles				
Robotics (consider Bee-Bots and Pro-Bots for younger students, building to advanced robotic kits such as Lego Mindstorms for upper primary and secondary)				
Assistive technology (for students with special needs)				
Other …				

Word Processing Skills

Most computer users feel they have reasonable, if not excellent, word processing skills—and no doubt they often do. However, even the most confident computer users will know that their word processor has features they are less familiar with or have never used. Here we list goal ideas that range from very basic skills to using more advanced features.

Resource 56 | **Table 6.4**   Word processing skills goal-setting scaffold

Core skills	Taking it further
Create and save a word processing document.	Use hyperlinks to create clickable worksheets.
Enter text and use different fonts, sizes, and colors.	Insert a comment (like a yellow sticky note).
	Insert a footnote into your document.
Cut, copy, and paste using at least two methods.	Insert a table of contents based on heading levels.
Undo the last action that you did.	Use text boxes to position graphics or text.
Print a document or part of a document.	Use WordArt (for Microsoft Word).
Use find and replace.	Insert page breaks or section breaks.
Create a bulleted or a numbered list.	Change one section of a document from portrait to landscape orientation.
Use the word count feature.	
Align your text to the left, right, or center.	Format bullets as different symbols.
Create headers and footers.	Use the Format Painter tool (for Microsoft Word).
Change the margins of a document.	
Use the spell checker, grammar checker, and thesaurus.	Use track changes.
	Use forms to create interactive worksheets.
Insert automatically generated page numbers.	Format a document or parts of a document with multiple columns (you need to use section breaks to achieve this).
Insert graphics into documents using clip art and other graphics files.	
Insert a table into your document.	Know how and when to use Rich Text Format (RTF) files.
Format the borders and shading of a table; resize and merge table cells.	Customize toolbars.
	Insert a sound.
Indent a paragraph of text using the ruler.	Use the drawing features, including grouping elements.
Format line spacing to be 1.5–line or double-spaced.	

Resource 56 | **Table 6.4** *(Continued)*

Implementing and integrating	
Your skills	**Students' skills**
Format students' worksheets creatively. Word process your programming documents—try more advanced formatting, such as hyperlinking to other files and websites. Try marking some students' work electronically using comments, track changes, highlighting, and/or sound annotations. Produce clickable or interactive worksheets (using either hyperlinks or forms). Try out some voice recognition software (e.g., Dragon Dictation).	Keep encouraging more advanced formatting in all students' typed work. Have students learn one new word-processing feature and teach it to others in the class (including you!). Have students produce a class newspaper using formatting techniques modeled from a real print newspaper (e.g., callouts, columns, headings, and graphics). Set a research task requiring students to produce a poster or brochure. Have students produce clickable or interactive worksheets for each other. Use drawing tools to have students name shapes or mark lines of symmetry.

World Wide Web Skills

Undoubtedly, any teachers with access to an Internet connection will have basic skills in using the web. However, most computer users only learn to do the basics and can remain oblivious to many other beneficial skills. It is also not uncommon for individuals to have misunderstandings or knowledge gaps in some important areas. Challenging teachers to move up a few rungs of the ladder in terms of web use can be beneficial—and lots of fun.

There is so much to learn about using the web that we have separated the goal-setting scaffold into two sections. The first section is termed Web 1.0 (although this term is used loosely) and covers the essential skills of consumption on the web—reading, receiving, and researching. The second section focuses on what have come to be termed Web 2.0 technologies—tools for contributing, collaborating, and creating (Hargadon, 2010).

Resource 57 | **Table 6.5** Web 1.0 skills goal-setting scaffold

Core skills	Taking it further
Understand what a web browser is.	Conduct an image, movie, or audio search using a common search engine (e.g., Google).
Connect to a specific URL (web address).	Know how to tell if a website is secure or not (e.g., for online payments).
Know how to follow links and use forward/back buttons.	Export, save, and back up your bookmarks/favorites.
Create browser bookmarks/favorites.	Find out what Boolean operators are and how to use them to improve search results (Hint: AND, OR, NOT, or "+" and "–" are common; also the wildcard "*").
Organize browser bookmarks/favorites into folders.	
Locate a search engine and perform a basic search.	
Conduct a phrase search (Hint: use "…").	Create a shortcut to a website on your desktop (very valuable for classroom use!).
Save text or images from the web to your desktop or hard drive.	Customize your browser using preferences/options (e.g., change your homepage to be your most visited website).
Compare different search engines/directories and identify their strengths and weaknesses.	Know what plug-ins are and why and how to use them.
Try some child-friendly search engines (e.g., Twurdy, which indicates the wordiness of the results).	
Try using online map tools (e.g., Google Earth or Google Maps).	

Implementing and integrating	
Your skills	**Students' skills**
Gain access to the Internet from home or investigate alternative Internet Service Providers (ISPs).	Try using a kid-specific search engine with your class.
Find out about the filtering policies and practices at your school.	Try a WebQuest with your class (see later in this chapter).
Look up some websites related to your recreational interests and passions.	Have students create a puzzle or quiz from their spelling list or from topic terms they are studying, using one of the many websites designed for this.
Try some online shopping.	
Try planning your next vacation online.	Teach students to use Boolean operators to conduct more effective searches.
Locate some lesson plan websites.	

Resource 58 | **Table 6.6**   Web 2.0 skills goal-setting scaffold

Core skills	Taking it further
Find out what a blog is. Find out what a wiki is. Explore the Flickr website. Find out what Twitter is and become aware of the many discussions you can follow this way (e.g., professional groups, TV shows, politicians). Explore YouTube and identify some educational videos for use in the classroom. Find out which of your friends, relatives, and colleagues use Facebook, LinkedIn, or other social media sites. Have a look at some examples of social bookmarking sites (e.g., Delicious). Learn what cloud computing is.	Set up a blog using websites such as WordPress or Blogger (you can always delete it later). Set up a wiki using sites such as PBWorks or Ning (you can always delete it later). Set up your own Facebook page, find some friends, and "like" some groups or websites. Find out about course management systems (e.g., Moodle) and talk to your ICT staff about what can be used in your school. Set up a Flickr account and upload some images. Set up a Twitter account. Try using Google Drive and learn how to share documents and collaborate with others.

Implementing and integrating	
Your skills	**Students' skills**
Set up a wiki site or a Facebook page for a recreational or professional group or for your class. Create a class social bookmarking site to support topics you are researching.	As a class, try using a blog (e.g., for a progressive story or a journaling activity). As a class, try using a wiki (e.g., for groups of students to report on a research project or for a whole-class website). Have students create a video to upload to YouTube.

Communication Applications Skills

Asynchronous communication is communication where the sending and receiving of messages occurs at different times; synchronous communication refers to communication that occurs roughly at the same time. For example, a telephone conversation is synchronous, whereas a letter (snail mail) is asynchronous. Email is asynchronous while instant messaging (or chat) is synchronous. Online communication can be asynchronous or synchronous, and it can be one-way, two-way, one-to-one, or one-to-many.

Any of these communication technologies can be used to support the global projects that are discussed later in this chapter.

Resource 59 | **Table 6.7** Communication applications skills goal-setting scaffold

Core skills	Taking it further
Asynchronous	
Send, receive, and delete an email.	Synchronize the address book from your mobile phone with your personal computer (if possible).
Reply to an email so the original message appears below your reply; reply to all so everyone can see your response.	Know what spam is and be aware of preventative measures to ensure you aren't at risk of viruses.
Create a mailbox (or folder) and file email into it.	Filter email.
Know what CC and BCC mean and how to use them.	Explore the preferences/options area of your email program.
Create a signature.	Set up your own blog.
Send and receive an attachment.	Access email from your mobile phone (if possible).
Create an address book entry.	
Synchronous	
Participate in a text-based chat session (e.g., MSN Messenger, Yahoo Messenger, or Facebook Chat).	Try some online conferencing software such as Google Hangouts, Elluminate Live, Adobe Connect, or GoToMeeting.
Try Internet telephony (e.g., Skype).	Learn to use SkypeOut to make standard telephone calls (to save on your phone bills).
Use a webcam to participate in a video chat.	Explore a virtual world such as Second Life.
Implementing and integrating	
Your skills	Students' skills
Check your email daily and increase its use for both personal and professional communication.	Implement keypals, travel buddies, or virtual bookclub, or participate in a book rap (see global projects later in this chapter).
Subscribe to a mailing list (e.g., to provide ICT resources).	Communicate with community groups as part of a current topic.
Send a favorite website address to your teaching colleagues.	Set up a class email address and join an online group discussing current issues (e.g., www.abc.net.au/btn).
Email a friend or family member and send them a digital photograph.	As a class, write iterative stories with another class via a wiki or blog.
Let students' parents know your email address and tell them when and for what purposes you would be happy to receive messages from them.	As a class, email someone famous or have someone do a virtual guest lesson via videoconferencing.
Try Skype with a friend or family member living overseas or at a distance.	Discuss cybersafety issues and cyberbullying.

Spreadsheet Software Skills

Spreadsheets are an incredibly useful category of software, yet many teachers know little about them or only know the very basics. Their uses are diverse, and it is as important for students to learn about spreadsheets as it is for them to learn to use a word processor. Students from the early years onward can gain much from using spreadsheets, especially if teachers become more confident with using them as well. This is a key area for teachers' goal setting.

Resource 60 | **Table 6.8** Spreadsheet software skills goal-setting scaffold

Core skills	Taking it further
Recognize the parts of a spreadsheet (worksheets, rows, columns, cells, etc.).	Copy (or fill) a function/formula to other cells.
Enter data into cells and move from one cell to another.	Know how to find advanced functions.
Enter labels.	Sort data.
Select a range of cells.	Select nonadjacent columns or rows.
Insert rows or columns and change column widths.	Use multiple sheets.
Use mathematical operators (+, –, *, /) to construct formulas.	Apply filters on data.
Use basic functions such as SUM, AVERAGE, MAX, MIN, and COUNT.	Know how to freeze panes for large spreadsheets.
Print an area of a spreadsheet.	
Create a chart.	

(Continued)

Resource 60 | **Table 6.8** *(Continued)*

Implementing and integrating	
Your skills	**Students' skills**
Create a teacher's log for recording day-to-day class information (including test results, permission slips, field trip payments, behavior management, etc.).	Create a simple survey across the class, grade, or school; graph the results (e.g., transportation to school, types of pets owned, diet, or awareness of current issues).
Set up a spreadsheet to manage your personal finances or taxes.	Run a guessing competition and graph students' responses (e.g., colors of candy in a jar).
Organize some information or a roster related to a community group for which you are involved.	Research data on a topic students are studying and present the data in a graphic format (e.g., rates of population growth, rainforest deforestation, or health issues).
	Try some online interactive spreadsheets for teaching math concepts, such as estimation.
	Play battleship to learn coordinates.

Presentation Software Skills

As with word-processing skills, teachers readily pick up the basics of using presentation software, such as Microsoft PowerPoint. Students also are frequently encouraged to produce presentations—for example, to report on their project work. But as with other software, teachers and students often do not push their skills beyond the basics, and the creative potential of presentation software is often not realized. Technology Together provides an opportunity to challenge teachers to move beyond their comfort zones.

We would like to make a particular note about interactive stories. There are an ever-increasing number of websites and commercial software packages providing access to stories with animations and sound. Many of these websites also include quizzes to build comprehension. The Ziptales site (www.ziptales.com) is one such example. Although such interactive websites are excellent, a great ICT integration activity relevant to any grade, is having students create their own talking or interactive stories by using presentation or multimedia software. Students can use presentation software, such as PowerPoint or flipchart software, or other multimedia software, such as Kid Pix or Kahootz, to combine text and images over a series of screens, then record an audio narration to play as the story is read. The text may be linear and traditional, fiction or nonfiction, or it can take the form of a "choose your own adventure" that uses hyperlinks to provide interactivity. When students are involved in creating talking stories, they develop skills in reading, writing, and speaking, as well as planning, designing, and communicating appropriately for a target audience. Sharing stories with other students creates a collaborative and fun dimension to learning. Even senior students can productively use these strategies to create stimulus for learning poems, plays, and quotes from literature.

Resource 61 | **Table 6.9** Presentation software skills goal-setting scaffold

Core skills	Taking it further
Create a basic presentation.	Print in different formats/layouts.
Insert graphics and sound.	Create a self-running presentation.
Apply transitions.	Record a narrative.
Apply animations.	Know about PowerPoint Viewer (so anyone without access to PowerPoint can view presentations).
Understand about different views.	
Use the notes area.	Explore alternative presentation programs, including cloud-based software such as Prezi.
Use a data projector.	

Implementing and integrating	
Your skills	**Students' skills**
Create a presentation to introduce a topic to your class.	Have students produce a presentation on a topic that they have researched (older students should use the notes area).
Use presentation software to present a model, diagram, or flowchart.	Create a "talking greeting card" for a friend or family member.
For younger students, create a presentation that reviews new words, letters of the alphabet, or math concepts.	Create "talking," or interactive, stories (those that incorporate sound) and share them with another class; try to make them self-running.
Create a presentation for a family event or gathering.	Extend the interactive story by using hyperlinks to create a choose-your-own-adventure story.
Create a presentation for a school assembly.	Create a presentation to recount a class field trip.
	Create class portfolios.
	Discuss issues in the use of PowerPoint, particularly its suitability for its audience.

Multimedia Skills

Technology starts to become lots of fun once you get into areas of multimedia. Although many people readily try their hand at digital photography, not everyone ventures into other exciting areas, such as audio and video, or more creative and original multimedia endeavors, such as animation and creating 3-D virtual worlds.

Resource 62 | **Table 6.10**   Multimedia skills goal-setting scaffold

Core skills	Taking it further
Insert a graphic from clip art into a document.	Download and try graphics editing software (e.g., GIMP).
Know how to locate and save graphics from the web.	Save a graphic into different formats.
Use a painting program (such as Microsoft Paint).	Know how to download a video from a website for offline viewing.
Use the drawing features in your word processor or presentation software to create a diagram.	Download and try Audacity (freeware for audio editing).
Record a sound.	Save a sound into different formats.
Resize and crop a graphic.	Record and do basic editing on a video.
Know how to rip a sound track from a CD to MP3 format (note legal issues in this regard).	Learn to record television on a personal computer (you will need a TV receiver).
Learn to use a media library program (e.g., iTunes or Windows Media Player).	Try music notation software (e.g., Sibelius, Finale, or Canorus).
Try mind-mapping software such as FreeMind, Cmap, or Inspiration/Kidspiration.	Try music composition software (e.g., GarageBand).
	Try some animation software such as Pivot Stickfigure Animator or Stop Motion Pro (which can be used for clay animation).

Resource 62 | **Table 6.10**   *(Continued)*

Implementing and integrating	
Your skills	**Students' skills**
Take digital photos or video at a family event and compile them into an album.	Try any of the applications listed in this table with your students.
Install iTunes or similar software and digitize some or all of your music collection.	Have students take digital photos of each other and manipulate them to create self-portraits.
Explore some of the legal music download sites.	Take digital photos on a school field trip/excursion and display them to the class.
Investigate MP3 players.	Record a story in audio format.
Listen to some podcasts, such as posted on the websites of your favorite local public radio station or international news channel.	Create original artwork for a digital class exhibit or to illustrate a story your class is reading.
Investigate and consider trying Kahootz (for creating 3-D worlds).	Create a video of a class play.
Create a DVD from your digital photos.	Listen to podcasts related to topics being studied (particularly for older students).
Create a thumbnail image of yourself (or an avatar) to use on social networking sites.	Create a podcast and upload and share it.
	Use technology to create scenery for your next school play or production.
	Produce a class video, starting from storyboarding the ideas, and then filming, editing, producing/exporting, and screening for family and friends.
	Use Kahootz with your class to create a collaborative story.

Database Software Skills

Perhaps no software category receives as little attention from teachers as databases. This is unfortunate because databases are a pervasive part of society and an important area for students' knowledge and skills development, particularly in the later schooling years. Databases can be used to teach many concepts and to develop critical skills, such as information literacy and organizational capacity.

A challenge teachers face is finding the appropriate database software for their student age group. For example, Microsoft Access, the database application included with professional versions of the Microsoft Office suite, is a complex program and not necessarily appropriate for younger students—or for less confident teachers. However, several companies produce student-friendly database software applications and these are ideal for primary school environments. Database concepts can also be integrated in other ways using existing databases that have already been set up and are accessible to you and your students. Developing database software skills may not be a goal-setting area for everyone, but for those seeking a challenge it can be both rewarding and enjoyable.

Resource 63 | **Table 6.11**   Database software skills goal-setting scaffold

Core skills	Taking it further
Understand the terms *database*, *record*, and *field*. Perform a search in an existing database. Set up an address book, such as that included with your email program. Sort and find records in an existing database.	Set up a simple database (such as in Access) using templates. Examples include a student or class database, assets, invoices, plants, photographs, books, music, video collections, or recipes. Discriminate between form (layout) view and list view.
Implementing and integrating	
Your skills	**Students' skills**
Find out more about your school's database systems (e.g., for student records, staffing, finances, or the library). Try a web search on a particular topic you are teaching and include "+ database" as a search term to see what you find. Note that when using Google, quotation marks now serve the same purpose—for example, music + database OR music "database". Set up an asset management database for your home, class, or school. Download list software (or a mobile app) and set up a database that includes all your to-do lists or passwords (note the need for a password-protected database for the latter); examples include ListPro or Keeper Password & Data Vault.	Talk about the structure and uses of commonly accessed databases (e.g., library catalogs, electronic encyclopedias, dictionaries, or other reference resources). Use an existing online database as the basis of a lesson with your students. Examples include the following: address databases, world flag databases, nutrition databases (which show the nutritional value of various foods), or book publisher or bookstore databases. Note that the best databases are those where the fields display in an obvious way and can be searched separately. Set up a database with your students. Examples might include the following: explorers, animals, pets, the periodic table or chemicals, poets, artists and their works, timbers, food groups, diseases, sports, authors and their works, careers, endangered species, historical landmarks, planets, scientists, cities around the world, or survey information.

Interactive Whiteboard Skills (Flipchart Software)

An interactive whiteboard (IWB) is essentially a large whiteboard-like surface that acts as an input device to a computer. When combined with a data projector that displays the computer monitor's image onto the board's surface, the IWB functions as a touch-sensitive screen. Any software that runs from the attached computer can be interacted with via the IWB. However, there is a category of software specifically designed for schools, which we more generally term "flipchart software." Such programs typically act like presentation software but include a range of specific functions to facilitate lessons. Each of the major IWB manufacturers produce and distribute their own proprietary version of this flipchart software (e.g., Smart Notebook, ActivInspire, or Easiteach).

Resource 64 | **Table 6.12** Interactive whiteboard skills goal-setting scaffold

Core skills	Taking it further
Find out how to get started with using an IWB in your school.	Screen capture (e.g., from a word processing document or website) to include on the flipchart page.
Learn how to calibrate the whiteboard.	
Start the flipchart software.	Link to other documents or websites.
Write and draw on multiple screens/pages.	Use templates such as quiz starters to customize a lesson.
Insert an object or image from the clip-art gallery.	Store/embed other resources in your flipchart file.
Drag and drop (to move objects around).	Use the video recorder to record a lesson.
Use color/shading/highlighting for emphasis.	Use layering (where available).
Insert a video, audio, or flash file from the gallery.	Use actions such as hide/show/contain (where available).
Convert handwriting to typed text (character recognition).	
Use interactive tools (e.g., protractor, dice).	

(Continued)

Resource 64 | **Table 6.12**   *(Continued)*

Implementing and integrating	
Your skills	**Students' skills**
Search online for pre-made IWB lesson resources.	Have students create some resources for each other on topics they are learning about.
Use premade IWB lessons downloaded by you or your colleagues.	Use the flipchart software to create a class interactive story or choose-your-own adventure story.
Modify premade IWB lessons downloaded by you or your colleagues.	
Create your own IWB lessons and share them with your immediate colleagues.	
Create your own IWB lessons and upload and share them online.	

Mobile Applications Skills

Mobile applications, or apps, developed for iPhones and iPads, together with apps developed for Android, Windows Mobile, and other systems, are rapidly finding their way into classrooms. An ever-increasing number of apps are being developed either specifically for educational use or for adaptation to classroom learning. The availability of apps is constantly growing and changing; we provide here a list representing an indicative selection of the scope of such apps and their potential in classrooms.

Resource 65 | **Table 6.13** Mobile apps skills goal-setting scaffold

English	Mathematics
Talking Tom or Talking Ben (for aural language)	iCut
Jumbline	Animals Count
Puppet Pals (for creating stories)	Cloud Math
Wattpad	Column Addition
WordWeb (Dictionary)	Math Magic
ABA Flash Cards—Actions	Mathtrain
ABC Phonics	Quick Graph
Chicktionary for iPad	Multiplication Rap
Sentence Builder	Math Helper
W.E.L.D.E.R.	Everyday Mathematics
StoryKit	Times Tables
Wide range of children's e-books	ArithFit

Science	Creative Arts
Planets	Color Splash
3D Cell Simulation and Cell Stain Tool	GarageBand
Mitosis	Fold-Man
NASA App	Chord Tutor
Periodic Table of the Elements	Doodle Buddy
Science360	Art App—Ultimate Scratch

Health and Personal Development	Social Science
MyNetDiary (record nutrition and exercise)	TapQuiz Maps
Touch and Learn—Emotions	Globe for iPad
Wide range of fitness apps	Google Earth

(Continued)

Resource 65 | **Table 6.13** *(Continued)*

General Purpose Apps	For you (or your students) just for fun!
iAnnotate PDF (for PDF reading and markup)	ArtPuzzles
SoundNote	Draw Something Free
Pages, Numbers, and Keynote	Call of Atlantis
Calculator	World of Goo
Whiteboard	Doodle Find
Dragon Dictation	Simply Find It

Other	
Second language learning—there are lots of apps available for learning a wide range of languages	Little Things
	Words with Friends
iRewardChart	
Special education apps, such as Proloquo2Go	
SimpleMind+ (mind mapping)	

Pedagogy Goals

The ultimate outcome of teachers' ICT learning is for them to integrate ICT into their teaching practices. In the previous sections on software applications, we suggested a range of ways in which technology skills could be put to immediate use in the classroom.

However, there are many integration ideas that do not specifically relate to software applications or hardware skills. Many of the most exciting educational applications of ICT are valuable because they represent innovations to classroom pedagogy and draw together a wide range of hardware and software to support good constructivist or connectivist learning experiences.

In Chapter 5, we provided six strategies for challenging teachers to reflect on their pedagogical values, attitudes, beliefs, and practices. The goal-setting ideas in this section provide the stimulus to implement such teaching philosophies in the classroom.

Our goal-setting scaffold for this section reflects two areas of challenge. First, we prompt teachers to consider the classroom management strategies they currently use and those they might use more often. We then prompt teachers to try some authentic connectivist lesson ideas, such as WebQuests or global projects.

Classroom Management

The management techniques that teachers employ when using ICT in their classrooms will reflect their teaching style and classroom culture. Of course, ICT resources vary greatly between schools. Some schools have excellent facilities, while others are more restricted. Some schools place one or more computer(s) in each classroom, while others rely on computer laboratories. And some schools are fortunate enough to have access to laptops—perhaps even one per student—or other mobile technologies, such as iPads.

Although not comprehensive, the following list (**Resource 66** | **Form 6.3**) provides some general structures for classroom management and can serve as a basis for prompting teachers to set goals to manage their ICT integration in different, new, or creative ways.

Resource 66 | **Form 6.3** Classroom management goal-setting scaffold

Strategy	I do this a lot.	I do this sometimes.	I aim to do this more.
Whole-class demonstration. Can be via a data projector or IWB. This approach is ideal for introducing something new or for whole-class discussions of content being covered.			
Individual rotation. Individual students use a computer or other device on a roster basis while the class continues with other activities.			
One-to-one. May be undertaken in a computer lab or using laptops or other mobile device.			
Buddy systems. Two students sit at a computer. While one is operating it, the other is playing an alternative role, such as recording, helping, or reading. Both swap roles.			
Peer or cross-age tutoring. Students assume a teaching role with others.			
Small groups. Three to four students work together. Ideal for problem-solving activities (such as WebQuests). Encourages cooperative problem solving and helps develop positive social behavior. It is good to allocate and rotate roles, such as leader, note taker, keyboard operator, or researcher.			
Roster systems. Individuals might work on an activity then check their names off the list and select someone else to take a turn. Groups can also circulate around different technology (e.g., IWB, laptops, iPads) on a roster system.			
Contract activities. Students are set a series of tasks to complete in the order of their choice. Allows teachers to cater to students of various abilities by setting different tasks. One or several contract activities can be technology based. Students with home computer access may do technology aspects of contract work as homework, freeing classroom technology for those without home access.			
Parent helpers. Parents assist individuals or small groups, working as troubleshooters, tutoring, doing demonstrations, or assisting students with research and information skills.			
Scaffolded link sites. A website, wiki, blog, or even a word-processing document provides directions for students and potentially links to resources to scaffold self-directed learning.			

Authentic, Connectivist Online Learning

In Chapter 5, we suggested six strategies to challenge and support teachers' teaching. In particular, we discussed the value of constructivist and connectivist approaches, and problem-based, authentic learning experiences. In this section, we provide some ideas for very practical goals that teachers can use to put these ideas into action in their classrooms. We focus on five key types of learning experiences, namely WebQuests, global projects (which include interpersonal exchanges, online information collection and analysis, and problem-solving projects), and simulations. Use the table (**Resource 67** | **Form 6.4**) as a way of prompting teachers to learn more about these ideas and to try them.

Resource 67 | **Form 6.4** Authentic and constructivist online learning goal-setting scaffold

Strategy	Learn more and investigate existing examples.	Try an existing resource with my class.	Adapt/create one myself or collaborate with other teachers.
WebQuests			
Global projects **Interpersonal exchanges** (including keypals, travel buddies, global classrooms, book raps, electronic appearances, telementoring, question and answer, impersonations, and virtual gatherings)			
Online information collection and analysis (including information exchanges, pooled data analysis, database creation, electronic publishing, and virtual field trips)			
Problem-solving projects (including scavenger hunts, parallel problem solving, social action projects, global WebQuests, and online competitions)			
Simulations			

WebQuests

WebQuest is a term widely used in education and other contexts to refer loosely to web-based research activities. However, the original (and we argue still the best) WebQuest takes a particular form. WebQuests are student-centered, problem-based activities where students work collaboratively on a real-life task with each member of the group assuming a specific responsibility. Although students use the web as a resource, WebQuests are not the same as simple online research projects. As they were first conceptualized by Bernie Dodge (way back in 1997, http://webquest.sdsu.edu/about_webquests.html), WebQuests consist of the following critical parts:

- An **introduction** that grabs students' attention and provides background information to the activity.
- An authentic **task** that is doable and interesting and is generally problem-based, in that students have to solve or do something;
- Links to **information** sources that are generally available online. Because pointers to resources are included, the learner is not left to wander and waste time;
- A description of the **process** learners need to engage in to accomplish the task, broken down into clear steps;
- Some **guidance** on how to organize or present the information acquired;
- A **conclusion** that reminds learners what they have learned and encourages them to extend their new knowledge or skills to other domains.

WebQuests are most engaging when they are scenario-based and provide students with particular roles to play (e.g., scientist, detective, or reporter), working toward a shared solution to the problem. WebQuests are thus great group learning activities.

There are many WebQuests available online, but the quality of them will vary, and they can get out of date if not maintained. Encourage teachers to search for WebQuests on topics that they are planning to cover (for example, "water conservation" +webquest; "Australian animals" +webquest) and see what they find. Some international websites also provide links to WebQuests.

Even if you find something of interest that is not quite right for your class, you can adapt the ideas and create a customized WebQuest for your students. WebQuests can be created using a wiki site or simply developed as a word-processed document and made accessible to your class via the school server.

Global Projects

The web is rich with informational websites relating to almost any topic your students might be studying. However, many available online resources move beyond the web as an information source and provide students with authentic, and constructivist online learning experiences—those that extend beyond the search for facts and figures to provide very different types of learning experiences. Global Projects harness the potential of online communication technologies to bring your class in contact with other students and adults from around the world. They open your classroom up to new ideas and new experiences that excite and inspire students.

The framework that we use in this section is based on that originally created by Judi Harris in the 1990s and still being used and discussed to this day (see, for example, Harris, Mishra, & Koehler, 2009). Not all of the specific examples Harris originally referred to still exist, but some do, and many new ones have arisen, taking advantage of newer technological possibilities.

Teachers might set a goal to learn more about one or two of these types of learning activities and investigate examples relevant to their own teaching area or topics being studied. Alternatively, they might set a goal to create an online learning experience along these lines and collaborate with other classes in the school, neighboring schools, or even create a national or international global project. Note that we do not provide web addresses for all examples, particularly where they are likely to change rapidly. Use your web-searching skills to locate the most current sites.

Interpersonal Exchanges

Interpersonal exchanges take place when individuals, groups, or whole classes communicate with others to exchange information or resources. There are a number of such types of learning experiences:

Keypals are like electronic penpals and can use a range of technologies, from email to blogs, wikis, synchronous text, or voice-based chat. Keypals can be beneficial for all ages to support literacy development as well as cross-cultural education and even second-language learning. There are numerous online sites (e.g., ePals) that help you match your class up with another of a similar age and/or interest area, or simply start the project yourself with a teacher you know.

Travel buddies or **travel friends** are a variation on keypals, often for younger students. A class in one school (or country) exchanges a toy with a class in another country, and the toy becomes the stimulus for all sorts of activities and communication, both technology-based and nontechnology-based.

Global classrooms are where two or more classes, located anywhere in the world, study a common topic and interact with each other to share their learning. There are many of these examples online—some are large multinational projects, others small and locally organized. Almost anything can be made of these experiences with a wide range of technologies used to communicate and share learning.

Book raps or **book chats** are like an online book club where students in different classes in different schools discuss certain books. They might use email, blogs, or wikis to communicate. Some education authorities and library associations organize these on a larger scale for their members, so talk to your school librarian. A variation on this idea is the official Flat Stanley Project (www.flatstanley.com) that has been going since 1995 and is now available on Facebook and as an iPhone/iPad app.

Electronic appearances are where special guests correspond with your students about a particular topic. These types of opportunities tend to be time limited, with the event occurring for a particular period of time (e.g., athletes communicating with students in the lead-up to the Olympic Games). Other regular examples include scheduled sessions with NASA astronauts or scientists at the Antarctic. Again, any communication technology may be used, but a webcam really brings the experience to life! The arrangement might be international (like these examples) or simply arranged between a single classroom teacher and a contact he or she might have in the community.

Telementoring is a more structured variation of the electronic appearances and is where subject-matter specialists from universities, businesses, or other areas share their expertise with students. Some such experiences become true mentoring relationships, particularly with older secondary school students. The Jason Project is one example that has been going since 1989—it "connects students with scientists and researchers in real- and near-real time, virtually and physically, to provide mentored, authentic and enriching science learning experiences" (www.jason.org/about, para. 1).

Question and answer is similar to telementoring; however, the relationship with the outside experts revolves around the students' ability to ask questions and get answers. These sites vary widely and their longevity relies on the ways they are staffed, which is usually a voluntary affair and often run through universities or other professional networks. Look for examples in the area of science (such as Ask Wendell) and legal studies.

Impersonations are a little less common but lots of fun! This is where some or all of the participants adopt the character of a fictitious or historical character. This may involve persons external to a school taking on a persona and corresponding with students, or it may involve students adopting a whole series of characters in online role-playing. Imagine the potential here when studying novels, plays, or periods of history.

Virtual gatherings are synchronous online get-togethers in which participants from different geographic locations gather by electronic means to address common issues or to engage in common activities. They can be like online conferences. QuestAtlantis (atlantis.remixed.org) uses a 3-D multiuser environment to bring students together.

Online Information Collection and Analysis

Online information collection and analysis is where students use technology to help them locate, collect, and analyze information, usually with a creative, international, and collaborative dimension. A few types are as follow:

Information exchanges offer opportunities for students to collaborate with students and classes around the world as they collect and share information on a particular project. One very well-known and long-running example is the Global Grocery List Project, where students share local grocery prices and build a growing table of data to be used in social studies, science, health, mathematics, and other curriculum areas. Other examples include wildlife surveys and weather recording.

Pooled data analysis involves participants collecting information on the same theme or question from a wide variety of sources and then pooling the resultant data. Gruesome as it sounds, the RoadKill project (which appeals to many students, if not teachers) has been going since 1992. The idea has sparked other more regional projects, such as the Save the Tasmanian Devil Program.

Database creation is similar to the pooled data analysis but focuses on information being sorted and organized so that it may be readily accessed by others, thus building either spreadsheet or database skills in the process.

Electronic publishing is so much easier than it used to be; there is no reason why all teachers cannot get involved. This type of online project involves students working together to create an online publication or exhibit. Some such projects focus on publishing e-zines within and between schools. Others involve putting together an online art exhibit. Some publications contain an element of peer feedback, and students might even revise and resubmit work based on this feedback (such as a writers-in-electronic-residence program).

Virtual field trips can get really exciting! They involve using technology to take your students on an excursion, a field trip—usually to somewhere they might never have the opportunity to go in person. These types of experiences vary considerably. Some field trips may simply be a series of digital images to guide students through an excursion experience, but others are interactive, virtual-world experiences. Most synchronous experiences require you to plan and book ahead of schedule—others are simply a matter of navigating through a website. The best are run by established organizations or government departments and are well resourced. Consider visiting the Great Barrier Reef, the Louvre, or Mawson Station in Antarctica. Try searching for virtual tours and field trips on whatever topic, country, or location you are studying.

Problem-Solving Projects

Problem-solving projects build on all the global networking possibilities alluded to already, but are particularly focused on problem-based learning—students collaborate online to solve problems. A few common project types are as follow:

Scavenger hunts are information searches where students must solve clues or answer questions, typically by using the web. Sometimes they are a race to see who finds the information first. Other times they are less competitive. An Australian favorite in this category is Where's Collie—Collie being a mischievous garden gnome who travels and gets involved in activities, usually without telling anyone where he is going or what he is doing. Students are asked to respond to Collie's weekly challenges, and the website provides teacher notes and resources.

Parallel problem solving is where students at a variety of different websites are given the same problem, asked to solve it, and then asked to share their solutions. Examples include designing a mousetrap, a land yacht, or a Popsicle-stick bridge. Parallel problem solving may include an element of competition and judging—something that is usually guaranteed to motivate young people!

Social action projects have elements of many of the previously mentioned problem-solving activities, but they focus particularly on a social issue or campaign, where groups of students commit to a cause and, through online activities, try to further that cause. The activities students engage in might be really diverse, from video or animation production to taking up global campaigns at a local level. Again, social action project websites come and go throughout the year. Many environmental examples might be cited such as Earth Hour or www.350.org.

Global WebQuests are very specific types of online problem-solving projects that were mentioned earlier in this section. WebQuests are not always global projects, in that they do not need to involve interaction beyond your classroom—but they certainly can!

Online competitions. From time to time, a range of online competitions occurs. Examples include designing websites or making videos or animations. The ThinkQuest International Competition (www.thinkquest.org/competition) and Doodle4Google (www.google.com/doodle4google) are just two examples. Other online competitions take the form of social networking games where students compete online against each other. The Mathletics site (www.mathletics.com), for example, sees students in hot competition with each other over math problem solving.

Simulations

Simulations are a different category of learning experience—one that arguably meets the criteria of promoting authentic and problem-based learning. Although many simulations take the form of games (e.g., SimCity, Civilization), much learning can also be gained from such programs. Flight simulators are an evident example as they are used to train real pilots. Many senior students in business and economics classes benefit from playing sharemarket simulation games (e.g., The ASX Sharemarket Game). Consider also the value of other virtual simulations, from rat dissections and physics and chemistry experiments through driver education and global issues, such as population levels and resource management. Some simulation software requires you to purchase a full installable program, while other smaller simulations are available as learning objects online.

Showcasing and Celebrating Achievements

In Chapter 3, we emphasized that schools should plan how they will showcase and celebrate teacher and student learning. This priority can also be part of a teacher's goal-setting process. By identifying initiatives that they can implement, teachers can be encouraged to plan ahead and work toward a celebratory finale for the ICT initiative. For example, rather than students simply creating a video, plan to screen it to an audience. **Resource 68** | Box 6.1 presents some ideas:

Resource 68 | **Box 6.1**   Ideas for showcasing and celebrating student achievements

- Electronically publish students' work in a class or school newsletter, or on a wiki or website.
- Take photos of students' work or a class field trip and involve students in using a data projector to present the photos at a school assembly.
- Put together a virtual art exhibition for parents.
- Create a digital exhibition displayed on class computers as screen savers or desktop images.
- Use students' digital audio productions for the school's on-hold phone message.
- Sell students' creations as part of a school fund-raiser.
- Have students create digital portfolios and take them home at the end of the year as a memento to show family and friends.

CHAPTER **7**

Bringing It All Together and Making IT Happen

In the previous six chapters, we have introduced you to the philosophy, principles, practical suggestions, and scaffolds that make up the Technology Together process. Throughout we have emphasized the key issues we feel are central in successfully planning, implementing, and evaluating the process. In this final chapter, we synthesize these ideas, bringing together all our advice and guidance to help ensure the successful implementation of Technology Together at your school.

This final chapter has three sections. First, we discuss implementation scheduling over a school year, including the importance of remaining flexible and refining the process as you go. Next, we provide some advice from the front line, sharing tips from teachers who have been involved in how to avoid potential problems. Finally, we consider the value of sustaining the process at your school so that Technology Together remains part of your school culture.

Scheduling into the School Year

At this point you may be feeling that we have covered many concepts and suggested lots of ideas, and that there is much for you to discuss with your staff. How do you put all this into action in your school? How can you fit these discussions into a school year?

As mentioned in Chapter 3, we recommend that you set aside regular time, most likely in staff meetings, to discuss key elements of the process. As illustrated in Chapters 4 and 5, as little as five to ten minutes can be effective to support teacher learning and keep Technology Together foremost in their minds.

Resource 69 | **Table 7.1** provides a guide for the activities that you might schedule over the course of a four-quarter or two-semester school year. **Table 7.2** provides a schedule for a three-term school year (trimester). We emphasize activities that may be facilitated and managed by the core Technology Together team (facilitator, companion mentors, and school executives) and that might form the focus for whole-staff learning. By setting a learning theme, most weeks you will gently and gradually expose staff to many of the metacognitive concepts, allowing them time to reflect on and apply the ideas to their own learning, classroom practice, and general interactions with students.

Although we provide some ways to order and flow these weekly themes, we do not suggest they be set in stone, nor that you give teachers a structure ahead of time. Rather, we suggest that facilitators and companion mentors (CMs) use this table (**Resource 69** | **Table 7.1** or **Table 7.2**) as a rough guide that can vary in response to staff needs and be adapted to respond to issues that arise during each school semester (**Table 7.1**) or term (**Table 7.1** or **7.2**). This flexibility will also add an element of surprise for staff, as well as make the issues and themes as relevant as possible.

Resource 69 | **Table 7.1** Suggested schedule for implementing Technology Together in a four-quarter year

Weeks	Facilitation and management	Focus for staff learning
Last quarter of the prior year		
1–4 (First month)	Decision to implement Technology Together, with whom and when (see Chapter 3, Step 1). Decision whether you will seek an external partner (see Chapter 3, Step 4)	Introduce Technology Together to your school and invite participation (Chapter 3, Step 2). Discuss ICT vision (Chapter 3, Step 3).
5–7 (Second month)	Allocate roles (Chapter 3, Step 4). Conduct the school analysis (Chapter 3, Step 3).	Staff involved in school analysis (Chapter 3, Step 5)
8–10 (Last month)	Involve key staff in planning other aspects of project (Chapter 3, Steps 6–10).	Keep staff informed of plans for the following year.
Cycle 1 (First quarter or Semester 1, first half)		
1–3 (First weeks)	Consolidate plans for implementation and clarify roles and meeting times.	Staff development day—at a minimum introduce the eight foundational pillars (Chapter 2), Competency/Capability (Chapter 4), and involve staff in Cycle 1 goal setting (Chapter 6).
4–9	Implement mentoring strategies. Conduct regular team meetings.	Perceived usefulness (Chapter 4). Role models and pathways to learning (Chapter 4). Self-efficacy (Chapter 4). Exploratory learning and playfulness (Chapter 4). Discuss whether students need to be taught computer skills.
10 (Last week)	Evaluate Cycle 1. Revise plans for Cycle 2.	Sharing and celebrating achievements. Reflecting on learning

(Continued)

Resource 69 | **Table 7.1** *(Continued)*

Weeks	Facilitation and management	Focus for staff learning
Cycle 2 (Second quarter or Semester 1, last half)		
1 (First week)	Consolidate plans for implementation.	Cycle 2 goal setting (Chapter 6)
2–9	Implement mentoring strategies. Conduct regular team meetings.	Support, encouragement, and use by others (Chapter 4) Learned helplessness and attribution (Chapter 4) Anxiety (Chapter 4) Students as digital natives (Chapter 5) Memory and retention (Chapter 4) Help seeking (Chapter 4)
10 (Last week)	Evaluate Cycle 2. Revise plans for next cycle (Cycle 3).	Sharing and celebrating achievements Reflecting on learning
Cycle 3 (Third quarter of 4-term year or Semester 2, first half)		
1 (First week)	Consolidate plans for implementation.	Cycle 3 goal setting (Chapter 6)
2–9	Implement mentoring strategies. Conduct regular team meetings.	Objectivism, constructivism, and connectivism (Chapter 5) Problem solving and volition (Chapter 4) Approaches toward time (Chapter 4) Cultures of teaching and learning (Chapter 5) Learning with and from students (Chapter 5)
10 (Last week)	Evaluate current cycle (Cycle 3). Revise plans for final cycle (Cycle 4).	Sharing and celebrating achievements Reflecting on learning

Resource 69 | **Table 7.1** *(Continued)*

Weeks	Facilitation and management	Focus for staff learning
Cycle 4 (Final quarter of 4-term year or last half-semester of the year)		
1 (First week)	Consolidate plans for implementation.	Final cycle (Cycle 4) goal setting (Chapter 6)
2–7	Implement mentoring strategies. Conduct regular team meetings.	How ICT can transform teaching (Chapter 5) Authenticity in teaching and learning (Chapter 5) Developing students' metacognition
8–10 (Last month)	Evaluate outcomes of Technology Together.	Sharing and celebrating achievements Reflecting on learning

If your school runs on a three-term (trimester) year, there is a single mid cycle rather than two, and the focus elements for staff learning are divided among three terms rather than four, as shown in **Table 7.2**.

Table 7.2 Suggested schedule for implementing Technology Together in a three-term year (trimester year)

Weeks	Facilitation and management	Focus for staff learning
Last term (Term 3) of the prior year		
1–4 (First month)	Decision to implement Technology Together, with whom and when (see Chapter 3, Step 1) Decision whether you will seek an external partner (see Chapter 3, Step 4)	Introduce Technology Together to your school and invite participation (Chapter 3, Step 2). Discuss ICT vision (Chapter 3, Step 3).
5–7	Allocate roles (Chapter 3, Step 4). Conduct the school analysis (Chapter 3, Step 3).	Staff involved in school analysis (Chapter 3, Step 5)
8–12 (Last month)	Involve key staff in planning other aspects of project (Chapter 3, Steps 6–10).	Keep staff informed of plans for the following year.
First cycle: Term 1 of 3-term year		
1–3 (First month)	Consolidate plans for implementation and clarify roles and meeting times.	Staff development day—at a minimum introduce the eight foundational pillars (Chapter 2), Competency/Capability (Chapter 4), and involve staff in first cycle goal setting (Chapter 6).
4–11	Implement mentoring strategies. Conduct regular team meetings.	Perceived usefulness (Chapter 4) Role models and pathways to learning (Chapter 4) Self-efficacy (Chapter 4) Exploratory learning and playfulness (Chapter 4) Discuss whether students need to be taught computer skills. Support, encouragement, and use by others (Chapter 4) Learned helplessness and attribution (Chapter 4)
12 (Last week)	Evaluate first cycle. Revise plans for next cycle (mid cycle).	Sharing and celebrating achievements Reflecting on learning

Table 7.2 *(Continued)*

Weeks	Facilitation and management	Focus for staff learning
Mid cycle: Term 2 of 3-term year		
1 (First week)	Consolidate plans for implementation.	Mid-cycle goal setting (Chapter 6)
2–11	Implement mentoring strategies. Conduct regular team meetings.	Anxiety (Chapter 4) Students as digital natives (Chapter 5) Memory and retention (Chapter 4) Help seeking (Chapter 4) Objectivism, constructivism, and connectivism (Chapter 5) Problem solving and volition (Chapter 4) Approaches toward time (Chapter 4)
12 (Last week)	Evaluate mid-cycle. Revise plans for final cycle.	Sharing and celebrating achievements Reflecting on learning
Last cycle: Final term of 3-term year		
1 (First week)	Consolidate plans for implementation.	Final cycle goal setting (Chapter 6)
2–9	Implement mentoring strategies. Conduct regular team meetings.	Cultures of teaching and learning (Chapter 5) Learning with and from students (Chapter 5) How ICT can transform teaching (Chapter 5) Authenticity in teaching and learning (Chapter 5) Developing students' metacognition
10–12 (Last month)	Evaluate outcomes of Technology Together.	Sharing and celebrating achievements Reflecting on learning

Remaining Flexible and Refining the Process

We would like to reemphasize that Technology Together is intended to be implemented through a number of successive cycles, with each cycle involving conscious planning and evaluating processes. The evaluation process might range from an informal meeting among key staff to a consolidated collection and analysis of participant feedback.

In any case, at the end of each school semester, teachers should be encouraged not only to share and celebrate their achievements (see Chapter 3), but also to reflect in a summative sense on what they have learned. **Resource 70 | Form 7.1** provides a simple scaffold for this process—one that teachers can include in their journals.

Facilitators, CMs, and school administrative leaders should meet and evaluate what worked well and what did not and take the opportunity to modify plans for the following cycle. **Resource 71 | Form 7.2** poses some key evaluative questions that might prompt your evaluation.

The following story from one Technology Together school provides an example of how such critical reflection and discussion can shed light on what is working well and not so well in a school.

> *When the staff began, they were instructed in the large group. The mentors felt this was the best approach as there would be no singling out anyone as being different from anyone else, and it was hoped that people would be comfortable in this situation. Through discussion it was found that the majority of teachers found the situation threatening and didn't want others to know what little computer skills/knowledge they had or didn't have, so they were not completely honest during some staff discussions. A lot got under the radar because of this factor. The mentors quickly learned that because of the wide spectrum of ability and people's lack of confidence, this was not the approach to take for this group.*
>
> *Many in the group decided that individual instruction would be more valuable to them as they all had different needs/problems. This decision, however, caused a dependency on the mentors. After much discussion at the mentor level, this type of instruction was deemed necessary at first, but with the view to helping people to become more independent and to learn that they were able to try things. Eventually through this program, the staff was led to some degree of independence. Once confidence was built up, teachers were encouraged to "have-a-go," problem solve, discuss with peers, and try to fix it themselves. Mentors would pose the question, "What do you think you can do to change this situation/or to solve this problem?" This became a very positive outcome for the project.*

Resource 70 | **Form 7.1** End-of-term reflection scaffold

\multicolumn{2}{c}{**Things I can do now**}
\multicolumn{2}{c}{(Remember to add achievements, no matter how big or how small!)}
1	
2	
3	
4	
5	
6	
7	
8	
9	
10	
\multicolumn{2}{c}{**Things I want to learn next term**}
1	
2	
3	
4	
5	
6	
7	
8	
9	
10	
\multicolumn{2}{l}{Other comments about your goals}
\multicolumn{2}{l}{What helped or impeded you in achieving your goals?}
\multicolumn{2}{l}{What did you discover about the way you learn? What strategies best support your long-term learning outcomes?}
\multicolumn{2}{l}{List other feedback about the Technology Together process.}

Resource 71 | **Form 7.2** End-of-term evaluative questions for facilitators, CMs, and school administrative leaders

Are we managing to engage all school staff?   Are we building a sense of collegiality and mutual support?   How might we best motivate those who might not be on board?
Are there elements identified through our school analysis which are impacting on how ICT is being integrated and how teachers are learning?   What can we do about these issues?
Are the strategies we are using to mentor staff consistent with the metacognitive approach?   Are the strategies achieving what we hoped?   How might we do things differently?
Are teachers carrying through on their goals?   Are they implementing useful initiatives in their classrooms?   How can we prompt teachers to embrace more challenging goals in the next cycle and take another step up the learning ladder?
Is our approach developing capability as well as competency?   Are staff evidencing that they understand the difference?   Where might we focus our efforts to enhance capability?
Do we need to vary our strategies to keep staff motivated?   What different ways can we engage them in reflection and discussion?
What, if anything, do we need to do or change to support each other as a coordinating team?

Advice from the Front Line

The success of Technology Together rests not on any prescription that we can provide, but rather on recognizing the diverse ways in which you can adopt and adapt the process to your school culture and context. We don't want to imply the journey will always be smooth sailing. Our Technology Together schools experienced many highs and lows.

In this section, we provide some advice from the front line of the change process, allowing Technology Together participants the opportunity to share their suggestions for what you can do to avoid potential problems and ensure your school's success. In particular we address eight issues:

- Overestimating staff skills and readiness,
- Dealing with reluctance to learn,
- Working with teachers who resist trying new strategies,
- Avoiding overdependency,
- Maintaining focus on metacognition,
- Overcoming resistance to reflection,
- Confronting the often-mentioned obstacle of time, and
- Maintaining enthusiasm as a Technology Together leader.

Overestimating Staff Skills and Readiness

Some companion mentors (CMs) reflected that they expected too much too soon from the teachers they worked with. They acknowledged that they had overestimated existing skills and ICT knowledge of many staff. These mentors emphasized that it may be better to focus initial support at a very foundational level, even if staff quickly tell you that they can "do that already," as this will affirm their existing abilities. The goal-setting resources in Chapter 6 begin with an acknowledgment of foundational skills because teachers are likely to feel good if they are "ticking off" these basics.

So don't be overambitious to start off. With realistic initial expectations and gentle and steady goal setting, staff are more likely to exceed your (and their!) expectations. Keep referring to the metaphor of the ladder and encouraging everyone to take continual upward steps!

Dealing with Reluctance to Learn

Occasionally mentors encountered individuals who were particularly reluctant to learn or simply unwilling to take on new or ambitious goals. In such instances, mentors came to recognize that they needed to be a bit more assertive. Some CMs found it useful to emphasize that students pay the price if teachers don't integrate ICT and described this as "a strong motivator and reality check!" Find a gentle way to interest them, such as a focus on recreational uses of ICT. Draw attention to good things people are doing and partner "resisters" with a compatible "other"—someone they respect who can interest and excite them with activities that they are doing and learning.

Stories emerged from some schools of teachers whose image (and self-image) was built around not being good with computers and, in some instances, how these perceptions were perpetuated by the school community and teachers themselves:

> *Once a person had taken up a pessimistic attitude to the computer, usually quite vocally, then it nearly seems a weakness on their part to succumb to trying again.*

Confronting these beliefs and substituting alternative positive discourses was an important mentoring strategy.

Working with Teachers Who Resist Trying New Strategies

Some teachers insist that they want to learn in ways they feel most comfortable with, rather than challenging themselves to try new and potentially more effective strategies. Some staff's expectations about skills training are firmly established, and it can be a difficult balancing act to challenge these expectations without causing frustration, loss of motivation, or lowering their self-efficacy.

It cannot be presumed that teachers will adopt or even try new strategies without lots of support and encouragement. However, a fine line exists between such support and training. Discussing past, present, and preferred strategies can stimulate teachers to recognize, even in small ways, how they need to gradually change to become more independent:

> *Teachers were asked to make notes on, and observe, how their students learn best with new technology. How do students solve problems when on the computer? Teachers stated that their students were great risk takers and clicked here and there*

until they reached where they wanted to be. This was a freedom many adults didn't allow themselves to have.... The reflection process gave teachers a lot of insight into how they (themselves) learn. It saw teachers realizing that their strategies influenced their achievements and developing a "can do" attitude.... Through the Technology Together process, we have allowed ourselves to become more like this type of learner, allowing ourselves the right to make mistakes, explore, and find out.

Some schools adopted very skillful and successful strategies that proved effective in moving reluctant teachers outside their initial comfort zones. Success partly relied on the schools' implementation plans, but it largely came down to individual CMs' interpersonal skills and understanding of the metacognitive approach. CMs needed to figure out why individuals might resist increased independence and to think creatively about what could be done to encourage independence. Perseverance and patience was needed and a key to their success.

Avoiding Overdependency

Ready access to technical assistance within a school can diminish teachers' willingness to take the small steps required to develop their problem-solving skills. Sometimes CMs inadvertently find themselves in a situation where staff too readily turn to them to solve all problems, as expressed by one Technology Together facilitator:

I felt that this actually hindered the metacognitive path of some people's journey, as they continually relied on the mentor for the solution to specific problems instead of exploring alternative problem-solving strategies. Sometimes the role of the mentor is to say that you don't know how to do something and to model problem solving to try and work through issues together. Also, knowing when to walk away is a key point. Teachers will often fiddle around and problem solve on their own, and this breaks down the reliance on the mentor.

Those schools where help seeking, problem solving, and exploratory learning were explicitly discussed evidenced changes in teachers' attitudes. Strategies such as modeling, prompting, and providing tips also proved useful. Importantly, CMs need to be cautious and have clever strategies up their sleeve to prevent teachers becoming overdependent, as evidenced in the following story.

Resource 72 | **Box 7.1**   Building teachers' independence: A story from the front line

> One Year 3 teacher, Heather, approached her companion mentor, John, and indicated that she was interested in doing something with digital photography. John suggested that she might consider using Microsoft Photo Story. He sat with Heather for five to ten minutes, indicating that he did not have long to show her the software, emphasizing that she could pick up some skills and then explore with her class to find anything she was unable to do.
>
> Heather was very hesitant about the activity and wanted to get Emma, a teacher's aide, to teach the students how to use the software during computer lab time first. John nudged Heather to set it as a challenge for herself—to try exploring with her class and see what happened with the lesson. He told her to have students open the program, and he promised that they would then be able to work things out. John also suggested that Heather use the "Ask three, then me" (explore first, ask three other students, and then ask me) policy and tell students that if they don't know how to figure out the software, then the class can explore it together.
>
> When John asked how the lesson went, Heather said that students had been a bit noisy, but she was really happy with how the learning went.

Maintaining Focus on Metacognition

A key to successfully implementing Technology Together lies with the ability of facilitators and CMs to maintain focus on the metacognitive approach. Much relies on their deep understanding of the foundations of this approach and on their interpersonal skills as they work with teachers. Sometimes the best metacognitive mentoring happens spontaneously in response to everyday happenings. It is difficult to prepare yourself to respond most productively when spontaneous opportunities arise, but the following story illustrates the benefits such interactions can have.

Resource 73 | **Box 7.2** Carrying metacognition into the classroom: A story from the front line

> A teacher related that she encountered problems during a lesson because she had forgotten the steps needed to show students. The teacher was assuming that she needed to teach a specific ICT skill so that students would learn it. After further discussion, I asked the teacher to try something new.
>
> I suggested that next time she could give students a goal to achieve and indicate that she would still be in the room but that students would be expected to help each other solve problems and achieve the goal. She'd emphasize that success depended on everyone being able to complete the task. The teacher would be a part of the process, but she would be asking for help just as much as the students.
>
> The results were interesting, as the teacher's subsequent journal entry indicates:
>
> > *I really had to let go of my gut instincts today, but the results were very positive. I let the kids discover the solution to the web paging activity without much intervention from me. I was making my own web page along with the kids, so I really learnt a lot. The room was very chaotic, but the talk was all task oriented, and ideas were flowing thick and fast.... We had a discussion at the end of the lesson and instead of the usual discussion about ICT skills and how we made something happen on the computer, we discussed how much we felt people learnt, and how that lesson was different from those in the past.*
>
> This journal entry indicated that this teacher was on the way to realizing that students can learn skills independently, and help and support each others' learning. Metacognitive approaches to teaching and learning are also evident.

Overcoming Resistance to Reflection

Despite the fact that teachers have been discussing reflection in their professional practice for many years, the degree to which teachers actually appreciate its benefits cannot be overestimated. As one companion mentor reflected, teachers "live their lives by the bell" and "will always find something more immediate to do." Teachers often find it a challenge to be active in driving and monitoring their own learning, and this difficulty may manifest itself as resistance and/or negativity toward reflection. We are not saying that you should abandon reflection strategies altogether, but there are some tips to be aware of to avoid potential problems.

First, some degree of routine and strong encouragement (perhaps even assertiveness) can help maintain momentum in the process. There needs to be an expectation that staff participate. Time needs to be allocated for reflection, whether as part of mentoring or staff meeting time.

> *From 15–20 minutes were set aside at the beginning of staff meetings every week—not at the end when everyone is tired and looking at the clock. After teachers got used to it, they quite enjoyed it, and the process built its own momentum.*

Large schools can find whole-school discussion more difficult, and in these cases breaking into smaller groups (perhaps by department or grade) is more productive. In some schools, getting teachers to write is difficult, and staff need encouragement to realize they have things worth recording and sharing. Providing examples of reflection may be valuable if teachers are struggling, and the range of reflective quotes throughout this book may be useful to share. Voluntary sharing of written reflections can also make this process more meaningful.

Some schools identified that they were predominantly verbal cultures, so for them, discussion was more appropriate than written reflection. Regardless of the approach, enthusiasm can wane, so try varying strategies regularly (e.g., use a journal during one term, reflective scaffolds in another, and small-group discussion in another). Some schools have experimented with group reflective discussions that were recorded using a laptop and data projector so that all staff could see the notes being kept. Much incidental learning occurred through this process, with skills being demonstrated and questions flowing. Another suggestion is to assign teachers a topic each week for leading the collective reflection and discussion.

Reflection will only be successful if school executives, facilitators, and mentors see its value and are committed to making it work. Many of the schools involved in the development of Technology Together reflected that, in retrospect, they wished they had encouraged more reflection, and earlier on.

Resource 74 | **Reflection 7.1**   Reflecting on a spreadsheet integration lesson

> *My knowledge of spreadsheets was very rudimentary, but I followed the lesson plan to count colors of Smarties. I gave children direct instruction on spreadsheet basics, then went over details again to consolidate facts.*
>
> *Children responded well, especially as they were able to eat the Smarties at the conclusion of the task. Children first counted their own Smarties, recorded details, and constructed a graph using the chart wizard. During the second week, children entered the data from all four classes, used the copy and paste functions, calculated totals, and constructed a pie graph for the whole stage.*
>
> *This task required attentive listening as well as exploratory learning. On occasions, the pie graph did not appear as it should. Children were asked to investigate why this happened and how this situation could be remedied. They invariably came up with the correct answer: the area had not been selected, too much information had been provided, or not enough information was provided.*
>
> *In all cases, much discussion took place, and peer assistance was available. It totally engaged their learning, and it was extremely satisfying for me as a teacher. Discussion then took place regarding the uses and purposes of spreadsheets. It was a fantastic exercise and held their attention to the task's conclusion.*

Confronting the Often-Mentioned Obstacle of Time

The most difficult attitude to change is probably teachers' attitudes toward time. Here, the metacognitive approach challenges teachers not to see time as an excuse but, rather, to reflect on matters of prioritization. In other words, the approach focuses on attitudes and beliefs about time. As we have already emphasized, despite teachers' repeated claims that their learning is limited by time, simply providing them release time is not in itself a solution. As recommended in Chapter 3, if you do have release time available, be clever in how it is allocated.

In some schools, teachers demonstrate great willingness to spend after-school time on their learning, although it is rare for all teachers in a school to be willing or able to do so. Typically, those teachers who most need to be involved are not. Although strategies such as providing food and drink have proved successful in coaxing along more reluctant teachers and building staff cohesiveness and collaboration, school administrative leaders need to balance such strategies with scheduled sessions during school hours.

Teachers may not be used to managing their own professional learning process and, when busy, they may forget their goals. In such cases, one strategy that may prove useful is increasing teachers' willingness to learn with and from their students in the classroom (see Chapter 6)—a strategy that can be effectively integrated into teachers' day-to-day responsibilities.

Maintaining Enthusiasm as a Leader

It is critically important for your coordinating team of facilitators and companion mentors to maintain enthusiasm and excitement about the process. It can be easy for companion mentors or other key staff to become disillusioned or frustrated, or for frictions to emerge between mentees and mentors or even among the core team. These issues will be exacerbated if mentors are overcommitted or do not have sufficient release time to juggle multiple commitments.

Some mentors in Technology Together schools experienced tensions while performing their roles. For example, those who were released regularly to work with staff ran a risk of feeling distanced from their classes. Mentors who were not in leadership positions, or who were younger or less experienced, at times experienced tensions in their sense of authority, ability, or acceptance by other staff (although such concerns were often internal and not substantiated through experience). Issues also arose in a few schools where CMs approached their roles from the vantage of showing off their skills or pushing their personal agendas within the school. Such instances needed to be quickly identified and circumvented early—something that did not always occur.

Most importantly, mentors need to maintain confidence in the importance and value of their role. If you are not necessarily a confident ICT user yourself, take strength from the following comment from one Technology Together CM:

> *Something my mother told me many years ago (she was a very effective primary school teacher) … : a teacher should never teach her best subject but teach her worst because she understands the barriers that subject presents and often how to overcome them.*

Where to Go from Here: Sustaining the Process

As we indicated in Chapter 1, Technology Together is an ongoing process rather than a project to be completed. The principles and practices underpinning the process can become an ongoing part of a school's culture. Schools will most likely focus on the activities that comprise the process for 12 to 18 months. However, our aim is that schools continue to see themselves as Technology Together schools after this initial time period, sustaining the values, beliefs, and strategies that Technology Together helped develop.

> *The impact upon our school's culture has been significant, yet it really has only just begun. The process this year has empowered most staff with the confidence to embrace what technology has to offer. Teachers have seen that computers do significantly enhance teaching and learning in the classroom, and more noticeably reduce behavioral issues. The process this year has really been an attitude-changing journey with the commencement of skill acquisition. It is believed that with further nurturing and fostering, the application of technology will only blossom.*

The nonfinite nature of the process has been seen positively by most schools. As one school expressed:

> *Rather than the end of the year signifying closure for the project, we can see that this year has been the beginning of a new chapter in teaching and learning at our school.*

Many of the Technology Together schools and teachers set themselves ongoing future goals, while others committed to continue taking time at staff meetings for discussion and to share discoveries of activities they trialed, problems they faced, and *aha* moments they experienced. We hope that such a sustainable outcome will result in your school.

It is fitting to conclude with the summative reflections from one Technology Together school:

> *Change is a process, not an event. The change process has started at our school. We have felt uncomfortable, frustrated, intimidated, and overwhelmed. We have experienced failure. However, now we know that we are not alone. We know that there are others who can help us, and there is more than one way to solve a problem. We have also felt success, we have been innovative, and we are excited by the progress we have made this year.*

APPENDIX A

List of Resources

Throughout this book we reference a wide range of resources that can be used to promote professional discussion and reflection by teachers. These resources include forms, diagrams, tables, goal-setting scaffolds, surveys, and thought-bubble displays. Some resources can be found in this book and others are available on the Technology Together website (http://technologytogether.scu.edu.au). The following list provides the location of each resource mentioned in the book. Resources mentioned specifically in this book are indicated by a page number (or ✓ if available on the Technology Together website). Many PowerPoint presentations for use in staff meetings are also available on the website. These are indicated by an asterisk (*).

Chapter 2 Resources

	ITEM	DESCRIPTION	LOCATION Page	Website
Resource 1	Figure 2.1	The visual model of the metacognitive approach to technology learning	43	✓

Chapter 3 Resources

	ITEM	DESCRIPTION	LOCATION Page	Website
Resource 2	Table 3.1	School analysis scaffold	61	✓
Resource 3	Form 3.1	Simple student survey	66	✓
Resource 4	Table 3.2	Possible mentoring strategies	70	—
Resource 5	Table 3.3	Potential approaches to allocation of release time.	75	—
Resource 6	Reflection 3.1	Example of a reflection scaffold	79	✓
Resource 7	Table 3.4	Strategies for showcasing and celebrating successes	84	—
Resource 8	Form 3.2	Checklist for implementation planning	85	✓

APPENDIX A | List of Resources

Chapter 4 Resources

*PowerPoint resources

ITEM		DESCRIPTION	LOCATION	
			Page	Website
Resource 9	Thought bubble 4.1	Competency/capability thought-bubble display	90	✓
Resource 10	Figure 4.1	Competency/capability model	—	✓
Resource 11	Table 4.1	Competency/capability: Ideas for engagement	92	*
Resource 12	Table 4.2	Competence and capability in a school context: A comparison	92	✓
Resource 13	Table 4.3	Self-efficacy: Ideas for engagement	96	*
Resource 14	Thought bubble 4.2	Self-efficacy thought-bubble display	—	✓
Resource 15	Table 4.4	Anxiety: Ideas for engagement	98	*
Resource 16	Form 4.1	Confronting anxieties scaffold	98	✓
Resource 17	Table 4.5	Support and encouragement: Ideas for engagement	100	*
Resource 18	Table 4.6	Learned helplessness and attribution: Ideas for engagement	102	*
Resource 19	Thought bubble 4.3	Attribution thought-bubble display	—	✓
Resource 20	Table 4.7	Comparison of ICT as a set of skills to be taught or a tool to enhance learning	105	✓
Resource 21	Table 4.8	Perceived usefulness: Ideas for engagement	105	*
Resource 22	Table 4.9	Pathways to learning: Ideas for engagement	111	*
Resource 23	Table 4.10	Advantages and disadvantages of various pathways to learning	112	✓
Resource 24	Table 4.11	Exploratory learning: Ideas for engagement	116	*
Resource 25	Box 4.1	Tips for exploratory learning	117	✓
Resource 26	Table 4.12	Memory and retention: Ideas for engagement	119	*

List of Resources | APPENDIX A

	ITEM	DESCRIPTION	Page	Website
Resource 27	Table 4.13	Problem solving and volition: Ideas for engagement	121	*
Resource 28	Table 4.14	Help seeking: Ideas for engagement	122	*
Resource 29	Thought bubble 4.4	Help seeking thought-bubble display	—	✓
Resource 30	Table 4.15	Confronting the time issue: Ideas for engagement	123	*
Resource 31	Thought bubble 4.5	Approaches to time thought bubble display	—	✓

Chapter 5 Resources

ITEM		DESCRIPTION	LOCATION	
			Page	Website
Resource 32	Table 5.1	Contrasting directed, constructivist, and connectivist teaching approaches	130	✓
Resource 33	Thought bubble 5.1	Constructivism thought-bubble display	—	✓
Resource 34	Table 5.2	Considering constructivism and connectivism: Ideas for engagement	131	*
Resource 35	Figure 5.1	Cultures of teaching and learning	133	✓
Resource 36	Table 5.3	Cultures of teaching and learning: Ideas for engagement	134	*
Resource 37	Table 5.4	Hawkes' generational comparison	135	✓
Resource 38	Table 5.5	Students as digital natives: Ideas for engagement	137	*
Resource 39	Table 5.6	Do students need to be taught technology skills: Ideas for engagement	138	*
Resource 40	Table 5.7	The pedagogical potential of ICT: Ideas for engagement	139	*
Resource 41	Box 5.1	Norton and Wiburg's framework	140	✓
Resource 42	Box 5.2	Richardson's "10 big shifts" in understanding how best to teach	142	✓

APPENDIX A | List of Resources

Resource 43	Table 5.8	Developing students' metacognition: Ideas for engagement	144	*
Resource 44	Box 5.3	Strategies to develop students' metacognition in practice	144	✓
Resource 45	Table 5.9	Learning with and from students: Ideas for engagement	147	*
Resource 46	Reflection 5.1	Learning with and from students—journal excerpts	148	✓

Chapter 6 Resources

ITEM		DESCRIPTION	LOCATION	
			Page	Website
Resource 47	Figure 6.1	Goal-setting pie chart	151	*
Resource 48	Table 6.1	The goal-setting matrix	152	✓
Resource 49	Form 6.1	Goal-setting scaffold	154	✓
Resource 50	Table 6.2	General goal-setting approaches	155	✓
Resource 51	Goals list 6.1	Examples of metacognitive goals	156	✓
Resource 52	Goals list 6.2	Examples of leadership goals	157	✓
Resource 53	Goals list 6.3	Examples of recreational goals	158	✓
Resource 54	Table 6.3	Foundational computer skills goal-setting scaffold	159	✓
Resource 55	Form 6.2	Hardware skills goal-setting scaffold	161	✓
Resource 56	Table 6.4	Word processing skills goal-setting scaffold	162	✓
Resource 57	Table 6.5	Web 1.0 skills goal-setting scaffold	164	✓
Resource 58	Table 6.6	Web 2.0 skills goal-setting scaffold	165	✓
Resource 59	Table 6.7	Communication applications skills goal-setting scaffold	166	✓
Resource 60	Table 6.8	Spreadsheet software skills goal-setting scaffold	167	✓

Resource 61	Table 6.9	Presentation software skills goal-setting scaffold	169	✓
Resource 62	Table 6.10	Multimedia skills goal-setting scaffold	170	✓
Resource 63	Table 6.11	Database software skills goal-setting scaffold	172	✓
Resource 64	Table 6.12	Interactive whiteboard skills goal-setting scaffold	173	✓
Resource 65	Table 6.13	Mobile apps goal-setting scaffold	175	✓
Resource 66	Form 6.3	Classroom management skills goal-setting scaffold	178	✓
Resource 67	Form 6.4	Authentic and constructivist online learning goal-setting scaffold	179	✓
Resource 68	Box 6.1	Ideas for showcasing and celebrating student achievements	186	✓

Chapter 7 Resources

ITEM		DESCRIPTION	LOCATION	
			Page	Website
Resource 69	Table 7.1	Suggested schedule for implementing Technology Together	189	—
Resource 70	Form 7.1	End-of-term reflection scaffold	195	—
Resource 71	Form 7.2	End-of-term evaluative questions for facilitators, CMs, and school administrators	196	✓
Resource 72	Box 7.1	Building teachers' independence: A story from the front line	200	—
Resource 73	Box 7.2	Carrying metacognition into the classroom: A story from the front line	201	—
Resource 74	Reflection 7.1	Reflecting on a spreadsheet integration lesson	203	—

APPENDIX B

Student and Teacher Surveys

Student Surveys

The student surveys are available in this book, in print, and are also downloadable from the Technology Together website, http://technologytogether.scu.edu.au.

Student Survey 1

SIMPLE STUDENT SURVEY, SUITABLE FOR MOST AGES

The print version of this survey appears in Chapter 3 as **Resource 3** | Form 3.1.

Length: 1 page
Suggested script for teachers:

> *Teachers in our school will soon be learning lots more new things about technology. We are very interested to know more about what YOU think about computers! To help us find this out I will give each one of you a sheet with some questions on it. Your answers are private and you are not asked to give your name.*

Student Survey 2

SURVEY SUITABLE FOR VERY YOUNG STUDENTS

The print version of Survey 2 appears in this appendix on page 215.

Length: 1 page
Suggested script for teachers:

> *Teachers in our school will soon be learning lots more new things about technology. We are very interested to know more about what YOU think about computers! To help us find this out I will give each one of you a sheet with some questions on it. I will help by reading the question. You do not need to give your name.*

APPENDIX B | Student and Teacher Surveys

Student Survey 3

SURVEY SUITABLE FOR OLDER STUDENTS

The print version of Survey 3 appears in this appendix following Survey 2.

Length: 3 pages

Note: This version of the survey is particularly beneficial where students themselves are to be engaged in the metacognitive process.

Suggested script for teachers:

> *Our school is implementing a program called "Technology Together" where we will be learning about new ways we can use computer technology to support teaching and learning. We are very interested to know more about what YOU think about technology and the role it plays in helping you learn. The following survey will help us find out your ideas. Your responses are confidential and you are not asked to provide your name.*

Student Survey 2
SURVEY SUITABLE FOR VERY YOUNG STUDENTS

Script for teachers — Teachers in our school will soon be learning lots more new things about technology. We are very interested to know more about what YOU think about computers! To help us find this out I will give each one of you a sheet with some questions on it. I will help by reading the question. You do not need to give your name.

Are you a boy or a girl?

Boy **Girl**

How much do you like using computers?

Do you think using computers helps you to learn?

How much would you like to use computers in class?

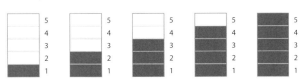

Do you use a computer at home?

Yes **No**

The following can serve as the basis of a verbal discussion with young children.

What do you like most about using computers at school?

What don't you like about using computers at school?

What would you like to see done differently with computers at school?

APPENDIX B | Student and Teacher Surveys

Student Survey 3
SURVEY SUITABLE FOR OLDER STUDENTS

Note: We have used the term *technology* to refer to lots of different types of computer technology—both software and hardware, such as desktops, laptops, tablets, mobile/cell phones, and MP3 players.

Are you? ☐ Male ☐ Female	
How old are you? _____ What grade/year are you in? _____	
Do you have access to a computer at home? ☐ Yes ☐ No	
How often do you use the computer at home?	☐ Every day … How many hours a day? _____ ☐ Two or three times a week ☐ Once every couple of weeks ☐ Never
Do you have access to the Internet at home? ☐ Yes ☐ No	
Are you allowed to go on the Internet?	☐ Yes, anytime I like ☐ Yes, but with restrictions. Please explain _____ ☐ No
What do you use your computer at home for? (Mark all that apply.)	☐ Playing educational games (e.g., math or science) ☐ Playing non-educational games ☐ Writing stories ☐ Using email ☐ Using social networking sites such as Facebook ☐ Digital photos ☐ Listening to music ☐ Researching information ☐ Other (please give examples)
Which of these technologies do you have regular access to? (Mark all that apply.)	☐ Mobile/cell phone ☐ iPad or similar ☐ MP3 player ☐ Wii, Nintendo, or similar ☐ Digital camera ☐ Smartphone with Internet access ☐ Digital video camera

Student and Teacher Surveys | APPENDIX B

Please respond to the next 25 questions using the following scale, where **1**= strongly disagree and **5**= strongly agree.	Strongly Disagree 1 2 3 Strongly Agree 4 5
1. I have been encouraged to use technology by my family.	1 2 3 4 5
2. I like to play around with technology.	1 2 3 4 5
3. I have been encouraged to use technology by my teachers.	1 2 3 4 5
4. I think it is easy learning about new technology.	1 2 3 4 5
5. I would choose to use technology in my spare time.	1 2 3 4 5
6. If I need assistance in using technology this assistance is easy to get.	1 2 3 4 5
7. When I succeed with a technology task it is because I know what to do.	1 2 3 4 5
8. My teachers are able to help me if I have difficulties with a computer task.	1 2 3 4 5
9. Using technology makes me more popular with people my own age.	1 2 3 4 5
10. I am more motivated by lessons that involve use of technology.	1 2 3 4 5
11. Learning to use technology will enhance my future job prospects.	1 2 3 4 5
12. I often think about the way I go about learning new technology.	1 2 3 4 5
13. I like to explore the features of software.	1 2 3 4 5
14. Once I get on the computer I find it hard to stop using it.	1 2 3 4 5
15. I give up easily when problems occur when using technology.	1 2 3 4 5
16. Using technology helps me to learn.	1 2 3 4 5
17. When something goes wrong with a computer, I generally see it as happening because of something I've done.	1 2 3 4 5
18. I prefer to be shown by someone else what to do on the computer.	1 2 3 4 5
19. Having to learn something new with technology isn't scary.	1 2 3 4 5
20. It is OK if teachers don't know how to do something with technology because we can figure it out together.	1 2 3 4 5
21. When I can't do something with technology it is because I haven't been shown how to.	1 2 3 4 5
22. Using technology helps me feel more confident.	1 2 3 4 5
23. If I was given a new piece of software or a new technology gadget that I'd never seen before, I could use it even if there was no one around to tell me what to do.	1 2 3 4 5
24. If a teacher doesn't know how to do something with technology, students can help the teacher.	1 2 3 4 5
25. I think I am an effective technology learner.	1 2 3 4 5

TECHNOLOGY **TOGETHER** | Whole-School Professional Development for Capability and Confidence

How confident would you be doing the following tasks:	Strongly Disagree 1 2 3 4 5 Strongly Agree
1. Start up a computer and open a document or program	1 2 3 4 5
2. Move, copy, or organize files	1 2 3 4 5
3. Install software from a CD or from online	1 2 3 4 5
4. Set up a computer by plugging it all together	1 2 3 4 5
5. Use the Help function of a program	1 2 3 4 5
6. Use more than one program at once (multitasking)	1 2 3 4 5
7. Teach a computer skill to others	1 2 3 4 5
8. Use a scanner	1 2 3 4 5
9. Use a digital camera	1 2 3 4 5
10. Find a website given a specific URL (web address)	1 2 3 4 5
11. Set up an address book in your e-mail program	1 2 3 4 5
12. File e-mails into mailboxes or folders	1 2 3 4 5
13. Perform a web search for specific information	1 2 3 4 5
14. Save images from the web	1 2 3 4 5
15. Modify the appearance of a photograph using a graphics program	1 2 3 4 5
16. Use a spreadsheet	1 2 3 4 5
17. Set up a blog	1 2 3 4 5
18. Create and edit a digital video	1 2 3 4 5
19. Problem solve when something goes "wrong" with technology	1 2 3 4 5
20. Record a digital audio file	1 2 3 4 5
21. Use an avatar to move around in a 3-D virtual environment	1 2 3 4 5
22. How would you score your overall confidence with technology skills?	1 2 3 4 5

What do you like most about using technology at school?

What don't you like about using technology at school?

What would you like to see done differently with technology at school?

Teacher Survey

The teacher survey is available in this book, in print, and is also downloadable from the Technology Together website, http://technologytogether.scu.edu.au. The print-based version of the survey can be used by schools choosing to collect and analyze the data themselves. The online teacher survey offers the opportunity to register your school online and provide feedback directly to the authors:

> As developers of Technology Together, we are eager to learn from those involved in the program. To this end we invite you to also share your anonymous responses with us for the purpose of research and program improvement.
>
> By registering your school online and having teachers complete the survey online, we are able to return a collated report on the data via email.
>
> R. Phelps and A. Graham

It is suggested that you invite your teachers to complete the print or online survey before implementing Technology Together at your school, and then after it has been running for approximately 12 months.

Note that there may be some minor differences between the version of the survey provided here and the online version of the survey.

APPENDIX B | Student and Teacher Surveys

Teacher Technology Use Survey: Initial teacher survey

Please respond openly to the survey items, giving each question reasonable thought.

Note: We have used the term *technology* to refer to diverse forms of computer technology, including desktops, laptops, tablets, mobile/cell phones, and MP3 players.

Name/Pseudonym/unique identifier (or leave blank):		No. of years teaching experience:	
☐ Male ☐ Female	Age: ☐ 21–25 ☐ 26–30 ☐ 31–35 ☐ 36–40 ☐ 41–45 ☐ 46–50 ☐ 51–55 ☐ 56–60 ☐ 60+		
School			

Please circle the option below that is most appropriate to your current circumstances

1. As a general rule, how frequently would you use technology in your classroom?
   Never Monthly Weekly Daily
   1 2 3 4 5 6 7

2. On average, how long would you spend using technology each day in your classroom?
   0 1 2 3 4 5 6+
   No. of hours

3. On average, how long would your students spend using technology each day in your classroom?
   0 1 2 3 4 5 6+
   No. of hours

4. How many computers do you own at home?

5. Which of the following technologies do you own and use personally?
   ☐ Desktop computer
   ☐ Laptop computer
   ☐ Mobile/cell phone
   ☐ Tablet computer

Please respond to the following questions using this scale, where **1** = strongly disagree and **5** = strongly agree.

Strongly Disagree Strongly Agree
1 2 3 4 5

1.	I have been encouraged to use technology by friends or family.	1	2	3	4	5
2.	I like to play around with technology.	1	2	3	4	5
3.	I would choose to use technology in my spare time.	1	2	3	4	5
4.	I have been encouraged to use technology by my supervisor at school.	1	2	3	4	5
5.	I reflect regularly on my attitude toward technology.	1	2	3	4	5
6.	I feel at ease learning about technology.	1	2	3	4	5
7.	I have been encouraged to use technology by fellow teachers.	1	2	3	4	5
8.	When I succeed with a technology task it is because of my knowledge or skills.	1	2	3	4	5

9.	If I need assistance in using technology, this assistance is easy to get.	1	2	3	4	5
10.	Using technology enhances my standing with peers.	1	2	3	4	5
11.	My fellow teachers are a good source of support regarding technology.	1	2	3	4	5
12.	Integrating technology in my teaching will motivate students.	1	2	3	4	5
13.	I reflect regularly on the effectiveness of my strategies for learning about new technology.	1	2	3	4	5
14.	Using technology will enhance my career prospects.	1	2	3	4	5
15.	I like to explore the features of software.	1	2	3	4	5
16.	I like working with technology.	1	2	3	4	5
17.	When a problem occurs with technology there is generally nothing I can do to change the situation.	1	2	3	4	5
18.	Once I get on the computer I find it hard to stop using it.	1	2	3	4	5
19.	I am the type to do well with technology.	1	2	3	4	5
20.	Technology provides access to information that helps me as a teacher.	1	2	3	4	5
21.	I like the challenge of learning new technology skills.	1	2	3	4	5
22.	I prefer to use a computer to prepare lesson material.	1	2	3	4	5
23.	I regularly set myself new learning goals with technology.	1	2	3	4	5
24.	I would choose to use technology in my teaching.	1	2	3	4	5
25.	I do not feel threatened by the impact of computer technology.	1	2	3	4	5
26.	When something goes wrong with a computer, I generally see it as something I've done.	1	2	3	4	5
27.	Using technology enables me to be more efficient in my teaching.	1	2	3	4	5
28.	I prefer to be shown by someone else what to do on the computer.	1	2	3	4	5
29.	Integrating technology into my teaching assists in meeting syllabus requirements.	1	2	3	4	5
30.	The thought of using technology is not frightening.	1	2	3	4	5
31.	Integrating technology into my teaching improves student learning outcomes.	1	2	3	4	5
32.	When I use technology I feel a sense of fun and discovery.	1	2	3	4	5
33.	When I can't do something with technology it is because I haven't been shown how to.	1	2	3	4	5
34.	Using technology helps me feel more confident teaching my students.	1	2	3	4	5
35.	I give up easily when problems occur when using technology.	1	2	3	4	5
36.	Using technology gives me a sense of accomplishment.	1	2	3	4	5
37.	I reflect regularly on the learning approaches adopted by other technology users.	1	2	3	4	5
38.	I think I am an effective technology learner.	1	2	3	4	5

APPENDIX B | Student and Teacher Surveys

Imagine you were required to use a new software package to support learning in your classroom. It doesn't matter what this software does, only that it is intended as a key element of the curriculum. The following questions ask how confident you would be to use this unfamiliar software under a variety of conditions, using the scale:

```
      Not                Totally
   Confident            Confident
   |_____|
   1    2    3    4    5
```

I could use this unfamiliar software package …

1.	… if there was no one around to tell me what to do as I go	1	2	3	4	5
2.	… if I had only the software manuals for reference	1	2	3	4	5
3.	… if I had seen someone else using it before trying it myself	1	2	3	4	5
4.	… if I could call someone for help if I got stuck	1	2	3	4	5
5.	… if I had a lot of time to complete the job for which the software was provided	1	2	3	4	5
6.	… if I only had the built-in help facility for assistance	1	2	3	4	5
7.	… if someone showed me how to use it first	1	2	3	4	5
8.	… if there was someone giving me step-by-step instructions	1	2	3	4	5

Please respond to the following questions using this scale, where **1** = strongly disagree and **5** = strongly agree.

```
   Strongly            Strongly
    Agree              Disagree
   |_____|
   1    2    3    4    5
```

1.	Teachers know a lot more than students; they shouldn't let students muddle around when they can just explain the answers directly.	1	2	3	4	5
2.	Learning that occurs when students interact *informally* with each other and with adults is less important than learning that happens in class.	1	2	3	4	5
3.	Teachers need to feel confident about technology skills themselves before they can teach these skills to students.	1	2	3	4	5
4.	It is better when the teacher—not the students—decides what activities are to be done.	1	2	3	4	5
5.	Young people are already good at using computers—schools don't need to spend time on technology learning.	1	2	3	4	5
6.	Teaching should be built around problems with clear, correct answers, and around ideas that most students can grasp quickly.	1	2	3	4	5
7.	It is more important for students to access information that is factual and accurate than be exposed to diverse opinions and views.	1	2	3	4	5
8.	Students won't learn the subject matter unless you go over it in a structured way. A teacher's job is to explain and show students how to do the work.	1	2	3	4	5
9.	Students don't like taking responsibility for learning. They want the teacher to tell them what to do.	1	2	3	4	5

10.	While student motivation is useful, it should not drive what students study.	1 2 3 4 5
11.	Teachers will lose students' respect if they admit that they don't know how to do something.	1 2 3 4 5
12.	Teachers know more than students. Students learn from teachers not the other way around.	1 2 3 4 5

How confident would you feel doing the following:

Not Confident 1 2 3 4 5 Totally Confident

1.	Start up a computer and open a document or program	1 2 3 4 5
2.	Move, copy, or organize files	1 2 3 4 5
3.	Print a document	1 2 3 4 5
4.	Install software	1 2 3 4 5
5.	Set up a computer (plugging it all together)	1 2 3 4 5
6.	Use the Help function of a program	1 2 3 4 5
7.	Use more than one program at once (multitasking)	1 2 3 4 5
8.	Teach a computer skill to others	1 2 3 4 5
9.	Use a scanner	1 2 3 4 5
10.	Use a digital camera	1 2 3 4 5
11.	Find a website given a web address	1 2 3 4 5
12.	Create a browser bookmark (Favorite)	1 2 3 4 5
13.	Set up an email address book	1 2 3 4 5
14.	File emails into mailboxes or folders	1 2 3 4 5
15.	Perform a web search for specific information	1 2 3 4 5
16.	Save images from the web	1 2 3 4 5
17.	Modify the appearance of a photograph using a graphics program	1 2 3 4 5
18.	Use a spreadsheet to record marks or grades for your class	1 2 3 4 5
19.	Create a presentation (for example, using PowerPoint)	1 2 3 4 5
20.	Use a data projector	1 2 3 4 5
21.	Create an interactive whiteboard lesson	1 2 3 4 5
22.	Set up a blog (web log)	1 2 3 4 5
23.	Create and edit a digital video	1 2 3 4 5
24.	Problem solve when something goes "wrong" with technology	1 2 3 4 5
25.	Create a wiki for use by your class	1 2 3 4 5

26.	Record a digital audio file	1	2	3	4	5
27.	Locate an app and install it on a mobile/cell phone or tablet	1	2	3	4	5
28.	Use an avatar to move around in a 3-D virtual environment	1	2	3	4	5
29.	Run a lesson using a personal response system (e.g., student "voting")	1	2	3	4	5
30.	How would you score your overall confidence with technology skills?	1	2	3	4	5

Please share your thoughts or reflections in response to the following questions.

1. What do you see as the benefits of using technology to support your teaching?

2. What factors have helped the integration of ICT in your classroom?

3. What factors have hindered the integration of ICT in your classroom?

4. List the achievements you are most proud of in your use of technology (at home or at school).

APPENDIX C

NETS for Coaches (NETS·C)

National Educational Technology Standards for Coaches (NETS·C)

All technology coaches should be prepared to meet the following standards and performance indicators.

1. **Visionary Leadership**
   Technology Coaches inspire and participate in the development and implementation of a shared vision for the comprehensive integration of technology to promote excellence and support transformational change throughout the instructional environment. Technology Coaches:

   a. contribute to the development, communication, and implementation of a shared vision for the comprehensive use of technology to support a digital-age education for all students

   b. contribute to the planning, development, communication, implementation, and evaluation of technology-infused strategic plans at the district and school levels

   c. advocate for policies, procedures, programs, and funding strategies to support implementation of the shared vision represented in the school and district technology plans and guidelines

   d. implement strategies for initiating and sustaining technology innovations and manage the change process in schools and classrooms

2. **Teaching, Learning, and Assessments**
   Technology Coaches assist teachers in using technology effectively for assessing student learning, differentiating instruction, and providing rigorous, relevant, and engaging learning experiences for all students. Technology Coaches:

   a. Coach teachers in and model design and implementation of technology enhanced learning experiences addressing content standards and student technology standards

   b. Coach teachers in and model design and implementation of technology-enhanced learning experiences using a variety of research-based, learner-centered instructional strategies and assessment tools to address the diverse needs and interests of all students

c. Coach teachers in and model engagement of students in local and global interdisciplinary units in which technology helps students assume professional roles, research real-world problems, collaborate with others, and produce products that are meaningful and useful to a wide audience

d. Coach teachers in and model design and implementation of technology-enhanced learning experiences emphasizing creativity, higher-order thinking skills and processes, and mental habits of mind (e.g., critical thinking, meta-cognition, and self-regulation)

e. Coach teachers in and model design and implementation of technology-enhanced learning experiences using differentiation, including adjusting content, process, product, and learning environment based upon student readiness levels, learning styles, interests, and personal goals

f. Coach teachers in and model incorporation of research-based best practices in instructional design when planning technology-enhanced learning experiences

g. Coach teachers in and model effective use of technology tools and resources to continuously assess student learning and technology literacy by applying a rich variety of formative and summative assessments aligned with content and student technology standards

h. Coach teachers in and model effective use of technology tools and resources to systematically collect and analyze student achievement data, interpret results, and communicate findings to improve instructional practice and maximize student learning

3. **Digital Age Learning Environments**
Technology coaches create and support effective digital-age learning environments to maximize the learning of all students. Technology Coaches:

a. Model effective classroom management and collaborative learning strategies to maximize teacher and student use of digital tools and resources and access to technology-rich learning environments

b. Maintain and manage a variety of digital tools and resources for teacher and student use in technology-rich learning environments

c. Coach teachers in and model use of online and blended learning, digital content, and collaborative learning networks to support and extend student learning as well as expand opportunities and choices for online professional development for teachers and administrators

d. Select, evaluate, and facilitate the use of adaptive and assistive technologies to support student learning

- e. Troubleshoot basic software, hardware, and connectivity problems common in digital learning environments
- f. Collaborate with teachers and administrators to select and evaluate digital tools and resources that enhance teaching and learning and are compatible with the school technology infrastructure
- g. Use digital communication and collaboration tools to communicate locally and globally with students, parents, peers, and the larger community

4. **Professional Development and Program Evaluation**

    Technology coaches conduct needs assessments, develop technology-related professional learning programs, and evaluate the impact on instructional practice and student learning. Technology Coaches:

    - a. Conduct needs assessments to inform the content and delivery of technology-related professional learning programs that result in a positive impact on student learning
    - b. Design, develop, and implement technology-rich professional learning programs that model principles of adult learning and promote digital-age best practices in teaching, learning, and assessment
    - c. Evaluate results of professional learning programs to determine the effectiveness on deepening teacher content knowledge, improving teacher pedagogical skills and/or increasing student learning

5. **Digital Citizenship**

    Technology coaches model and promote digital citizenship. Technology Coaches:

    - a. Model and promote strategies for achieving equitable access to digital tools and resources and technology-related best practices for all students and teachers
    - b. Model and facilitate safe, healthy, legal, and ethical uses of digital information and technologies
    - c. Model and promote diversity, cultural understanding, and global awareness by using digital-age communication and collaboration tools to interact locally and globally with students, peers, parents, and the larger community

6. **Content Knowledge and Professional Growth**

    Technology coaches demonstrate professional knowledge, skills, and dispositions in content, pedagogical, and technological areas as well as adult learning and leadership and are continuously deepening their knowledge and expertise. Technology Coaches:

    a. Engage in continual learning to deepen content and pedagogical knowledge in technology integration and current and emerging technologies necessary to effectively implement the NETS•S and NETS•T

    b. Engage in continuous learning to deepen professional knowledge, skills, and dispositions in organizational change and leadership, project management, and adult learning to improve professional practice

    c. Regularly evaluate and reflect on their professional practice and dispositions to improve and strengthen their ability to effectively model and facilitate technology-enhanced learning experiences

© 2011 International Society for Technology in Education (ISTE), www.iste.org. All rights reserved.

Glossary

This glossary acts as a ready reference, summarizing some of the key terms and ideas covered throughout this book. We have also included the meaning of acronyms or abbreviations used throughout.

action learning. A form of collective, self-reflective inquiry undertaken by participants to improve their own social or educational practices, their understanding of these practices, and the situations in which these practices are carried out. (Kemmis & McTaggart, 1988)

action research. A form of collective self-reflective inquiry, as per action learning, but with a greater emphasis on making an original contribution to knowledge.

action research cycles. A process of planning to do something, acting on that plan, observing and documenting what happens, and then reflecting on what you have learned. Typically this is repeated by subsequent cycles of planning, acting, observing, and reflecting.

active experimentation or **exploratory learning.** A process of learning whereby an individual identifies a need or motivation to learn, tries things out for themselves, usually through exploration, seeking help if and when required.

affects. Our feelings, attitudes, values, beliefs, and assumptions.

appropriate attribution. The ability to accurately determine whether the cause of success or lack of success is external or internal, for example, due to yourself or to factors outside your control.

attribution. An explanation for the cause of an event. Individuals who have an internal attribution predominantly believe that the reason for success or failure resides within themselves. Individuals who have an external attribution predominantly believe that the reason for success or failure is due to influences outside themselves.

bifurcation point. See **tipping point.**

capability. The ability to perform in varied, familiar, and unfamiliar circumstances.

CMs, companion mentors. Companion mentors is a term used by some Technology Together schools to refer to those who are undertaking the main role in mentoring and supporting staff.

competency. The ability to perform specific skills within a predictable and controlled environment.

complexity science. A relatively new, cross-disciplinary theory which helps to understand evolving and changing systems and the big consequences of little things.

computer anxiety. Irrational emotional distress experienced by an individual when using or considering the use of computer technology.

computer self-efficacy. An individual's beliefs about what he or she is capable of doing on a computer, not about what he or she can already do.

connectivist pedagogy. A belief that learning is collaborative and occurs not only within individuals but also within and between networks of people.

constructivist pedagogy. A belief that learning is about individuals constructing their own understandings.

directive-style training. A training approach that focuses predominantly on the teacher providing step-by-step instructions to participants as they learn particular skills.

exploratory learning or **active experimentation.** A positive learning strategy to promote computer capability. Essentially, a give it a try, hands-on approach to learning.

external partner. An outside partner involved in the Technology Together implementation process. The external partner brings a fresh perspective and acts a critical friend who can ask the more-difficult questions. The external partner might be from a university, another school, an educational district office, or an outside organization.

futures studies. Interdisciplinary field that actively engages individuals in envisaging and discussing possible, probable, and preferred futures. It acknowledges the limitations of prediction and recognizes the importance of exploring alternative and plural futures rather than arriving at one monolithic future.

goal orientation. The capacity or willingness of an individual to identify, articulate, and pursue personally relevant goals.

graffiti board. An area where teachers or students can freely write messages in a spontaneous and informal manner. May take the form of a whiteboard surface or a large sheet of paper or cardboard, ideally positioned in a high-traffic area, such as a staff room or next to a photocopier.

homeostasis. The tendency of a system to maintain a stable, constant condition in the face of changing circumstances.

ICT. ICT (information and communication technology) is used in this book to refer to a broad range of electronic technologies (beyond computers and software), including devices such as DVD players, MP3 players, and mobile devices. At times we abbreviate it to *technology* or to *IT* (information technology).

ICT integration. An instructional decision by teachers to deliberately incorporate ICT into their teaching curriculum, including to introduce, reinforce, extend, enrich, assess, and remediate students' achievement of learning objectives (informed by Hamilton, 2007).

IWB. Interactive whiteboard

just-in-time learning. Learning that occurs in response to an immediate need or problem.

KLA. Key learning area is an Australian term for curriculum areas, for example, English, mathematics, science, physical education, creative arts, and so on.

learned helplessness. When learners faced with challenges or difficulties abandon any problem-solving strategies and fail to help themselves.

like-to-like (nonexpert) mentoring. A learning partnership that occurs between two individuals with similar levels of technology skills, typically two nonexperts.

memory and retention of learning. Learning that involves a degree of difficulty and leads to long-term learning outcomes.

metacognition. Thinking about thinking or learning about learning. Reflection lies at the heart of metacognitive learning.

metacognitive approach to technology learning. Assumes that learning is influenced by three key components: affects, motivation, and strategies. Engages learners in actively thinking about their thinking in order to become better technology learners.

motivation. Motivation can be either extrinsic (driven by factors outside the individual) or intrinsic (driven by factors within the individual).

objectivist (or behaviorist) pedagogy. A belief that learning is about transmitting knowledge from one person to another.

perceived usefulness. One's feeling of benefiting from using technology whether the technology actually does benefit the person or not. Pedagogical perceived usefulness pertains to one's feelings toward technologies used in the classroom as being beneficial, whereas personal perceived usefulness pertains to technologies used in one's own professional or recreational life.

perceptions of time. How one perceives time has a significant impact on the ability to be a good technology learner.

PMI process. A strategy for brainstorming or discussing the pluses, minuses, and interesting points (PMI) about a given situation or circumstance.

problem solving. Probably the most important opportunity for learning about computers is while solving problems.

proximity paralysis. When an individual feels "frozen" or unable to function properly, generally due to nervousness, when working or learning alongside another person.

role models. Positive (or negative role) models can be used to actively construct our ideal or possible selves based on our needs and goals.

self-directed learning. The ability to make conscious and informed choices about sources and strategies for help and support. Does not mean learning in isolation.

self-efficacy. An individual's belief in his or her own capacity to perform on a particular task.

support, encouragement, and use of computers by others. Can be a positive and/or negative influence on someone's computer self-efficacy.

technophrenic. Someone who likes and is not anxious about using technology.

technophobic. Someone who dislikes and/or has a phobia or anxiety about using technology.

thinking aloud strategy. Sometimes referred to as cognitive modeling. Occurs when mentors verbally explains the thought processes that they go through as they work through a task or problem.

tipping point or **bifurcation point.** A critical point where a system changes significantly from one form or characteristic to another, often in a dramatic way.

volition. Willfulness or dogged perseverance in pursuit of difficult goals.

Additional glossary terms can be found in Chapter 6 under Interpersonal Exchanges, Online Information Collection and Analysis, and Problem-Solving Projects.

Interpersonal Exchanges

The following terms are defined in Chapter 6 under Interpersonal Exchanges:

- Book raps or book chats
- Electronic appearances
- Global classrooms
- Impersonations
- Keypals
- Question and answer
- Travel buddies or travel friends
- Telementoring
- Virtual gatherings

Online Information Collection and Analysis

The following terms are defined in Chapter 6 under Online Information Collection and Analysis:

- Database creation
- Electronic publishing
- Information exchanges
- Pooled data analysis
- Virtual field trips

Problem-Solving Projects

The following terms are defined in Chapter 6 under Problem-Solving Projects:

- Global WebQuests
- Online competitions
- Scavenger hunt
- Parallel problem solving
- Social action projects

Bibliography

This bibliography consists of References that correspond to material cited in the text and Further Reading.

References

American Association of Colleges for Teacher Education (AACTE) Committee on Innovation and Technology (Ed.). (2008). *Handbook of technological pedagogical content knowledge (TPCK) for educators.* New York: Routledge.

Bjork, R. (1994). Memory and metamemory considerations in the training of human beings. In J. Metcalfe & A. P. Shimamura (Eds.), *Metacognition: Knowing about Knowing* (pp. 185–205). Cambridge, MA: MIT Press.

Cairns, L. (2000, April). *The process/outcome approach to becoming a capable organisation.* Australian Capability Network Conference, Sydney. (1–14).

Carroll, T. G. (2000). If we didn't have the schools we have today, would we create the schools we have today? *Contemporary Issues in Technology and Teacher Education, 1*(1), 117–140.

Compeau, D. R., & Higgins, C. A. (1995). Computer self-efficacy: Development of a measure and initial test. *MIS Quarterly, 19*(2), 189–211.

Davidson, J. (2003). A new role in facilitating school reform: The case of the educational technologist. *Teachers College Record, 105*(5), 729–752.

Davis, B., & Sumara, D. (2005). Complexity science and educational action research: Toward a pragmatics of transformation. *Educational Action Research, 13*(3), 453–466.

Dodge, B. (1997). *Some Thoughts About WebQuests.* Retrieved from http://webquest.sdsu.edu/about_webquests.html

Doll, W. E. (1989). *A post-modern perspective on curriculum.* New York: Teachers College Press.

Downes, T., Fluck, A., Gibbons, P., Leonard, R., Matthews, C., Oliver, R., et al. (2001). *Making better connections: Models of teacher professional development for the integration of information and communication technology into classroom practice.* Canberra, ACT, Australia: Commonwealth Department of Education, Science and Training.

Dwyer, J. (2007). Computer-based learning in a primary school: Differences between the early and later years of primary schooling. *Asia-Pacific Journal of Teacher Education, 35*(1), 89–103.

Ertmer, P., Conklin, D., Lewandowski, J., Osika, E., Selo, M., & Wignall, E. (2003). Increasing preservice teachers' capacity for technology integration through the use of electronic models. *Teacher Education Quarterly, 30*(1), 95–112.

Ertmer, P., & Ottenbreit-Leftwich, A. (2010). Teacher technology change: How knowledge, confidence, beliefs, and culture intersect. *Journal of Research on Technology in Education, 42*(3), 255–284.

Ertmer, P., Ottenbreit-Leftwich, A., & York, C. (2006–07). Exemplary technology-using teachers: Perceptions of factors influencing success. *Journal of Computing in Teacher Education, 23*(2), 55–60.

Fullan, M. (2007). *The new meaning of educational change* (4th ed.). New York: Teachers College Press.

Gibson, D. (2002). Role models in career development: New directions for theory and research. *Journal of Vocational Behavior, 65*(1), 134–156.

Goddard, D., Hoy, W., & Hoy, A. (2004). Collective efficacy beliefs: Theoretical developments, empirical evidence, and future directions. *Educational Researcher, 33*(3), 3–13.

Hamilton, B. (2007). *IT's elementary! Integrating technology in the primary grades*. Eugene, OR: International Society for Technology in Education (ISTE).

Hargadon, S. (2010). Web 2.0: The essential ingredient in education. *Education Technology Solutions,* (37), 46–56.

Hargreaves, A. (1998). Pushing the boundaries of educational change. In A. Hargreaves (Ed.), *International handbook of educational change* (pp. 281–294). Dordrecht, Netherlands: Kluwer Academic Publishers.

Harris, J., Mishra, P., & Koehler, M. J. (2009). Teachers' technological pedagogical content knowledge and learning activity types: Curriculum-based technology integration reframed. *Journal of Research on Technology in Education, 41*(4), 393–416.

Hawkes, T. F. (2006, November). Teaching the millennial boy. Keynote presented at IES Boys' Education Conference, "Best Practices—What works in schools," Australian Technology Park Conference Centre, Sydney, Australia.

Hew, K., & Brush, T. (2007). Integrating technology into K–12 teaching and learning: Current knowledge gaps and recommendations for future research. *Educational Technology Research and Development, 55*(3), 223–252.

Howard, S. (1999, November). *Mentoring: Transforming school cultures.* Paper presented at the Annual Conference of Australian Association for Research in Education, Melbourne, VIC, Australia. Retrieved from www.aare.edu.au/99pap/how99257.htm.

Igbaria, M., & Iivari, J. (1995). The effects of self-efficacy on computer usage. *Omega International Journal of Management Science, 23*(6), 587–605.

Judson, E. (2006). How teachers integrate technology and their beliefs about learning: Is there a connection? *Journal of Technology and Teacher Education, 14*(3), 581–597.

Kauffman, S. (1995). *At home in the universe: The search for laws of complexity.* London: Penguin.

Kemmis, S., & McTaggart, R. (1988). *The action research planner.* Geelong, VIC, Australia: Deakin University Press.

Lakoff, G., & Johnson, M. (1980). *Metaphors we live by.* Chicago, IL: University of Chicago Press.

Lee, M. (2001). Chaotic learning: The learning style of the net generation? In *New Millennium, New Horizons: Information Services in Schools 2000 Online Conference Proceedings.* Wagga Wagga, NSW, Australia: Charles Sturt University, Centre for Studies in Teacher Librarianship.

Levin, T., & Wadmany, R. (2006–2007). Teachers' beliefs and practices in technology-based classrooms: A developmental view. *Journal of Research on Technology in Education, 39*(2), 157–181.

Lloyd, M., & Yelland, N. (2003). Adaptation and avoidance: Observations of teachers' reactions to information and communication technologies in the classroom. *Change: Transformations in Education, 6*(1), 81–96.

Loader, D. (2007). *Jousting for the new generation: Challenges to contemporary schooling.* Camberwell, VIC, Australia: ACER Press.

Lombardi, M. (2007). *Authentic learning for the 21st century: An overview.* Educause Learning Initiative ELI Paper 1. Retrieved from http://www.educause.edu/ELI/AuthenticLearningforthe21stCen/156769

Lundin, R. (2002). The state of technology in education: A reality check. *The Practising Administrator,* (1), 10–13.

Ministerial Council on Education, Employment, Training and Youth Affairs (MCEETYA), ICT in Schools Taskforce. (2005). *Learning in an online world: Pedagogy strategy.* Carlton South, VIC, Australia. Retrieved from http://icttaskforce.edna.edu.au/icttaskforce/webdav/site/icttaskforcesite/users/root/public/learning_online_pedagogy_05.pdf

Mishra, P., & Koehler, M. J. (2006). Technological pedagogical content knowledge: A framework for teacher knowledge. *Teachers College Record, 108*(6), 1017–1054.

Mitra, S., Dangwal, R., Chatterjee, S., Jha, S., Bisht, R. S. & Kapur, P. (2005). Acquisition of computing literacy on shared public computers: Children and the "hole in the wall." *Australasian Journal of Educational Technology, 21*(3), 407–426.

Moyle, K. (2006). *Leadership and learning with ICT: Voices from the profession.* Canberra, ACT, Australia: Teaching Australia.

Norton, P., & Wiburg, K. (2003). *Teaching with technology: Designing opportunities to learn.* Belmont, CA: Thompson/Wadsworth.

Papaleontiou-Louca, E. (2003). The concept and instruction of metacognition. *Teacher Development, 7*(1), 9–30.

Papert, S. (1996). *The connected family: Bridging the digital generation gap.* Atlanta, GA: Longstreet Press.

Passey, D., Rogers, C., Machell, J., & McHugh, G. (2004). *The motivational effect of ICT on pupils.* Great Britain Department of Education and Skills. Retrieved from www.dfes.gov.uk/research/data/uploadfiles/RR523new.pdf

Phelps, R. (2002). *Mapping the complexity of computer learning: Journeying beyond teaching for computer competency to facilitating computer capability* (Doctoral dissertation). Lismore, NSW, Australia: Southern Cross University.

Phelps, R. (2005). The potential of reflection in studying complexity "in action." *Complicity: An International Journal of Complexity and Education, 2*(1), 37–54.

Phelps, R. (2007). The metacognitive approach to computer education: Making explicit the learning journey. *AACE Journal, 15*(1), 3–21.

Phelps, R., & Ellis, A. (2002a, December). *Helping students to help themselves: Case studies from a metacognitive approach to computer learning and teaching.* Paper presented at 2002 International Conference on Computers in Education. Auckland, New Zealand. Retrieved from doi:ieeecomputersociety.org/10.1109/CIE.2002.1186143

Phelps, R., & Ellis, A. (2002b, September). *A metacognitive approach to computer education for teachers: Combining theory and practice for computer capability.* Paper presented at Linking Learners: Australian Computers in Education Conference. Hobart, TAS, Australia. Retrieved from www.pa.ash.org.au/acec2002/

Phelps, R., Graham, A., & Kerr, B. (2004). Teachers and ICT: Exploring a metacognitive approach to professional development. *Australasian Journal of Educational Technology, 20*(1), 49–68.

Prensky, M. (2001). Digital natives, digital immigrants: Part 1. *On the Horizon, 9*(5), 1–5. Retrieved from www.marcprensky.com/writing/Prensky - Digital Natives, Digital Immigrants - Part1.pdf

Redmond, P., & Brown, K. (2004). Are we there yet? The journey of ICT integration. *Professional Educator, 3*(4), 14–16.

Richardson, W. (2010). *Blogs, wikis, podcasts, and other powerful web tools for classrooms.* Thousand Oaks, CA: Corwin Press.

Roblyer, M. D. (2004). *Integrating educational technology into teaching* (3rd ed.). Upper Saddle River, NJ: Pearson/Merrill/Prentice Hall.

Russell, G., Finger, G., & Russell, N. (2000). Information technology skills of Australian teachers: Implications for teacher education. *Journal of Information Technology for Teacher Education, 9*(2), 149–166.

Selwyn, N. (2009). The digital native: Myth and reality. *ASLIB Proceedings: New Information Perspectives, 61*(4), 364–379.

Siemens, G. (2005). Connectivism: A learning theory for the digital age. *International Journal of Instructional Technology and Distance Learning, 2*(1). Retrieved from www.itdl.org/Journal/Jan_05/article01.htm

Stacey, R. D., Griffin, D., & Shaw, P. (2000). *Complexity and management: Fad or radical challenge to systems thinking?* London: Routledge.

Strudler, N. (2010). Perspectives on technology and educational change. *Journal of Research on Technology in Education, 42*(3), 221–229.

Tapscott, D. (1998). *Growing up digital: The rise of the net generation.* New York: McGraw-Hill.

Waldrop, M. (1992). *Complexity: The emerging science at the edge of order and chaos.* London, UK: Penguin.

Webster, J., & Martocchio, J. J. (1995). The differential effects of software training previews on training outcomes. *Journal of Management, 21*(4), 757–787.

Further Reading

If you are interested in reading more about the research underpinning Technology Together, or about the metacognitive approach to technology learning in general, you may want to consult these publications. Many are available from http://works.bepress.com/renata_phelps.

Phelps, R. (2002). Mapping the complexity of computer learning: Journeying beyond teaching for computer competency to facilitating computer capability. (Unpublished doctoral dissertation). Lismore, NSW, Australia: Southern Cross University.

Phelps, R. (2005). The potential of reflection in studying complexity "in action." *Complicity: An International Journal of Complexity and Education, 2*(1), 37–54.

Phelps, R. (2007). The metacognitive approach to computer education: Making explicit the learning journey. *AACE Journal (International Forum on Information Technology in Education), 15*(1), 3–21.

Phelps, R., & Ellis, A. (2002, September). *A metacognitive approach to computer education for teachers: Combining theory and practice for computer capability.* Paper presented at the Linking Learners: Australian Computers in Education Conference. Hobart, TAS, Australia.

Phelps, R., & Ellis, A. (2002, December). *Helping students to help themselves: Case studies from a metacognitive approach to computer learning and teaching.* Paper presented at the International Conference on Computers in Education. Auckland, New Zealand. Retrieved from http://icce2002.massey.ac.nz/

Phelps, R., & Ellis, A. (2002, December). *Overcoming computer anxiety through reflection on attribution.* Paper presented at the Winds of Change in the Sea of Learning: Charting the Course of Digital Education: Australian Society for Computers in Learning in Tertiary Education (ASCILITE). Auckland, New Zealand. Retrieved from www.unitec.ac.nz/ascilite

Phelps, R., Ellis, A., & Hase, S. (2001). The role of metacognitive and reflective learning processes in developing capable computer users. In *Meeting at the Crossroads: Proceedings of the Australian Society for Computers in Learning in Tertiary Education (ASCILITE)*. Melbourne, VIC, Australia.

Phelps, R., & Hase, S. (2002). Complexity and action research: Exploring the theoretical and methodological connections. *Educational Action Research, 10*(3), 503–519.

Phelps, R., Hase, S., & Ellis, A. (2005). Competency, capability, complexity and computers: Exploring a new model for conceptualising end-user computer education. *British Journal of Educational Technology, 36*(1), 67–84.

Phelps, R., & Graham, A. (2007). *Developing Technology Together together: Consolidated report on an investigation of the metacognitive influences on teachers' use of information and communication technology (ICT) and the implications for teacher professional development.* Lismore, NSW, Australia: Southern Cross University.

Phelps, R., & Graham, A. (2007). *Developing Technology Together together: Final report on an investigation of the metacognitive influences on teachers' use of ICT and the implications for teacher professional development.* Lismore, NSW, Australia: Southern Cross University.

Phelps, R., & Graham, A. (2007). Technology Together: A structured approach to effective ICT professional development and culture change for schools. *QUICK: Journal of the Queensland Society for Information Technology in Education, Winter* (103), 15–16.

Phelps, R., & Graham, A. (2008). Developing Technology Together, together: A whole-school metacognitive approach to ICT teacher professional development. *Journal of Computing in Teacher Education, 24*(4), 125–133.

Phelps, R., & Graham, A. (2010). Exploring the complementarities between complexity and action research: The story of Technology Together. *Cambridge Journal of Education, 40*(2), 183–197.

Phelps, R., Graham, A., Brennan, S., & Carrigan, C. (2006, October). *I can u can: Six strategies for building teachers' ICT confidence and capability through metacognitive discussion and reflection: Experiences from Technology Together.* Paper presented at the Australian Computers in Education Conference. Cairns, QLD, Australia. Retrieved from www.acec2006.info/confpapers/paperdetails.asp?pid=7213&docid=691

Phelps, R., Graham, A., & Kerr, B. (2004). Teachers and ICT: Exploring a metacognitive approach to professional development. *Australian Journal of Educational Technology, 20*(1), 49–68.

Phelps, R., Graham, A., & Thornton, P. (2006). Technology Together: Getting whole schools involved with ICT through a metacognitive approach. *The Australian Educational Leader, 28*(1), 22–24.

Phelps, R., Graham, A., Watts, L., & O'Brien, A. (2006, October). *Technology Together: Supporting whole-schools to become capable learning communities.* Paper presented at the Australian Computers in Education Conference. Cairns, QLD, Australia. Retrieved from www.acec2006.info/confpapers/paperdetails.asp?pid=7213&docid=690

Phelps, R., Graham, A., & Watts, T. (2011). Acknowledging the complexity and diversity of historical and cultural ICT professional learning practices in schools. *Asia-Pacific Journal of Teacher Education, 39*(1), 47–63.

Index

Page references followed by *f*, *t*, or *b* indicate figures (including reflections and thought bubbles), tables, or boxes, respectively.

A

ability, 38. *See also* capabiity
action learning, 25, 26, 49, 229. *See also* action research
action prompts, 92*t*, 96*t*, 98*t*, 100*t*, 102*t*, 105*t*, 111*t*, 116*t*, 119*t*, 121*t*, 122*t*, 123*t*, 131*t*, 134*t*, 137*t*, 138*t*, 139*t*, 144*t*, 147*t*
action research, 25, 26, 26*f*, 229
active experimentation, 229, 230
activities
    contract activities, 178*f*
    four-quarter school year schedule, 188, 189*t*–191*t*
    three-term (trimester) school year schedule, 191, 192*t*–193*t*
adaptation, 22
administrative leaders. *See* school executives
administrative staff, 48
advice from the front line, 197–204
affects, 37–38, 43*f*
    definition of, 229
    metacognitive approach focused on, 94, 94*f*
    mindfulness toward, 94–102
agendas for staff meetings, 77
anxiety, 114–115
    computer anxiety, 38, 97, 230
    ideas for engagement, 98*t*
    scaffold for confronting anxieties, 98*t*
    types of, 97
appropriate attribution, 101, 229
ARC. *See* Australian Research Council
Ask Wendell, 182
assemblies, 82–83, 84*t*
assistive technologies, 48
asynchronous communication, 158*t*, 165, 166*t*
attitudes, teacher, 32–33
    school analysis of, 63*t*
    about time, 122–123, 203–204
attribution
    appropriate, 101, 229
    definition of, 229
    dimensions of, 101
    ideas for engagement, 102*t*
    theory, 100, 101
Australian Research Council (ARC), xi
authentic learning, 131–133
    connectivist online learning, 179–185, 179*f*
    goal-setting scaffold for, 179*f*
authenticity, 131–133

B

baby boomers, 135*t*
beginning teachers, 8–9. *See also* teachers
behaviorist (or objectivist) pedagogy, 231
beliefs, teacher, 32–33, 63*t*
bifurcation, 24
bifurcation point, 24, 229
blaming others, 38, 100
book chats, 182
buddy systems, 178*f*
butterfly effect, 21

C

capability, 32, 89–91, 90*f*
    competency/capability model, 91
    definition of, xi, 12, 229
    learning strategies that promote, 40
    mentoring for, 88–92
    in school context, 92*t*–93*t*
    technology capability, 31–32, 89–90, 92*t*–93*t*
capability-based approaches, 14–15
celebrating achievements, 35, 82–83, 186
    ideas for, 186*b*
    planning for, 82–83
    strategies for, 83, 84*t*
change, 23
    as natural and evolutionary, 22
    openness to, 62*t*
    as process, 205
    resistance to trying new strategies, 198–199
    in school culture, 35–36, 62*t*
change agents, 8–9
checklists, 85
children teaching children, 146*b*
citizenship, digital, 227

INDEX

classroom(s)
    global, 182
    metacognition in, 92t, 96t, 98t, 100t, 102t, 105t, 111t, 116t, 119t, 121t, 122t, 123t, 131t, 134t, 137t, 201b
    story from the front line, 201b
    visits to, 73t
classroom management, 177
    goal-setting scaffold for, 178f
    strategies for, 178f
CMs. See companion mentors
coaches, 225–228
collecting information, 61
collective efficacy, 59–60
communication(s)
    asynchronous, 158t, 165, 166t
    synchronous, 158t, 165, 166t
communication applications skills, 158t, 165
    core skills, 166t
    goal-setting scaffold for, 166t
community demographics, 61t
companion mentors (CMs), xii, 34, 54–55
    definition of, 229
    end-of-term evaluative questions for, 194, 196f
    key role, 53–54
    maintaining enthusiasm, 204
    qualities to bring, 54
    risks for teachers as, 58
competency, 230
competency-based approaches, 14–15, 31
competency/capability, 32, 89–91, 90f
    ideas for engagement, 92t
    in school context, 92t–93t
    technology capability, 31–32, 89–90, 92t–93t
    technology competency, 31–32, 89–90, 92t–93t
competency/capability model, 91
competitions, online, 184–185
complexity science, 20, 21–22, 23–24, 230
computer anxiety, 38, 97
    definition of, 230
    mentoring to decrease, 97–98
    scaffold for confronting anxieties, 98t
computer self-efficacy, 38, 95–96, 230
computer skills. See also technology
    core skills, 159t
    foundational, 158t, 159, 159t–160t
    goal-setting scaffold for, 159t–160t
confidence, teacher, 32–33
confronting anxieties scaffold, 98t
connectivism, 129, 131t
connectivist online learning, 179–185
connectivist pedagogy, 230
connectivist teaching approach, 130t, 131t, 132, 133f
constructivism, 129, 140b
constructivist approaches, 106, 129, 130t, 132, 133f
    ideas for engagement, 131t
    online learning goal-setting scaffold, 179f
constructivist pedagogy, 230
content knowledge (CK), 10
    NETS for Coaches (NETS•C), 228
    TPACK (technological, pedagogical, and content knowledge) model, 10
contract activities, 178f
control: locus of, 101
cooperative learning, 146b
coordinating team, 58
creative arts apps, 175t
critical friends, 60
cultural encounters, 45
culture(s)
    of ICT use, 62t
    ideas for engagement, 134t
    of learning, 62t, 133f, 134t
    of meetings and discussion, 63t
    pedagogical, 62t
    school analysis of, 62t, 63t
    school culture, 33, 35–36
    teacher culture, 62t
    of teaching and learning, 133f, 134t
customized learning, 141b
cycles of planning, acting, observing, and reflecting, 49

D

data analysis, pooled, 183
data collection, 26
    goal-setting scaffold for, 179f
    online information collection and analysis, 179f, 183–184, 232
    resources available online, 27
    school analysis, 61
database creation, 183
database software skills, 158t, 171–172
    core skills, 172t
    goal-setting scaffold for, 172t
demonstration
    for goal setting, 156t
    whole-class, 178f
department goal setting, 156t
digital citizenship, 227
digital natives, 134–137, 137t
directed (or objectivist) approaches, 106, 129, 130t, 132, 133f

directive-style training, 230
discovery, 140*b*
discussion(s)
    culture of, 63*t*
    incidental, 82
    informal, 82
    school analysis of, 63*t*
    in staff meetings, 77–78
    strategies for, 76–82
    teaching as conversation, 142*b*
    whole-school, 202
discussion prompts, 92*t*, 96*t*, 98*t*, 100*t*, 102*t*, 105*t*, 111*t*, 116*t*, 119*t*, 121*t*, 122*t*, 123*t*, 131*t*, 134*t*, 137*t*, 138*t*, 139*t*, 144*t*, 147*t*
discussion starters, 140*b*–141*b*
displays, 81–82
diversity, 23
Dodge, Bernie, 180
Doodle4Google, 185

E

e-portfolios, 79, 80–81
    annotations to include, 81
    types of, 80–81
efficacy
    collective, 59–60
    mentoring to build, 95–96
    self-efficacy, 38, 59–60, 95–96
effort, 38
electronic appearances, 182
electronic publishing, 183
encouragement
    of computer use by others, 232
    ideas for engagement, 100*t*
    role of, 99
end-of-term evaluative questions, 194, 196*f*
end-of-term reflection scaffold, 195*f*
engagement: suggestions for, 92*t*, 96*t*, 98*t*, 100*t*, 102*t*, 105*t*, 111*t*, 116*t*, 119*t*, 121*t*, 122*t*, 123*t*, 131*t*, 134*t*, 137*t*, 138*t*, 144*t*, 147*t*
English apps, 175*t*
enthusiasm: maintaining, 204
evaluation
    end-of-term questions for, 194, 196*f*
    NETS for Coaches (NETS•C), 227
    of staff skills and readiness, 197
excursions, virtual, 184
executive, school, 52–54
experiential learning. *See* exploratory learning
experimentation, active, 229, 230
expert mentors, 70*t*
experts, ICT, 56
exploratory learning, 40
    advantages and disadvantages of, 113*t*
    definition of, 230
    encouraging, 114–116
    fostering, 115
    ideas for engagement, 116*t*
    mentoring to foster, 115–116
    self-directed, 113*t*
    tips for, 117*b*
external partners, 57, 60, 230

F

facilitators, 54
    end-of-term evaluative questions for, 194, 196*f*
    qualities to bring, 54
    teachers as, 141*b*
faculty/department goal setting, 156*t*
failure accepting, 38, 100
field trips, virtual, 184
financial issues, 63*t*
Flat Stanley Project, 182
flexibility, 194–195
flipchart software, 158*t*, 168
foundational computer skills, 158*t*, 159
    core skills, 159*t*
    goal-setting scaffold for, 159*t*–160*t*
foundational pillars, 11–12, 30–36
friends, critical, 60
future agendas, 62*t*
futures
    possible, 51
    preferred, 51
    probable, 51
futures studies, 51, 230

G

generation X, 135*t*
generational comparisons, 135*t*
global classrooms, 182
Global Grocery List Project, 183
global projects, 179*f*, 181–185
global WebQuests, 184
goal orientation, 39
    definition of, 230
    for developing metacognition, 145*b*
    modeling, 106–108

INDEX

goal setting, 39, 107, 143*b*
    approaches to, 155, 155*t*–156*t*
    areas for, 68
    by demonstration, 156*t*
    for developing metacognition, 145*b*
    facilitating, 67–68
    helping teachers with, 150–153
    independent, 155*t*
    whole-grade or faculty/department, 156*t*
    whole-school, 152–153
    whole-staff, 156*t*
goal-setting matrix, 152*t*
goal-setting pie chart, 151, 151*f*
goal-setting scaffolds, 27, 154, 154*f*, 159*t*–160*t*, 161*f*, 162*t*–163*t*, 164*t*, 165*t*, 166*t*, 167*t*–168*t*, 169*t*, 170*t*–171*t*, 172*t*, 173*t*–174*t*, 175*t*–176*t*, 178*f*, 179*f*
goal-setting structure, 151–152
goals, 149–186
    leadership, 152*t*, 157*t*
    metacognitive, 152*t*, 156, 156*t*
    pedagogy, 152*t*, 176–177
    recreational, 152*t*, 157–158, 158*t*
    skills-based, 152*t*, 158–159, 158*t*
    whole-school, 153
grade level-based meetings, 73*t*
graffiti boards, 81–82, 230
group instruction
    advantages and disadvantages of, 111*t*
    peer-group learning, 114*t*
group skills input sessions, 72*t*
growth, professional, 228

H

hardware, 160
    goal-setting scaffold for, 161*f*
    school analysis, 62*t*
Harris, Judi, 181–185
Hawkes' generational comparison, 135*t*
Health and Personal Development apps, 175*t*
help seeking, 41
    balancing, 121–122
    ideas for engagement, 122*t*
helplessness, learned, 38, 100–101
    definition of, 231
    ideas for engagement, 102*t*
history of ICT professional development, 62*t*
Hole-in-the-Wall website, 138
homeostasis, 23–24, 231

I

"I can–You can" motto, 14, 14*f*
ICT. *See* information and communication technology; technology learning; technology skills
impersonations, 183
implementation
    checklist for planning, 85
    four-quarter school year schedule, 188, 189*t*–191*t*
    planning for, 47–85
    three-term (trimester) school year schedule, 191, 192*t*–193*t*
    timing of, 48–49
    who to involve and when, 48–49
improvement, 26
incidental discussions, 82
independence building, 200*b*
individual goal setting, 155*t*
individual instruction, 113*t*
informal discussions, 82
information and communication technology (ICT)
    adoption of, 32–33
    definition of, 231
    ideas for engagement, 139*t*
    implementation of, 187–205
    metacognitive approach to learning, 36–41
    patterns and culture of use, 62*t*
    potential to transform teaching, 139, 139*t*, 140*b*–141*b*
    professional development in, 10, 24–25
    rationale for, 8
    school analysis, 62*t*
    school receptivity to, 59
    as skills to be taught, 105*t*
    as tool for learning, 105*t*
information and communication technology (ICT) experts, 56
information and communication technology (ICT) integration, 8, 32–33, 231
information and communication technology (ICT) vision, 51
information collection and analysis, 61
    goal-setting scaffold for, 179*f*
    online, 179*f*, 183–184, 232
information exchanges, 183
initial conditions, 21–22
initiatives, 149–186
inquiry learning, 25, 229

instruction
    group, 111*t*, 114*t*
    individual, 113*t*
    one-to-one, 178*f*
interactive multimedia learning environments, 146*b*
interactive stories, 168–169
interactive whiteboards (IWBs), 1, 158*t*, 173
    core skills for, 173*t*
    goal-setting scaffold for, 173*t*–174*t*
Internet
    connectivist online learning, 179–185
    online competitions, 185
    online information collection and analysis, 179*f*, 183–184, 232
    scaffolding link sites, 178*f*
    Web 1.0 skills, 163, 164*t*
    Web 2.0 skills, 163, 165*t*
interpersonal exchanges, 181–183, 232
    goal-setting scaffold for, 179*f*
    types of, 181–183
introducing Technology Together, 49
iPads, 174, 177, 178
iPhones, 174
IWBs. *See* interactive whiteboards

J

Jason Project, 182
journaling
    for developing metacognition, 146*b*
    journal excerpts, 148*t*
    reflective journals, 79–80
    for showcasing and celebrating success, 82–83, 84*t*
    weekly, 80
journey, traveling metaphor, 44–45
just-in-time learning, 73*t*, 231

K

Kahootz, 168
key learning areas (KLAs), 231
key project participants, 61*t*
keypals, 181
Kid Pix, 168
KLAs (key learning areas), 231
knowledge, technological, pedagogical, and content (TPACK) model, 10
knowledge
    meaningful, 142*b*
    social, collaborative construction of, 142*b*

L

laptop computers, 9, 137
leadership, 34
    maintaining enthusiasm, 204
    school, 52–54
    school analysis of, 62*t*, 63*t*
    taking part in, 57–58
    visionary, 225
leadership goals, 152*t*, 157*t*
learned helplessness, 38
    definition of, 231
    ideas for engagement, 102*t*
    recognizing, 100–101
learning. *See also* exploratory learning
    action learning, 25
    authentic, 131–133
    authentic, connectivist online, 179–185
    cooperative, 146*b*
    culture of, 62*t*, 133*f*
    customized, 141*b*
    as fun, 141*b*
    ICT learning, 20–25, 36–41
    as journey, 44–45
    just-in-time, 73*t*
    learning how to learn, 140*b*
    lifelong, 140*b*
    linear to hypermedia, 140*b*
    metacognitive approach to, 36–41
    NETS for Coaches (NETS•C), 225–226
    occasioning, 24–25
    ongoing, 142*b*
    pathways to, 40, 110
    reluctance to learn, 198
    retention of, 231
    school analysis of, 62*t*
    self-directed, 232
    with and from students, 146–147, 147*t*, 148*t*
    technology learning, 20–25, 36–41
    24/7, 142*b*
learning community, 17
learning environments
    digital age, 226–227
    interactive multimedia, 146*b*
learning goals. *See* goal setting
learning outcomes, long-term, 40
learning partners, 55. *See also* companion mentors (CMs)
learning pathways, 40, 110
    advantages and disadvantages of, 112*t*–114*t*
    ideas for engagement, 111*t*
    reflection on, 110

INDEX

learning strategies
    teacher, 32–33
    that promote capability, 40
lifelong learning, 13, 140b
like-to-like (nonexpert) mentoring, 71t, 231
locus of control, 101
luck, 38

M

management, 63t
management team, school, 52–54
maps, 45
mathematics apps, 175t
Mathletics, 185
meaningful knowledge, 142b
meeting times, 58
meetings
    culture of, 63t
    grade level-based, 73t
    resources for, 27
    school analysis of, 63t
    staff meetings, 77–78
    strategies for showcasing and celebrating success in, 82–83, 84t
memory, 40, 118–119
    definition of, 231
    ideas for engagement, 119t
memorization, learners who focus on, 118–119
mentoring, 34
    to build self-efficacy, 95–96
    to decrease computer anxiety, 97–98
    to develop appropriate strategies, 108–124
    to develop capability, 88–92
    with expert mentors, 70t
    to foster exploratory learning, 115–116
    to foster motivation, 102–108
    to foster problem solving, 120–121
    grade level-based meetings, 73t
    "how" approaches, 72t–73t
    just-in-time learning, 73t
    as keeping company, 34
    for learners who focus on memorization, 118–119
    like-to-like (nonexpert), 71t
    metacognitive approaches to, 87–125
    with mindfulness toward affects, 94–102
    planning, 69
    with several mentors, 70t
    strategies for, 69, 70t–73t
    strategies that foster capability, 91–92
    structured, 72t
    suggestions for, 99, 102
    telementoring, 182
    tips for, 125
    via group skills input sessions, 72t
    via visits to other classrooms, 73t
    "who" approaches, 70t–71t
mentors, 55. *See also* companion mentors (CMs)
    advice for, 124–125
    individual goal setting with, 155t
    maintaining enthusiasm, 204
    role of, 88
    tips for, 125
metacognition, 32, 36, 40–41
    in classroom, 92t, 96t, 98t, 100t, 102t, 105t, 111t, 116t, 119t, 121t, 122t, 123t, 131t, 134t, 137t, 138t, 201b
    definition of, 231
    development of, 144, 144t, 144b–146b
    ideas for engagement, 144t
    maintaining focus on, 200
    story from the front line, 201b
    strategies for development of, 145b–147b
metacognitive approach, 15, 17, 32–33
    benefits of, 36–37
    definition of, 231
    dimensions of, 37
    focused on affects, 94, 94f
    to mentoring, 87–125
    to problem solving, 120
    spin-offs for students, 37
    strategies, 39–41, 43f
    to technology learning, 36–41
    visual models of, 26f, 42, 43f, 109f
metacognitive goals, 152t, 156, 156t
metaphors, 21, 44, 49–50, 197
Millenials, 134, 135t
mindfulness toward affects, 94–102
Mitra, Sugata, 138
mobile apps, 158t, 174, 175t–176t
mobile devices, 9
modeling for developing metacognition, 146b
modeling goal orientation, 106–108
motivation, 38–39, 43f, 103f
    definition of, 231
    mentoring to foster, 102–108
    teacher, 32–33
multimedia, 158t, 168, 170
    core skills, 170t
    goal-setting scaffold for, 170t–171t
    interactive multimedia learning environments, 146b

N

National Educational Technology Standards for Coaches (NETS•C), 52, 225–228
Net generation, 134, 135*t*
Norton and Wiburg's framework, 139, 140*b*–141*b*

O

objectivist (or directed) approaches, 106, 129, 130*t*
objectivist (or behaviorist) pedagogy, 231
occasioning learning, 24–25
one-to-one instruction, 178*f*
online competitions, 185
online information collection and analysis, 179*f*, 183–184, 232
online learning, connectivist, 179–185
open content, 142*b*
openness to change, 62*t*
orientation, pedagogical, 106
overdependency, 199

P

parallel problem solving, 184
paralysis, proximity, 232
paraphrasing, 146*b*
parent helpers, 178*f*
Participants' Zone (Technology Together website), 27–28
participatory action research. *See* action research
partners. *See also* companion mentors (CMs)
    external partners, 57, 60, 230
    learning partners, 55
pathways to learning, 40, 110
    advantages and disadvantages of, 112*t*–114*t*
    ideas for engagement, 111*t*
    reflection on, 110
pedagogical culture, 62*t*
pedagogical knowledge (PK), 10
pedagogical orientation, 106
pedagogical perceived usefulness, 39, 104
pedagogy
    connectivist, 230
    constructivist, 230
    ideas for engagement, 139*t*
    objectivist (or behaviorist), 231
    strategies for challenging, 128–139
pedagogy goals, 152*t*, 176–177
peer-group learning, 114*t*
peer or cross-age tutoring, 178*f*
peer pressure, 99
perceived usefulness, 39
    definition of, 232
    fostering, 103–105
    ideas for engagement, 105*t*
    pedagogical, 104
    personal, 104
perceptions of time, 232
perseverance, 41. *See also* volition
personal perceived usefulness, 39, 104
planning
    checklist for implementation planning, 85
    cycles of, 49
    for implementation, 47–85
    key purpose in, 69
    resources available online, 27
    to showcase and celebrate achievements, 82–83
    steps that require close consideration, 48
planning and organizing strategy, 145*b*
planning checklists, 85
planning mentoring strategies, 69
playfulness, 40, 114–116
PMI process, 232
policy, 63*t*
pooled data analysis, 183
portfolios. *See* e-portfolios
possible futures, 51
PowerPoint, 168
preferred futures, 51
presentation software skills, 158*t*, 168–169
    core skills, 169*t*
    goal-setting scaffold for, 169*t*
pre-service teacher education, 8–9
principals. *See* school executives
probable futures, 51
problem solving, 119, 120
    definition of, 232
    for developing metacognition, 145*b*, 146*b*
    fostering, 119–121
    ideas for engagement, 121*t*
    metacognitive approach to, 120
    parallel, 184
problem-solving projects, 184–185, 232
    goal-setting scaffold for, 179*f*
    types of, 184–185
procrastination, 38, 100
professional development
    ICT, 10, 24–25
    NETS for Coaches (NETS•C), 227
    Technology Together as, 35–36
professional dialogue, 36, 76
professional growth, 228

professional learning, 59
professionalism, 35–36
program evaluation, 227
proximity paralysis, 232
publishing, electronic, 183

Q

QuestAtlantis, 183
question-and-answer, 182
questions: generating, 145*b*

R

Read/Write Web, 139
readers, 143*b*
readiness, staff, 197
Reconnector Workshop, xii
recreational goals, 152*t*, 157–158, 158*t*
redundancy, 23
reflection
    on action over time, 41–42
    on authenticity in teaching and learning, 131–133
    on connectivism, 129
    on constructivism, 129
    end-of-term, 194–195, 195*f*
    example on spreadsheet integration lesson, 203*b*
    list of resources, 207–211
    on objectivism, 129
    as part of ongoing learning, 42
    on pathways to learning, 110
    on potential of ICT to transform teaching, 139
    prompts for, 92*t*, 96*t*, 98*t*, 100*t*, 102*t*, 105*t*, 111*t*, 116*t*, 119*t*, 121*t*, 122*t*, 123*t*, 131*t*, 134*t*, 137*t*, 138*t*, 139*t*, 144*t*, 147*t*
    questions for, 41
    resistance to, 201–202
    scheduling time for, 202
    strategies for, 76–82
    on students as digital natives, 134–137
    summative, 205
    video reflecting, 82
reflection scaffolds, 78
    end-of-term reflection scaffold, 195*f*
    example, 79*f*
    resources available online, 27
reflection sheets, 78
reflective inquiry, 25, 229
reflective journals, 79–80

relationships. *See* partners
release time, 53, 71, 74–75
    advice for, 74–75
    approaches to allocation of, 75*t*–76*t*
    strategies for, 74
reluctance to learn, 198
research
    action research, 25, 26, 26*f*, 229
    for developing metacognition, 146*b*
resistance
    to reflection, 201–202
    to trying new strategies, 198–199
Resource 1 model, 42, 43*f*
resources
    further reading, 233–234
    list of resources, 207–211
    Participants' Zone, 27–28
    references, 235–239
retention, 40, 118–119
    definition of, 231
    ideas for engagement, 119*t*
Richardson's 10 big shifts, 139, 142*b*–143*b*
RoadKill project, 183
role models, 39–40, 109, 232
role playing, 146*b*
roles, 52
roster systems, 178*f*
rotation, individual, 178*f*

S

Save the Tasmanian Devil Program, 183
scaffolded link sites, 178*f*
scaffolds
    for authentic learning, 179*f*
    for classroom management, 178*f*
    for communication applications skills, 166*t*
    for computer skills, 159*t*–160*t*
    for confronting anxieties, 98*t*
    for database software skills, 172*t*
    end-of-term reflection scaffold, 194, 195*f*
    goal-setting scaffolds, 27, 154, 154*f*
    for hardware skills, 161*f*
    for information collection and analysis, 179*f*
    for interactive whiteboards, 173*t*–174*t*
    list of resources, 207–211
    for mobile apps, 175*t*–176*t*
    for multimedia skills, 170*t*–171*t*
    for online, constructivist learning, 179*f*
    reflection scaffolds, 78, 79*f*, 194, 195*f*
    resources available online, 27
    for school analysis, 60, 61*t*–63*t*

for software skills, 167*t*–168*t*, 169*t*
strategies for showcasing and celebrating success in, 83, 84*t*
for Web 1.0 skills, 164*t*
for Web 2.0 skills, 165*t*
for word processing, 162*t*–163*t*
scavenger hunts, 184
scheduling, 188–194
approaches to, 122–123
for reflection, 202
strategies for, 203–204
suggestions for four-quarter school year implementation, 188, 189*t*–191*t*
suggestions for three-term (trimester) school year implementation, 191, 192*t*–193*t*
school executives, 52–54
end-of-term evaluative questions for, 194, 196*f*
key role tasks, 53–54
school analysis, 59, 60
collecting information for, 61
of general school demographics, 61*t*
rationale for, 59–60
scaffold for, 60, 61*t*–63*t*
of school and ICT leadership, 62*t*, 63*t*
of school culture, 62*t*–63*t*
of students' technology use, 63*t*
of teachers' values, attitudes, beliefs, and skills, 63*t*
school culture, 33, 35–36, 62*t*–63*t*
school demographics, general, 61*t*
school executives, 52–54
school history, 61*t*
school leadership, 52–54
school management team, 52–54
school vision, 51
school year
four-quarter schedule, 188, 189*t*–191*t*
scheduling into, 188–194
three-term (trimester) schedule, 191, 192*t*–193*t*
science apps, 175*t*
self-directed learning
advantages and disadvantages of, 113*t*
definition of, 232
self-efficacy, 38, 59–60, 95
computer self-efficacy, 230
definition of, 230, 232
ideas for engagement, 96*t*
mentoring to build, 95–96
self-handicapping, 38, 100
self-reflective inquiry, 25, 229
sensitivity to initial conditions, 22
shortcuts, 117*b*

showcasing, 186
ideas for, 186*b*
planning for, 82–83
strategies for, 83, 84*t*
simulations, 179*f*, 185
skills
school analysis of, 63*t*
teachers' perceptions of, 63*t*
skills-based goals, 152*t*, 158–159, 158*t*
small groups, 178*f*
strategies for showcasing and celebrating success in, 83, 84*t*
social action projects, 185
social science apps, 175*t*
software skills, 158*t*
goal-setting scaffolds for, 167*t*–168*t*, 169*t*, 172*t*
school analysis, 62*t*
spreadsheet software skills, 158*t*, 167
core skills, 167*t*
goal-setting scaffold for, 167*t*–168*t*
reflection on spreadsheet integration lesson, 203*b*
stability, 101
staff, 48
discussions, 51
goal setting, 156*t*
skills and readiness, 197
staff meetings
agenda, 77
discussion in, 77–78
resources available online, 27
strategies for showcasing and celebrating success in, 83, 84*t*
storytelling, interactive, 168–169
strategic planning, 49
strategies: focus on, 109*f*
structured mentoring time, 72*t*
student assemblies, 82–83, 84*t*
student surveys
available surveys, 213–218
example, 66*f*
formats for, 65
impact of, 64
simple survey for most ages, 213
survey for older students, 214, 216–218
survey for very young students, 213, 215
students
behavior of, 146*b*
communication applications skills, 166*t*
database software skills, 172*t*
as digital natives, 134–137, 137*t*
foundational computer skills, 160*t*
general school demographics, 61*t*

interactive whiteboard skills, 174*t*
learning with and from, 146–147, 147*t*, 148*t*
multimedia skills, 171*t*
need to teach ICT skills to, 137–138
older, 214, 216–218
perspectives and vision of, 63*t*, 64–65
presentation software skills, 169*t*
school analysis of, 63*t*
showcasing and celebrating, 82–83, 84*t*, 186, 186*b*
spreadsheet software skills, 168*t*
teacher perceptions of, 63*t*
technology use by, 63*t*
very young, 213, 215
Web 1.0 skills, 164*t*
Web 2.0 skills, 165*t*
word processing skills, 163*t*
students with disabilities, 48
support
    for computer use by others, 232
    ideas for engagement, 100*t*
    role of, 99
support materials. *See also* resources
    Participants' Zone, 27–28
support staff, 48
surveys
    student surveys, 64, 65, 66, 213–218
    teacher surveys, 67, 219–224
sustainability, 205
synchronous communication, 158*t*, 165, 166*t*

T

tablet computers, 9. *See also* mobile devices
teacher culture, 62*t*
teacher surveys, 67, 219–224. *See also* surveys
    initial survey, 220–224
    purpose of, 67
Teacher Technology Use Survey, 220–224
teachers,
    adoption and integration of ICT by, 32–33
    attitudes toward time, 122–123, 203–204
    beginning, 8–9
    beliefs about time, 122–123
    building independence of, 200*b*
    capable, 92*t*–93*t*
    as change agents, 8–9
    communication applications skills, 166*t*
    as companion mentors, 58
    competent, 92*t*–93*t*
    database software skills, 172*t*
    as facilitators, 141*b*
    foundational computer skills, 160*t*
    general school demographics, 61*t*
    goal setting for, 150–153
    interactive whiteboard skills, 174*t*
    learning goals, 149
    learning strategies of, 32–33, 35
    multimedia skills, 171*t*
    pedagogical orientation, 106
    perceptions of students' knowledge and skills, 63*t*
    pre-service education for, 8–9
    presentation software skills, 169*t*
    professionalism of, 35–36
    release time for, 74–75, 75*t*–76*t*
    resistant to trying new strategies, 198–199
    school analysis of, 62*t*, 63*t*
    skills of, 63*t*
    spreadsheet software skills, 168*t*
    suggestions for engaging, 92*t*, 96*t*, 98*t*, 100*t*, 102*t*, 105*t*, 111*t*, 116*t*, 119*t*, 121*t*, 122*t*, 123*t*, 131*t*, 134*t*, 144*t*, 147*t*
    support for, 127–148
    as technology travelers, 45
    values, attitudes, and beliefs of, 15–16, 32–33, 63*t*
    Web 1.0 skills, 164*t*
    Web 2.0 skills, 165*t*
    word processing skills, 163*t*
    young, beginning, 8–9
teachers' aides, 48
teaching
    authenticity in, 131–133
    connectivist approaches, 129, 130*t*, 131*t*, 132, 133*f*
    constructivist approaches, 106, 129, 130*t*, 131*t*, 132, 133*f*
    as conversation, 142*b*
    cultures of, 133*f*
    learner-centered, 140*b*
    NETS for Coaches (NETS•C), 225–226
    objectivist (or directed) approaches, 106, 129, 130*t*, 131*t*, 132, 133*f*
    teacher-centered, 140*b*
    "10 big shifts" in understanding, 142*b*–143*b*
teams, coordinating, 58
technical support, 48
technological change, 9
technological, pedagogical, and content knowledge (TPACK) model, 10
technology
    assistive technologies, 48
    integration of, 45
    need to teach, 137–138
    perceived usefulness of, 103–105
    school analysis of, 63*t*

students' use of, 63t
training vs learning, 30–31
use by others of, 99
technology capability, 31–32, 89–90, 92t–93t
technology coaches, 225–228
technology competency, 31–32, 89–90, 92t–93t
technology learning
as complex process, 20–25, 33
as different from technology training, 30–31
metacognitive approach to, 42, 43f, 109f, 231
need for, 1–2, 8–11, 137–138
visual models of, 26f, 42, 43f
technology self-efficacy, 38
technology skills, 137–138, 138t
Technology Together, 1, 2
advice from the front line, 197–204
benefits of, 16–17
as evidence-based action-oriented practice, 25–27
foundational pillars, 11–12, 30–36
foundations, xi, 15–16
as framework, 11–14
at a glance, 5
implementation, 47–85, 187–205
introducing, 49–51
as learning journey, 44–45
mentoring, 88
planning for, 47–85
principles, 13
as professional development program, 35–36
rationale for, 7–28
research project, xi–xii
sustaining, 205
timing of, 48–49
tips for sustaining, 125
unique characteristics of, 18–19
website, 2, 27–28
Technology Together partners, 57, 60, 230
technophobics, 38, 97, 232
technophrenics, 38, 97, 232
telementoring, 182
"10 big shifts" in understanding teaching, 142b–143b
thinking aloud, 124
definition of, 232
for developing metacognition, 146b
ThinkQuest International Competition, 185
thought bubble displays
competency/capability, 90f
list of resources, 208–211
time
as investment, 122–123
as obstacle, 203–204
perceptions of, 232
teachers' beliefs about, 122–123, 203–204

time management
approaches to, 122–123
approaches to allocation of release time, 75t–76t
as challenging, 203–204
ideas for engagement, 123t
for reflection, 202
release time, 74–75
strategies for, 203–204
strategies for release time, 74, 75t–76t
time on/time off, 122–123
timetables. *See* scheduling
tipping points, 21, 24, 232
TPACK (technological, pedagogical, and content knowledge) model, 10
training
directive-style, 230
skills-based goals, 152t, 158–159, 158t
travel buddies or travel friends, 182
traveling metaphor, 44–45
tutoring, peer or cross-age, 178f
24/7 learning, 142b

U

usefulness, perceived, 39
definition of, 232
fostering, 103–105
ideas for engagement, 105t

V

values, teacher, 32–33, 63t
video reflecting, 82
virtual field trips, 184
virtual gatherings, 183
vision
ICT vision, 51
school analysis of, 63t
student, 63t, 64–65
visionary leadership, 225
visits to other classrooms, 73t
visual displays, 81–82
for engagement, 92t, 96t, 102t, 105t, 111t, 116t, 121t, 122t, 123t, 131t, 139t, 144t, 147t
visual models, 26f, 42, 43f
volition, 41, 120
definition of, 232
fostering, 119–121
ideas for engagement, 121t

INDEX

W

wall displays, 81–82
    for engagement, 92*t*, 96*t*, 102*t*, 105*t*, 111*t*, 116*t*, 121*t*, 122*t*, 123*t*, 131*t*, 139*t*, 144*t*, 147*t*
Web 1.0 skills, 163
    core skills, 164*t*
    goal-setting scaffold for, 164*t*
Web 2.0 skills, 163
    core skills, 165*t*
    goal-setting scaffold for, 165*t*
WebQuests, 180
    critical parts, 180
    global, 184
    goal-setting scaffold for, 179*f*
weekly journals, 80
Where's Collie, 184
whiteboards, interactive, 1, 158*t*, 173
    core skills for, 173*t*
    goal-setting scaffold for, 173*t*–174*t*
whole-grade or faculty/department goal setting, 156*t*
whole-school approach, 33–34
    development of, 8–11
whole-school goal setting, 152–153, 156*t*
whole-school teacher-learning model, 7–28
word processing skills, 158*t*, 162
    core skills, 162*t*
    goal-setting scaffold for, 162*t*–163*t*
World Wide Web skills, 158*t*, 163
writing, 143*b*

Z

Ziptales, 168